Pre-emptive Remedies in Europe

FOR LYDIA

Pre-emptive Remedies in Europe

General Editor:

Nicholas Rose
Partner in Field Fisher Waterhouse

© Nicholas Rose 1992

ISBN 0 85121 8199

Published by
Longman Law, Tax and Finance
Longman Group UK Ltd
21–27 Lamb's Conduit Street, London WC1N 3NJ

Associated offices
Australia, Hong Kong, Malaysia, Singapore, USA

A CIP catalogue record for this book is available from the
British Library.

Printed in Great Britain by Mackays of Chatham PLC, Chatham, Kent.

Contents

Foreword

The Freedom of Services Directive and the directive on the mutual recognition of diplomas have contributed, and one day the establishment directive will contribute, to opening up legal practice throughout the Community. A single market, to the achievement of which all Member States are firmly committed, will increasingly involve lawyers in looking after their clients' affairs in other Member States. They may or they may not want to get involved in the conduct of litigation in other Member States. Whether they do or not it will become increasingly necessary that they should have either knowledge of, or the means of access to, information about the remedies available in those States.

This book gives a detailed and practical account of the courts in which, the procedures by which, and the terms upon which, presumptive or interim relief can be obtained in the various Member States. The importance of such relief is underlined as a way not only of protecting claims which might otherwise be frustrated by the date of trial but also of focusing the parties' minds on the real issues in the case in a way which can often lead to a settlement. The potential importance of this is indicated in the Italian chapter which states that with a large number of cases awaiting trial in Rome the average duration of the case is some seven and a half years.

The chapters follow a broadly similar pattern in respect of each Member State. There are many differences of procedure—in some States there is an oral hearing, in others rarely; in some affidavit evidence is essential, in others it is not required; in some a 'freezing' order to protect assets is readily available, in others it seems difficult if not impossible to obtain—the Mareva injunction and the Anton Piller order are reflected in some but not in others. A cross-undertaking in damages is required not only in the United Kingdom but also in Denmark; it is not required in Belgium or in the Netherlands. It may be ordered but is rarely used in France. For many Member States examples are given of the types of situation in which injunctions or other forms of interim relief are available and on what terms.

The general conditions of interim relief appear to be broadly the same— an arguable case, urgency and the risk that irremediable damage will be suffered before trial. It is also noteworthy that in most Member States there are no rigidly codified rules as to the exercise of the jurisdiction. As is said in the chapter on Spain, 'it is necessary to take account of the development which is taking shape day by day through the judgments pronounced by the courts, for in the final analysis the judges are the ones who keep the law alive by constantly updating it'. The Danish chapter seems to say the same: 'Conventional jurisprudence cannot be relied on to provide suitable criteria in its literature for determining that there has been an event which would justify the implementation of an injunction'. Everywhere much depends on the discretion of the judge, which may be exercised in different ways in different States. Nowhere I suspect would there be any doubt, however, that an injunction should be granted even *ex parte* if 'the 2000 one-day old chicks would not become two-day old chicks' as in the Irish case cited.

This book will enable lawyers in the Community to see whether it is worthwhile going to another Member State for interim relief and what the procedures and financial risks are. The chapter on the United Kingdom will not only be useful to lawyers from other Member States, it is a statement of practice and procedure useful for English lawyers too.

Lord Slynn of Hadley, June 1992

Preface

This book provides a country-by-country study of the availability of injunctive relief in the courts of the European Community. It was originally conceived as a result of my personal experience in seeking advice from lawyers in other Member States on whether certain types of injunctive relief were available in their jurisdiction. Like all practitioners, I was conscious of the costs involved in seeking the advice of foreign lawyers when litigation spilt over into other jurisdictions. Further, in view of the international nature of commerce and as a commercial litigator I became aware of the need to possess a certain degree of knowledge of the basic mechanics of the legal systems of the other Member States. I hope this book will assist lawyers both inside and outside the Community in advising clients caught up in litigation in one or other of the EC Member States.

In addition to providing a description of the types of pre-emptive remedies available in Member States, I have offered an explanation of the structures of the courts, the legal team required, the procedures to be followed when applying for interlocutory relief within the Community jurisdictions, and the potential liability of the losing party for costs. This book will enable the litigant's lawyer to provide a client with basic advice before instructing lawyers in the Member State which has the conduct of the litigation, and to help the litigant's indigenous lawyer to co-ordinate strategy with, and interpret advice from, the foreign lawyer.

Notwithstanding the diversity and the origins of the various legal systems within the European Community, some being constitutional and others based on common law principles, I was struck by the remarkable similarity in the types of injunctions and the remedies available to protect legal rights in urgent situations. Where a speedy remedy is required the courts of all the Member States are able to respond and provide appropriate protection. In addition, the criteria in each State is almost identical—urgency and risk of irreparable harm to name but two. Again, the courts of all the Member States have jurisdiction to prevent the disposal of movable assets of a defendant wherever necessary and the equivalent of the Mareva injunction in England can be found in other Member States, albeit in a variety of forms, from the *attachment* in France to the judicial sequestration and temporary seizure available in Greece. However, no other Member State, with the exception of Ireland, has cultivated a remedy quite as draconian as the Anton Piller order which is available in the English courts, allowing one party to enter the other's premises and search for and seize specified categories of documents and other evidence.

My contributors are all experienced litigators with proven knowledge and experience of interlocutory litigation in their own jurisdictions. Each chapter is therefore tempered by a real experience of the problematic issues involved. However, the chapters do not set out to deal with complicated legal procedures or concepts in depth but only to describe the essential features of obtaining pre-emptive remedies within each Member State.

I have tried to remain faithful to 'foreign' jurisdictions' terminology and to the sometimes complex legal procedures being described by the contributor—even though this may mean in places that literary style has been sacrificed for accuracy.

I have included a chapter on the Brussels Convention of 1968 for two reasons. First of all, one needs to identify the appropriate jurisdiction in which to make the interlocutory application. For instance, should the application be made in the same jurisdiction in which the main action is being, or will be, conducted? Or should the court hearing the interlocutory application decide whether the defendant is domiciled in the jurisdiction? Secondly, if the defendant's assets are located in another Member State, it is important to know whether the injunction is enforceable in that jurisdiction. For instance, can *ex parte* injunctions be exported and registered and enforced in the courts of other Member States?

In the chapter dealing with the United Kingdom, I have dealt in more depth with the current state of the law relating to both Mareva injunctions and Anton Piller orders. This has been an active area in recent years and readers should be aware that this is a rapidly changing part of English law. I have therefore provided in the Appendices to that chapter a checklist of practical points to note in the case of both Marevas and Anton Piller orders in which those in urgent need will hopefully find some useful guidance.

The European Community comprises 12 countries, has a population of over 342,000,000 and covers over 2,363,000 square kilometres. It has come a long way from its original varied economic, cultural and political origins towards the single market which it aspires to today.

I started researching this project with the preconception that the less economically developed countries in the Community may lack the necessary sophisticated legal procedures for providing injunctive relief in urgent situations. However, I found this not to be the case. My overriding impression of the legal systems of the Community is that they are perhaps closer to harmonisation than the various economies, cultures and political systems of the constituent Member States. Faced with a company or individual seeking to dissipate his assets or delay the legal process, the courts of all the Member States are equipped with the means to provide urgent, pre-emptive injunctive relief. I hope this book will aid the international lawyer in deciding what action to take in the courts of the Community countries.

Nicholas Rose

Acknowledgements

I would like to thank my wife Fiona for her support and understanding during the many evenings and weekends I was immersed in this project; my secretary Molly Gavigan who is responsible for typing most of this book and for her tireless work in administering and co-ordinating all the contributions; Stephen Silber QC, for his valuable advice and all my contributors for the excellent summaries of the law in their own countries which they have provided and for their patience in dealing with my many queries during the course of the editing process.

Contributors

Contributor	Chapter	Firm
Nicholas Rose	The Brussels Convention 1968	Field Fisher Waterhouse
Nicole Van Crombrugghe	Belgium	Lafili & Van Crombrugghe
Jakob Poulsen	Denmark	Mazanti-Andersen, Korso Jensen & Partnere
Philippe Bessis	France	Philippe Bessis
Dr Klaus Gerstenmaier	Germany	Haver & Mailander
Yanos Gramatidis	Greece	Bahas, Gramatidis & Associates
Terry Leggett	Ireland	Eugene F Collins & Son
Fabio Gullotta	Italy	Studio Legale Gullotta
Alex Schmitt	Luxembourg	Bonn & Schmitt
Peter Eijsvoogel	The Netherlands	Loeff Claeys Verbeke
Cesar Bessa Monteiro	Portugal	Veiga Gomes, Bessa Monteiro, Marques Bom
Juan Barthe	Spain	Bufete Cuatrecasas
Nicholas Rose	UK: England and Wales	Field Fisher Waterhouse
David Walker	UK: Scotland	Brodies

The Brussels Convention 1968

Introduction

The Contracting States

One of the basic principles of the Treaty of Rome is that it prohibits any discrimination on the grounds of nationality against Member States nationals. Article 220 of the EC Treaty required the Member States to enter into negotiations with each other with a view to securing, for the benefit of their nationals, the simplification of formalities governing the reciprocal recognition and enforcement of judgments of courts and other tribunals. Negotiations between the six original Member States led to the signing of the Convention on jurisdiction and the enforcement of judgments in civil and commercial matters (including the Protocol annexed to that Convention) which was signed in Brussels on 27 September 1968 ('the Convention'). On 3 June 1971 a Protocol on the interpretation of the Brussels Convention by the European Court was signed in Luxembourg. The Brussels Convention came into force for the six original Contracting States on 1 February 1973.

The overall aim of the Convention was to achieve certainty, equality and simplification of procedures for litigants based in the EC, in the courts of all the Member States in which proceedings are brought. The Convention set out to unify and rationalise the jurisdiction rules of Contracting States as well as the principles of recognition and enforcement of judgments.

In 1978 an Accession Convention was signed by Denmark, Eire and the United Kingdom and the Convention came into force in Denmark on 1 November 1986, in the United Kingdom on 1 January 1987 (when the Civil Jurisdiction and Judgments Act 1982 came into force) and in Eire on 1 June 1988. Transitional provisions were contained in the Accession Convention of 1982 for Greece (art 12) and in the 1989 Accession Convention for Spain and Portugal (art 16). The Convention came into force in Greece on 1 October 1989 and in Spain on 1 February 1991. As for Portugal, it is not anticipated that the Portuguese Government will adopt the Convention in the near future. In this chapter those countries who have acceded to and adopted the Convention are referred to as Contracting States.

The objects of the Convention

The key feature of the Convention is that judgments obtained in one of the Contracting States are 'exportable' to other Contracting States with the minimum of formalities and conditions and with the scope for challenge of the judgment in the receiving country being very limited. The Brussels Convention contains a very wide definition for the term 'judgment' and includes any judgment given by a court or tribunal of a Contracting State, whatever the judgment may be called.

The Convention states that 'A judgment given in a Contracting State shall be recognised in the other Contracting States without any special procedure being required'. The judgment becomes immediately 'exportable'. A defendant cannot attack the merits of the judgment in the courts of the 'importing' country. Neither the findings of facts by the original court nor the substance of the judgment can be questioned. There are, however, limited instances where a judgment will not be recognised. For example, one of the most important of these is where a judgment is obtained in default of a defence being served by the defendant who can subsequently show that he has not been served with the documents which instituted the proceedings. In the English courts this will be, in most cases, a High Court writ or a county court summons. It will be for the defendant to prove that he has not been directly served and that he could not therefore prepare a defence. In most cases, however, recognition of the judgment will be automatic.

Recognition of a judgment under the Convention is not dependent on the defendant being a national of a Contracting State. For example, if the defendant is American but has assets in France, judgment can be enforced through the French courts against those assets. This will be the case unless the 'importing' state has agreed a Convention with the non-Contracting State not to recognise such judgments.

So far as pre-emptive remedies are concerned, the Convention means that interim injunctions obtained in one Contracting State can be enforced in other Contracting States. Therefore fast and effective enforcement of injunctions throughout the EC has been facilitated, as long as the injunction has not been obtained *ex parte* and is intended to be executed without notice (*Denilauder v SNC Couchet Freres* [1981] 1 CMLR 62). However, it seems that procedural orders which do not affect the legal relationship of the parties (eg for discovery of documents) are not within the scope of the Convention.

The procedure to enforce the judgment requires, for example, a certified copy of the judgment obtained in the English courts to be presented to the enforcement authorities in the French courts. Enforcement will then proceed in accordance with the procedure of that court. For example, if a foreign judgment is to be enforced through the English courts, it can be dealt with by the Sheriff of the High Court who can exercise his powers of seizure of the assets of a defendant.

The difficulty in seeking effective and easy enforcement lay in the complexity and diversity of national laws. Although bilateral enforcement treaties did exist between individual Member States these were largely divergent and incomplete.

Therefore the main objects of the Convention are to bring jurisdiction issues and the enforcement of judgments into line with the European Community's ideal of harmonisation. The basic functions of the Convention are:

(a) to standardise the conditions in which the courts of the EC States have jurisdiction in civil matters over claims against parties who are domiciled in the EC (and in a few cases who are not); and

(b) to enable all judgments of EC courts against non-EC domiciled parties to be recognised and enforced in other EC States.

The adoption of the Convention in the UK

The Civil Jurisdiction and Judgments Act 1982 in England and Wales ('the 1982 Act') provides one example of how a Member State has applied the provisions of the Convention and brought into play one single set of rules governing the enforcement of foreign judgments within the EC. This Act contains the necessary provisions to achieve the aims and objects of the Brussels Convention and is typical of similar national legislation passed in the other Contracting States. Schedule 1 of the 1982 Act sets out the Convention and Sched 4 sets out an amended version of the Convention applicable for England and Wales.

Section 3 of the 1982 Act provides that: 'Any question as to the meaning or effect of any provision of the Convention shall, if not referred to the European Court in accordance with the 1971 Protocol, be determined in accordance with the principles laid down by any relevant decision of the European Court.' It further provides that judicial notice will be taken of any decision or opinion expressed by the European Court on any question arising out of the Convention. Similar legislation has been passed in the other Contracting States.

The European Court is therefore competent to determine questions of interpretation of the Convention in the UK (as well as in the other Contracting States).

This chapter will examine in more detail the following areas covered by the Convention:

(a) the scope of proceedings;
(b) jurisdiction;
(c) recognition;
(d) enforcement; and
(e) the practical procedure for registration and enforcement in the UK.

The scope of proceedings

(1) The subject matter of the judgment must be civil and commercial.

(2) There must be the existence of a judgment which will include any decree, order or writ of execution, including an order for costs, in any national court. The Convention applies to money or non-money judgments.

(3) The judgment must be of a 'court or tribunal'.

(4) The foreign judgment should not be defective under the judgment state's law.

(5) The principal subject matter of proceedings must be within the Convention's scope. It is therefore necessary to analyse in every case whether the main claim, and not any incidental issues, falls within the Convention's scope. If the main claim is within the scope of the Convention then the incidental issues will also come under the umbrella of the Convention's rules. However, if the main claim is excluded, then incidental issues, which would otherwise have come within the Convention's scope, will also be excluded. An incidental matter is one which the court must determine in order to decide the main issue(s) in the action.

Article 1 states that the Convention shall not apply to:

(a) the status or legal capacity of natural persons, rights in property arising out of a matrimonial relationship, wills and succession;
(b) bankruptcy, proceedings relating to the winding-up of insolvent

companies or other legal persons, judicial arrangements, compositions and analogous proceedings;

(c) social security; and

(d) arbitration.

Jurisdiction

The grounds of jurisdiction can be divided into six categories:

(1) Jurisdiction based upon the situation of the defendant's domicile.

(2) Jurisdiction based upon submission to the jurisdiction by the defendant.

(3) Exclusive jurisdiction arising either from the terms of an agreement nominating the jurisdiction of one Contracting State to deal with disputes between the parties or alternatively exclusive jurisdiction arising in various stipulated circumstances which will be examined in more detail below.

(4) Special jurisdiction for example in matters relating to a tort whereby jurisdiction will be in the courts of the country in which the harmful event occurred.

(5) Jurisdiction rules in relation to applications for provisional and protective relief.

(6) Special rules apply to jurisdiction in matters relating to insurance and consumer contracts (ss 3 and 4 of Title 2 of the Convention). These contracts provide exclusive jurisdictional rules, in the insured's or consumer plaintiff's favour, irrespective of the domicile of the defendant.

An examination of these detailed rules is outside the scope of this chapter and specific reference should be made to Title 2 of the Convention when determining jurisdiction in relation to any insurance or consumer contract.

Generally, there must be a close connection between the litigation and the Contracting State accepting jurisdiction of the matter, which will be based either on the defendant's domicile, the nature of the case or the stated intention of the parties.

These grounds will now be examined in turn.

Domicile

The domicile of the defendant constitutes the principal jurisdictional factor for Convention purposes and so it is essential to determine its meaning.

Domicile of individuals

There is no Convention definition of domicile. There are differences in national law meanings of domicile and the drafters of the Convention were anxious to avoid placing too many difficulties in the path of adoption of the Convention by Member States and unification of the relevant laws.

Article 52 lays down Convention choice of law rules for the determination of an individual's domicile as follows:

In order to determine whether a party is domiciled in a Contracting State whose courts are seized of the matter, the court shall apply its internal law.

If a party is not domiciled in a state whose courts are seized of the matter, then, in order to determine whether the party is domiciled in another Contracting State, the court shall apply the law of that latter State.

The main purpose of Article 52 is to avoid the occurrence of positive and negative conflicts of jurisdiction.

Problems can, however, arise under art 52. For example, the courts of, say, France, applying the latter's domicile concept, may decide that a defendant is not domiciled in France and that the French courts are not, therefore, entitled to exercise jurisdiction under the Convention. The French courts may then consider whether the defendant is domiciled in another forum, say Germany, applying the relevant German law. If the French courts decided that the defendant was domiciled in Germany, the plaintiff might then try to bring the proceedings in Germany. If, however, although domiciled in Germany under France's interpretation of German law on domicile, the defendant was held by the German courts not to be domiciled in Germany by the latter's own concept, but in France or, alternatively, in The Netherlands, then the plaintiff would be unable to bring proceedings in France or Germany on the basis of the law of domicile in those Contracting States. If problems then arose in The Netherlands regarding domicile a situation can arise whereby the plaintiff would be unable to proceed in France or Germany or The Netherlands or conceivably any other Contracting State.

These problems can be avoided by the inclusion of a jurisdiction clause in a contract which, under art 17, will confer exclusive jurisdiction on the nominated Contracting State. This will be considered in greater detail below.

A brief account of the meaning of domicile for civil jurisdictional purposes under the laws of the Contracting States will show several differences in relation to the national laws of domicile.

The Netherlands Domicile is the place in which an individual has his home or effective residence, under art 10 of the Civil Code 1970. If, therefore, a person's centre of business and professional interests is situated in one place, but he lives with his family in another territory, then the latter will be his domicile according to an objective assessment.

Italy Domicile is situated in the place in which an individual has the chief centre of his interests and affairs under art 43(1) of the Civil Code. The test is an objective one.

France and Luxembourg Domicile is the place in which an individual's 'principal establishment' is situated being that of his usual residence and the centre of his family, economic and vocational interests. In order to bring about a change of domicile the individual is required to reside in a new place and to form an intention to make the latter his principal establishment.

Belgium As in France and Luxembourg domicile is an individual's 'principal establishment'. However, in Belgium the place in which the individual's name is entered upon the official population register is deemed to be the principal establishment under art 36 of the Judicial Code. The theory is that each person is to have the right to choose his principal establishment and is presumed to know the consequences of registration and the place of registration will take precedence over the individual's 'principal establishment' in the event of any conflict.

Germany Domicile exists where an individual has a fixed and stable establishment under art 7 of the Civil Code. Unlike the French and Italian concepts, the establishment required by German law need not be the principal centre of a person's personal or business affairs and the major difference, therefore, between the German concept and those of the other Contracting States is that under the former, a person may be domiciled in more than one place, or even nowhere at all when he shows an intention to abandon his existing domicile without establishing a new one.

England and Wales Section 41 of the 1982 Act states that an individual is domiciled in England or Wales if he is resident in England or Wales and the nature and circumstances of his residence indicate that he has a substantial connection with England or Wales. If an individual has been resident in England or Wales, or a part of England or Wales, for three months or more then the provisions of domicile will be presumed to be fulfilled unless the contrary is proved.

Eire   The Fifth Schedule to the Jurisdiction of Courts and Enforcement of Judgments (European Communities) Act 1988 defines an individual's domicile as follows:

(a) an individual is domiciled in the State, or in a State other than a Contracting State, if, but only if, he is ordinarily resident in the State or in that other State;

(b) an individual is domiciled in a place in the State, if, but only if, he is domiciled in the State and is ordinarily resident or carries on any profession, business or occupation in that place.

Denmark   Proceedings must be brought in the court of the defendant's place of residence which is the place in which he has an address. A person may have an address in several places in Denmark or in Denmark and abroad, in which case he may be sued in each of those places in Denmark. A person's address is the place in which he and his household have their permanent home, where their property is usually situated and where the person lives. In Denmark every person is obliged to report his address to a registration office in the community in which the address is situated. Any person who changes his address must notify his new address within five days of moving. A certificate of registration is not conclusive evidence of a person's address but it is important evidence.

As regards Danish nationals who are resident abroad, with no address in Denmark, if they are not subject to the jurisdiction of the courts of their country of residence then they may be sued in Copenhagen.

Spain   Article 40 of the Civil Code states that the domicile of individuals is the place of habitual residence.

Article 65 of the Law of Civil Procedure states that the legal domicile of any trader, in all matters relating to commercial actions and contracts and consequences deriving from them, shall be the town in which they have their centre of commercial operations. If a trader has a commercial establishment in different judicial districts then the plaintiff has the choice of suing the trader in the place where he has his principal establishment or the place in which the obligation occurred.

Portugal   Under Portuguese law an individual's voluntary domicile is the place in which a person has his fixed and permanent place of living. If there are several permanent places then he may be domiciled in any of them. In the absence of a permanent place of living, his place of domicile will be in his occasional place of living and, in the absence of that, a person's domicile is the place in which he is found. Portuguese law also incorporates certain special domicile rules: for example, in any judicial issues resulting from labour relations, an individual's domicile will be the place in which he carries out his work.

Greece   Domicile for all individuals in Greece will be the place in which an individual lives and intends to live in the future.

Domicile of companies
This is dealt with separately under the Convention and art 53 states as follows:

For the purposes of this Convention, the seat of a company or other legal person or association of natural or legal persons shall be treated as its domicile. However, in order to determine that seat, the court shall apply its rules of private international law.

The seat of a company is a concept used by continental legal systems which, before 1987, formed no part of English and Welsh law. The function of the seat of a company is similar to the concept of the place of incorporation under English and Welsh law.

There are two different concepts of a company's seat: the real seat doctrine and the statutory seat doctrine.

(1) The 'real seat' doctrine is the place of the company's central management, administration and control, the place in which corporate decisions are taken and general meetings of shareholders and directors' meetings are held. It should therefore be relatively easy to ascertain the real seat and the company should be subjected to the law and jurisdiction of the State in which the company actually organises its business activities.

(2) This can be contrasted to a 'statutory seat'. This is the place designated as the company's seat in its Statute or Memorandum and will therefore usually correspond with the place of incorporation. If this doctrine is applied then the statutory seat will overrule the location of the company's central management and control if it is located in a different State from that of the statutory seat.

The position regarding the Contracting States is as follows:

France   France will adopt the real seat doctrine unless the real seat moves abroad and the statutory seat remains in France;

Germany   applies the real seat doctrine;

Italy   Italian courts will follow the real seat doctrine when neither statutory nor real seat is situated in Italy. If either is so situated the real seat doctrine is preferred although reference may be made to the statutory seat if it is located in the State having forum;

Belgium and Luxembourg   apply the real seat approach when the real seat is located there;

The Netherlands   This is the only original Contracting State which will solely be concerned with the statutory seat of a company;

England and Wales   Section 42 of the 1982 Act states that the company will have its seat in England or Wales if and only if it was incorporated or formed under the law of a part of England or Wales and has its registered office or some other official address in England or Wales or its central management and control is exercised in England or Wales;

Eire   The Fifth Schedule to the 1988 Act in Eire states that a company's seat will be determined if it was incorporated or formed under the law of the State or if its central management and control is exercised in the State. Further, a company will have its seat in a particular place in the State if its registered office or other official address is at that place or its central management and control is exercised from that place or if it is carrying on business in that place;

Denmark   Companies have their domicile in the area in which the office is situated. In the absence of a head office, the domicile will be in the court area in which a member of the board of directors or the equivalent management organ has his address. This provision covers any type of association, regardless of its form or object. The head office or the main place of business is the place where the company or other association is managed by its management body. The constitution of a company must contain the information regarding the location of its head office.

Denmark has therefore adopted the real seat doctrine;

Spain   Spain applies the statutory seat doctrine. Article 66 of the Law of Civil Procedure states that the domicile of companies shall be in the place indicated in the articles of incorporation or the byelaws which govern them.

Only if this does not exist will domicile be in the place where the principal functions of the institution are carried out.

If a company has a domicile established in its articles of incorporation which is in a different place to its central administration and management, but both places are in Spain, third parties have the choice of suing the company in either of the two places. If a company has a domicile within Spanish territory in accordance with its articles of incorporation, but its central management is located in a different State, the company will, under Spanish law, be domiciled in Spain in accordance with the statutory seat doctrine;

Portugal The domicile of a company is the place in which the company has its head office which will be established under the constitution of the company. In the absence of any head office, a company will be domiciled in the place where its administration carries out its functions. If a company has its head office in a foreign country but carries out some of its activities in Portugal, its domicile will be the place in which it has its permanent place of business;

Greece In Greece the statutory seat doctrine is applied. Any company registered in Greece will be domiciled at the place of its registered office. If a company is registered abroad it will not be regarded as a Greek company and therefore cannot be domiciled in Greece.

In view of the differing national laws on domicile there is a need to replace art 52 with a uniform Convention concept of domicile in order to avoid the possibility of courts in different Contracting States reaching differing decisions with regard to the factual element concerning domicile.

It should be emphasised that the domicile rules in the Convention do not preclude the courts of a Contracting State from exercising its own national laws when determining jurisdiction issues if the only conflict of jurisdiction to be determined is between a Contracting State and a non-Contracting State.

For example, in the case of *Re Harrods (Buenos Aires) Ltd* [1991] 3 WLR 397; [1991] 4 All ER 334 the English High Court had to consider jurisdiction issues under the Convention in relation to a company incorporated in England, whose registered office was in England, but whose business was carried on and was managed and controlled exclusively in Argentina. Applying the national law of *forum non conveniens* it could be argued that the most appropriate forum for the trial of the case was in Argentina, despite the fact that, under the Convention, it could be argued that the company was domiciled in England. A conflict of jurisdiction therefore existed. The court had to decide whether the Convention's rules on jurisdiction and domicile applied or not. The dispute was between the two Swiss shareholders, proceedings were commenced in England but one shareholder sought a stay of the proceedings on the basis that the appropriate forum for the trial of the issues was in Argentina.

The High Court held that the court had a discretionary jurisdiction under the Convention to stay or dismiss proceedings properly served on a defendant domiciled in England on the ground that the case would be more appropriately heard elsewhere in circumstances where the conflict of jurisdiction was between the English courts and the courts of a non-Convention country. The purpose of the Convention was to establish an expeditious, harmonious and certain procedure for securing the reciprocal recognition and enforcement of judgments as between Convention countries and to regulate relations *only as between Convention countries*. Therefore, the domicile rules in the Convention do not require the national courts of a Contracting State to hear and determine proceedings commenced in that country on the basis of the defendant's domicile alone if there was a conflict of jurisdiction with the courts of a non-Contracting State. In this case the English court could apply the national laws of *forum non conveniens* and it retained jurisdiction under s 49 of the 1982 Act to stay or dismiss the English proceedings if it decided that the Argentine court was the more appropriate forum to decide the case.

Jurisdiction based upon submission by the defendant

Article 18 states that:

Apart from jurisdiction derived from other provisions of this Convention, a court of a Contracting State for whom a defendant enters an appearance shall have jurisdiction. This rule shall not apply where appearance was entered solely to contest jurisdiction, or where another court has exclusive jurisdiction by virtue of Article 16.

Therefore regardless of the rules relating to domicile, if a plaintiff issues proceedings in the jurisdiction of a Contracting State in which the defendant is not domiciled, but the defendant nevertheless acknowledges service of the writ he will be submitting to the jurisdiction of the courts of that Contracting State which will then have jurisdiction.

Exclusive jurisdiction

Article 16

There are five separate categories of exclusive jurisdiction under art 16. These five categories will apply irrespective of the situation of domicile or of the contractual choice of a different Contracting State by the parties, or in the event of submission by the defendant to the jurisdiction of another Contracting State's courts.

The exclusive jurisdiction categories set out under art 16 are based upon the connections between the subject matter of the litigation and a particular Contracting State. In these instances, the connections were considered to be so close as to justify jurisdictional exclusivity of the Contracting States forum.

The courts of a Contracting State shall therefore have exclusive jurisdiction in the following circumstances:

(1) In proceedings which have as their object rights *in rem* in, or tenancies of, immovable property: the courts of the Contracting State in which the property is situated.

(2) In proceedings which have as their object the validity of the constitution, the nullity or the dissolution of companies or other legal persons or associations of natural or legal persons, or the decisions of their organs: the courts of the Contracting State in which the company, legal person or association has its seat.

(3) In proceedings which have as their object the validity of entries in public registers: the courts of the Contracting State in which the register is kept.

(4) In proceedings concerned with the registration or validity of patents, trade marks, designs or other similar rights required to be deposited or registered: the courts of the Contracting State in which the deposit or registration has been applied for, has taken place or is under the terms of an international convention deemed to have taken place.

(5) In proceedings concerned with the enforcement of judgments: the courts of the Contracting State in which the judgment has been or is to be enforced.

The counterpart to art 16 is art 19 of the Convention which provides as follows:

Where a court of a Contracting State is seised of a claim which is principally concerned with a matter over which the courts of another Contracting State have exclusive jurisdiction by virtue of Article 16, it shall declare of its own motion that it has no jurisdiction.

It must be emphasised that art 16 confers exclusive jurisdiction over the principal proceedings and not any incidental matters. The categories of cases set out in art 16 must therefore form the principal subject matter of the action for art 16 to apply.

A good example of the sort of case which will fall within the ambit of art 16(2) is the recent case heard in March 1990 in the English High Court: *Newtherapeutics Ltd v Kats* [1991] Ch 226; 3 WLR 1183; [1991] 2 All ER 151. In that case the plaintiff was a company registered in England but managed exclusively outside the UK, mainly in France. The company commenced proceedings against two of its directors, one of whom was domiciled in France. The allegations related to the individual defendants entering into a contract on behalf of the company on terms unfavourable to the company. It was alleged that the directors had been in breach of their duty of acting in the utmost good faith to the company and that they had exceeded their authority as directors in signing the contract without first convening a meeting of the Board of Directors of the company. The proceedings were commenced in the English courts but the French defendant, on the basis that he was domiciled in France, claimed that under the 1968 Convention he ought to be sued in France.

The English courts held that under art 16(2) of the Convention exclusive jurisdiction was granted in 'proceedings which have as their object the validity of . . . the decisions of the organs of companies . . .'. In this context the 'object' of the proceedings referred to the subject matter of the proceedings. In this case the main claim against the French director related to the absence of a Board resolution and the need to have one. The subject matter of the proceedings therefore concerned the validity or invalidity of decisions of the company's organs and the matter therefore fell within art 16(2) and the English High Court determined that it had exclusive jurisdiction to hear the action against the French defendant.

Article 17
Article 17 states that:

If the parties, one or more of whom is domiciled in a Contracting State, have agreed that a court or courts of a Contracting State are to have jurisdiction to settle any disputes which have arisen or which may arise in connection with a particular legal relationship, that court or those courts shall have exclusive jurisdiction.

Any such agreement conferring jurisdiction must be in writing or evidenced in writing, or, in international trade or commerce, in a form which accords with practices in that trade or commerce of which the parties are or ought to have been aware. Where such an agreement is concluded by parties, none of whom is domiciled in a Contracting State, the courts of other Contracting States shall have no jurisdiction over their disputes unless the court or courts chosen have declined jurisdiction.

The court or courts of a Contracting State on which a trust instrument has conferred jurisdiction shall have exclusive jurisdiction in any proceedings brought against a settlor, trustee or beneficiary, if relations between these persons or their rights or obligations under the trust are involved.

Agreement or provisions of a trust instrument conferring jurisdiction should have no legal force if they are contrary to the provisions of Articles 12 or 15, or if the courts whose jurisdiction they purport to exclude have exclusive jurisdiction by virtue of Article 16.

If an agreement conferring jurisdiction was concluded for the benefit of only one of the parties, that party shall retain the right to bring proceedings in any other court which has jurisdiction by virtue of this Convention.

Therefore, in any contract, if one or more of the parties is domiciled in a Contracting State, and if jurisdiction is conferred on the courts of any Contracting State, then those courts will have exclusive jurisdiction and no disputes between the parties can be litigated in any other jurisdiction. The chosen court will have exclusive and mandatory jurisdiction under art 17.

Under art 17, businessmen have the ability, at the time of concluding contracts, to reduce the risk of jurisdiction disputes occurring at a later stage and to secure the resolution of any dispute in their chosen forum.

The various parts of art 17 need to be analysed independently.

Non-exclusive jurisdiction clauses If the parties to an agreement, one of whom is domiciled in a Contracting State, sign an agreement which contains a non-exclusive submission to the jurisdiction of a Contracting State, then this would still have the effect of excluding the jurisdictions which would otherwise be imposed on the parties by other Articles of the Convention. This rule was recently upheld in the English courts in the case of *Kurz v Stella Musical Veranstaltungs GmbH* [1991] 3 WLR 1046. In that case the defendant argued that the non-exclusive choice of a jurisdiction would not qualify for validity under art 17. However, the High Court held that art 17 did not mean 'unique' in that the parties were limited to using only a single jurisdiction. Article 17 meant only that their choice, whatever it was, should have the effect to exclude other jurisdictions.

Relationship of Article 17 to other Articles

(a) *Articles 12 and 15* Article 17, para 3, expressly states that an agreement conferring jurisdiction under art 17 shall have no legal force if it is contrary to the provisions of arts 12 and 15 relating to insurance and consumer contracts respectively. Therefore, even if the requirements of art 17, para 1, are satisfied, in normal circumstances they will not suffice in insurance and consumer transactions. The requirements of arts 12 and 15 must also be fulfilled for the choice of jurisdiction to be effective.

(b) *Article 16*   In accordance with art 17, para 3, the exclusive jurisdiction granted by art 16 should take precedence over any agreement conferring jurisdiction under art 17.

(c) *Article 18*   Article 18 also takes precedence over art 17. If the defendant enters an appearance to the plaintiff's action in one Contracting State then jurisdiction will be available in that Contracting State despite the fact that the parties may have previously agreed to litigate in the courts of another Contracting State, in accordance with art 17.

(d) *Article 24*   Article 24 also takes precedence over art 17. It is therefore possible for a party, in accordance with art 24, to apply for provisional and/or protective relief in the court of any Contracting State despite the existence of a clause in an agreement between the parties conferring jurisdiction on another Contracting State in accordance with art 17. In such circumstances art 17 will operate so as to confer jurisdiction as to the substance and merits of the case on the designated Contracting State. Article 24 is looked at in greater detail below.

The operation of Article 17, paragraph 4   This paragraph has the effect of precluding the exclusive jurisdiction otherwise conferred by art 17, para 1, if one party alone will have the benefit of the choice of the jurisdiction clause in the relevant agreement.

To ascertain 'benefit' in this context the courts must examine the joint intention of the parties at the time of the agreement. The court will not automatically assume that the choice of one party's domicile was concluded to the benefit of that party alone. The court will consider the terms of the jurisdiction clause itself, other indications in the contract as a whole and the circumstances in which the contract was concluded.

An example of such a jurisdiction clause conferring benefit would be a clause which indicated expressly the party for whose benefit the clause was concluded, or which gave one party a wider jurisdiction than the other when specifying the courts before which each party may commence proceedings. In the case of *Anterist v Credit Lyonnais* the jurisdiction clause conferred jurisdiction to the courts of the place of the 'relevant branch' of the bank and this was held to be an example of a clause conferring jurisdiction for the benefit of only one party: the bank.

Agreements between parties who are not domiciled in a Contracting State The final sentence of art 17, para 1, states:

Where such an agreement is concluded by parties, none of whom is domiciled in the Contracting State, the courts of other Contracting States shall have no jurisdiction over their disputes unless the court or courts chosen have declined jurisdiction.

The position, therefore, is that both national laws and the rules of the Convention are applicable in these circumstances. If the courts of a Contracting State are chosen by parties who are not domiciled in a Contracting State, then those courts do not have *mandatory* jurisdiction under the Convention.

For example, if the English courts are selected in these circumstances, there will be no obligation to accept jurisdiction and the courts will apply the usual rules of *forum non conveniens* in accordance with English and Welsh law in order to decide whether to hear, stay or strike out the proceedings before it.

Although the English courts will therefore apply national law in determining jurisdiction, the Convention is relevant because the courts of the other Contracting States cannot accept jurisdiction until the English courts have declined jurisdiction. The position therefore is that the English courts have *exclusive* jurisdiction, in relation to other Contracting States, until a decision is made by the courts whether to accept jurisdiction or not.

Choice of courts in a non-Contracting State Article 17 does not apply to the choice of courts in a non-Contracting State. The position is therefore uncertain as to whether such a jurisdiction clause may preclude the court of a Contracting State from exercising jurisdiction in circumstances whereby it would have jurisdiction under the Convention, for example if one of the parties was domiciled in a Contracting State or if the Contracting State had exclusive jurisdiction in accordance with art 16.

The different Contracting States may adopt different solutions to this problem. One solution would be for the courts of the Contracting State to decline jurisdiction until the chosen non-Contracting State's courts decided whether to refuse or exercise jurisdiction. Only if the non-Contracting State's courts refused jurisdiction would the Contracting State's courts then exercise jurisdiction under the rules of the Convention. This solution would at least take into account the parties' intentions as expressed in the jurisdiction clause and would also take account of the actions of the courts of the chosen non-Contracting State.

Special jurisdiction

Article 5 states that a person domiciled in a Contracting State may be sued in another Contracting State in certain situations. Examples are as follows:

(1) In matters relating to a contract, in the courts for the place of performance of the obligation in question.

(2) In matters relating to tort in the courts for the place where the harmful event has occurred. The infringement of intellectual property rights constitutes a tort and therefore the courts of the country where the infringement (the harmful event) occurred will have jurisdiction.

(3) In a civil claim for damages based on an act giving rise to criminal proceedings then, to the extent that the court has jurisdiction under its own law to entertain civil proceedings, the court seised of the criminal proceedings will have jurisdiction.

Article 6 also sets out situations in which the courts of a Contracting State may have special jurisdiction regardless of domicile. For example, if the person is one of a number of defendants, then that person may be sued in the courts of the place where any one of the defendants is domiciled. Another example would be in the case of a counterclaim arising from the same contract or facts on which the original claim was based, and the court in which the original claim is pending will have jurisdiction.

Examples of the application of the jurisdiction rules
A useful example is in the case of a party needing to protect its intellectual property rights. If the plaintiff wishes to take action to prevent an infringement of, say, its trade marks, the rules relating to jurisdiction will operate as follows:

(1) The plaintiff may sue the infringer in its country of domicile provided the domicile is in a Contracting State.

(2) Alternatively, by virtue of art 5 the infringer may be sued in the courts of the country where the infringement (the harmful event) occurred. The question then arises: what is the harmful event? The harmful act may be the application of the trade mark to the goods (in one Contracting State) and the importation of the goods bearing the infringing trade mark (into another Contracting State). It can be argued that the harmful act will be both the importation (probably by a distributor) and the application of the trade marks by the manufacturer. However, any action

against the manufacturer in respect of the application of the infringing trade mark to the goods will have to be issued in the jurisdiction of the manufacturer unless the manufacturer was a party to the importation of the goods into the distributor's jurisdiction.

(3) In the case of *Handelskwekerii Gj Bier BV v Mines de Potasse d'Alsace* (Case 21/76 [1977] CMLR 284) the European Court held that jurisdiction may be conferred on the courts of the country where both the harmful act was perpetrated and where the damage was suffered. For example, if a plaintiff in England or Wales wished to take action for infringement of its trade marks and the act of infringement took place in France he could commence proceedings in England or Wales if he was able to show actual financial loss incurred in England or Wales and a direct connection between the economic loss and the infringing act.

However, in such a case if the English courts did accept jurisdiction the question of infringement would have to be decided according to French law because the infringing act took place in France. The relevant law will be the law relating to the rights recognised in the jurisdiction where the harmful act occurred.

(4) In any proceedings concerning the registration or validity of trade marks the courts of the Contracting State in which, for example, the registration of the trade marks has been applied for, will have exclusive jurisdiction by virtue of art 16.

An exception to this rule, in the future, would be proceedings relating to the proposed Community Patent which, when it is implemented, will be valid for the whole Community.

The plaintiff should therefore consider commencing any action for infringement of its trade marks in the country where the rights are registered even if the defendant may not be domiciled in that Contracting State and even if the harmful act of infringement occurred in another Contracting State. If a plaintiff commences an infringement action in the jurisdiction where the harmful act occurred, and if the defendant challenges the validity of the trade mark, the defendant could argue that, in accordance with art 16, the proceedings should be referred to the courts in the country where the trade marks are registered thereby causing a substantial increase in the legal costs and a potential duplication of the litigation.

These are the jurisdiction rules which apply to all substantive proceedings. Different rules apply in relation to proceedings for provisional relief, including urgent protective relief.

Proceedings for interim relief

As has already been stated, the object of the Convention is to provide for a simpler and universal system of recognition of judgments. A judgment, even if it is enforceable in another Contracting State, is of no use if the defendant has already removed his assets from the Contracting State, so that execution of the judgment is frustrated.

To avoid this, art 24 provides that interim relief may be granted in a court other than that which has jurisdiction under the Convention. Thus interim measures can be obtained in Contracting States preventing, for instance, a defendant from removing his assets.

The Article states that:

Application may be made to the courts of a Contracting State for such provisional, including protective, measures as may be available under the law of that State, even if, under this Convention, the courts of another Contracting State have jurisdiction as to the substance of the matter.

In order to obtain interim relief, the following conditions in art 24 must be satisfied:

(1) The measures required must be provisional, and they can be, although they do not necessarily need to be, protective.

(2) They must be available under the law of the State in which they are being applied for.

(3) The measures must be 'under the Convention', ie the main subject matter in connection with which the provisional measure is being applied for, must fall within the Convention's scope.

(4) The courts of one of the Contracting States must have jurisdiction as to the substance of the matter in respect of which provisional relief is being applied.

Article 24 therefore creates an additional ground of jurisdiction. Once the criteria listed above are satisfied, a State has jurisdiction even if the defendant is not domiciled in that country, or that State does not have jurisdiction under any of the other provisions in the Convention. Article 24 may be used even if proceedings in another Member State are merely in contemplation; the main proceedings do not need to have been commenced.

Article 24 appears in Table II of the Convention and accordingly sets out the rules relating to jurisdiction. Enforcement of provisional orders is dealt with under Table III.

Each of these conditions is now looked at in turn.

Provisional, including protective, measures

The relief claimed under art 24 must be of a temporary nature and dependent for its continuance upon the outcome of proceedings in the main action. If the relief granted under art 24 would fully satisfy the plaintiff's cause of action then it is not provisional.

Also, one must differentiate orders which are simply variable, or revocable, from those which are of a truly temporary nature and dependent on further proceedings.

An example of a provisional remedy in England or Wales is the Mareva injunction preventing the removal of any assets from England or Wales. Similar orders are available in the other Contracting States. The relief in this context is not only limited to orders freezing or protecting assets. Any interlocutory injunction will be provisional, including orders restraining the infringement of intellectual property or the publication of defamatory statements or the enforceability of potentially invalid resolutions passed at shareholders' meetings.

The words 'including protective' suggest that the measures applied for do not necessarily need to be protective. For instance, an application under art 24 could be made to obtain samples, or to inspect property, both being provisional measures.

'Such . . . measures as may be available'

The issue here is whether all the remedies known to the national law of a State are available on an application under art 24 regardless of whether such remedies would be available in the courts of the Contracting State which has jurisdiction as to the substance of the case. The likely answer is that they are. Therefore, whether or not any particular Contracting State has the power to grant the provisional relief requested depends on its own national laws, even if such a provisional measure may be unavailable from the courts of the Contracting State hearing the main action. Regard must also be had for its relationship with any main proceedings which may not have been issued yet (for example, as to the time limit allowed for commencement of the main proceedings in the other Contracting State).

'The courts of another Contracting State must have jurisdiction "under this Convention"'

The substance of the claim must fall within the Convention's scope. The courts of Contracting States should only be required to enforce each other's provisional orders if the substance of the action falls within the Convention. For example, interim relief cannot be obtained and 'exported' in matrimonial matters.

However, a question arises as to the degree that the ancillary, provisional proceedings are linked with a main action, the subject matter of which is excluded from the Convention.

The issue is whether provisional proceedings ancillary to excluded main proceedings are automatically excluded from the Convention's scope or whether they are only so excluded if they concern or are closely connected with a subject matter excluded from the Convention.

It is the latter concept which has been suggested by the European Court in the *de Cavel* cases (1979 ECR 1055 and 1990 ECR 731): whether the ancillary proceedings are concerned or closely connected with subject matter excluded from the Convention. Although the court did not go on to clearly define this criteria, this approach was preferred to the automatic exclusion of the ancillary proceedings. It is likely therefore that there will be some consideration by the courts, hearing the application for interim relief, as to whether the ancillary proceedings relate to subject matter, in the main action, outside the scope of the Convention. For example, in a divorce case, which is outside the Convention's scope, it could be said that the ownership of property by the spouses relates to a prior legal relationship and prior property rights. Therefore any application to freeze one of the party's assets could be said to relate to subject matter not excluded from the Convention's scope, and does not relate to the divorce proceedings as such.

However, it is certain that if the main proceedings fall within the Convention an application for interim relief may be available under art 24.

'Even if . . . the courts of another Contracting State have jurisdiction'

If the courts of another Contracting State have jurisdiction in the main proceedings interim relief may be sought under art 24 in a different jurisdiction.

In the interests of creating a community wide system of enforcement of judgments, art 24 should be applicable both when the jurisdiction of the Contracting State in the main proceedings is determined by the Convention and also when it is decided under that State's national rules.

By contrast, art 24 will not apply if the proceedings of substance are taken in a non-Contracting State.

Ex parte decisions   It was decided by the court in the case of *Denilauler v Snc Couchet Freres* [1981] ECR 1553, that interim relief would not be enforceable in other Contracting States in cases where the judicial decision to grant it was made without:

(a) prior service on the defendant; and
(b) where the defendant was not summoned to appear at the hearing.

However, art 24 does not preclude provisional or protective measures ordered in the State of origin pursuant to provisional proceedings—even though by default of appearance—from being the subject of recognition and authorisation for enforcement. Therefore, in *inter partes* applications, where proceedings were served on the defendant, but he failed to attend the court hearing, any subsequent order is 'exportable' and can be enforced in other Contracting States.

Courts which are applied to *ex parte* for provisional, including protective, relief, should not have to determine whether they have jurisdiction under any ground other than art 24. Problems of proving jurisdiction, for example, based on the defendant's domicile, may arise in view of the fact that the defendant will not be appearing at court. For the court to require a full hearing as to the domicile of the defendant, would go against the spirit of the Convention as it would delay the granting of interim relief in cases where speedy action is necessary. The court may, therefore, base jurisdiction solely upon art 24.

Recognition

The essential principle is that any judgment given in a Contracting State will be recognised in the other Contracting States without any special procedure being required (art 26, para 1).

The scope for challenging the jurisdiction of the original court is extremely limited.

Article 28 of the Convention lays down certain rules in respect of recognition:

(a) in considering an allegation of lack of jurisdiction the national courts are bound by the findings of fact upon which the original court based its jurisdiction;
(b) a judgment will not be recognised if it conflicts with the jurisdictional rules under arts 7–12a of the Convention (insurance), 13–15 (consumer contracts) or arts 16 and 17 (exclusive jurisdiction);
(c) the jurisdiction of the court of the Contracting State in which the judgment was given may not be reviewed subject to (b) above.

In general the grounds upon which a judgment can be challenged are procedural rather than substantial. The following are five possible grounds under art 27 where a judgment may not be recognised and they are as follows:

(a) if such recognition is contrary to public policy in the State in which recognition is sought;

(b) where the judgment was given in default of appearance by the defendant, who was not duly served with the document which commenced the proceedings in sufficient time to enable him to arrange for his defence;

(c) if the judgment is irreconcilable with a judgment given in a dispute between the same parties in the 'importing' State;

(d) if the court of the State in which the judgment was given, in order to arrive at its judgment, has decided a preliminary question concerning the status or legal capacity of natural persons, rights in property arising out of a matrimonial relationship, wills or succession in a way that conflicts with a rule of the private international law of the State in which the recognition is sought, unless the same result would have been reached by the application of the rules of private international law of that State; and

(e) if the judgment is irreconcilable with an earlier recognisable judgment given in a non-Contracting State involving the same cause of action between the same parties.

In accordance with (a) above, fraud will be a ground for reviewing the foreign judgment.

The Convention has no application to proceedings for the recognition and enforcement of the judgments of non-Contracting States. In England and Wales therefore the Convention will not apply to proceedings under the Administration of Justice Act 1920 which relates to the reciprocal recognition of judgments with various non-Contracting States. This rule was upheld by the Court of Appeal in *Owens Bank Ltd v Bracco* (1991) *The Times*, 15 May. The court confirmed that the Convention was only concerned with the jurisdiction of the courts of Contracting States *inter se* and the reciprocal recognition and enforcement of their judgments. The Convention did not apply to proceedings for the recognition of a judgment of a non-Contracting State even if the defendant was domiciled in a Contracting State.

Enforcement

Lawyers in all Contracting States must first of all decide whether the Convention applies in relation to a foreign judgment before deciding whether to make an application, under the rules of the Convention, to register that judgment in the courts of the 'importing' State. For example, in the United Kingdom, there are currently four methods for the enforcement of foreign judgments in England. They are as follows:

(1) The Brussels Convention of 1968.

(2) Foreign Judgments (Reciprocal Enforcement) Act 1933: this covers a list of countries set out in the Act including some countries covered by the Convention. However, enforcement rules under the Convention will always apply to those countries which are also covered by the 1933 Act.

(3) Administration of Justice Act 1920: a list of countries covered by the 1920 Act is found in the Supreme Court Rules applicable to the High Court (Ord 71(1), (3)).

(4) Common law action which will cover the judgments given in countries not covered by the Convention or the above two Acts.

The Lugano Convention of 1988 is not yet in force but will in due course provide another convention for courts of the Contracting States to the Brussels Convention to take into account when determining the appropriate rules for the enforcement of judgments. The parties to the Lugano Convention are the EFTA Member States; namely Austria, Finland, Iceland, Norway, Sweden and Switzerland. The Lugano Convention will be scheduled to the Civil Jurisdiction and Judgments Act 1991 when it comes into force in the UK.

The Lugano Convention will contain similar provisions for EFTA Member States relating to jurisdiction, recognition and enforcement as in the Brussels Convention. The important rule is contained in art 54B(2)(c) of the Lugano Convention which provides that that Convention will only apply where either the country in which the original judgment was given, or the country in which the judgment is to be enforced, is not a member of the European Community. Therefore, a judgment given in the Italian courts against a company domiciled in Switzerland will be enforceable in the English courts pursuant to the provisions of the Brussels Convention and not those of the Lugano Convention. Similarly, a judgment given in the Swiss courts against a company domiciled in Germany would be enforceable in England pursuant to the provisions of the Lugano Convention because the country in which the judgment was given was an EFTA Member State.

Having determined whether or not the Brussels Convention will apply to the foreign judgment, then it is necessary to consider the enforcement provisions of that Convention. According to art 54, the Convention will only apply to:

(a) proceedings instituted after the entry into force of the Convention; or

(b) to judgments given after the date of entry into force of the Convention in proceedings instituted before that date, if jurisdiction was founded upon rules which accorded with those provided for in the Convention or in a similar convention between the 'exporting' State and the 'importing' State containing reciprocal enforcement provisions.

Article 31 provides that the judgment of a Contracting State, enforceable in that Contracting State, is enforceable in any other Contracting State if, on the application of any interested party, it is registered in the Contracting State where enforcement is sought.

The precise manner of giving expression for authorisation is a matter for the national procedure of each enforcement State. Some States require a separate order to be made following an *ex parte* application and in other States a copy of the judgment is merely stamped in order to register it.

In the UK the application for registration must be made to the High Court in England and in Northern Ireland and in Scotland to the Court of Accession. The reasonable costs or expenses incidental to its registration shall be recouperable as if they were sums recoverable under the judgment.

Interest on the judgment debt depends on the law of the Contracting State in which the judgment was issued. The rate and the date of interest will be fixed by the 'exporting' court. Although both the Convention and the Act are silent on this point, it seems clear that the judgment must be registered in the currency in which it was given.

In addition to the essential pre-conditions for the recognition of judgments described above, art 31 provides for one more important positive requirement for the actual registration of a judgment in a Contracting State and an enforcement order: the foreign judgment must be enforceable in the judgment State.

A judgment will still be enforceable even if it is capable of being subsequently varied, superseded or cancelled by a final judgment of a court of the judgment State, *provided* it is enforceable for the time being in the judgment State. For example, if an appeal has been lodged in the judgment State, and the judgment at least provisionally cannot be enforced in the judgment State, then the judgment cannot be enforced in any other Contracting State in which the defendant's assets may be located.

Other requirements which are likely to arise are as follows:

(a) a translation of the judgment (if necessary) should also be lodged in the registering court;
(b) if there is a dispute in the judgment State as to whether or not the judgment has been satisfied, then the judgment is unlikely to be enforced;
(c) the applicant for the enforcement must be 'an interested party'. This will apply in all Contracting States;
(d) certain documents must be produced including evidence showing that the foreign judgment was served on the defendant.

As mentioned above, fraud can be used as a defence to enforcement under the Brussels Convention (art 27(1)). If the foreign judgment was obtained by fraud and cannot be set aside by an application to the court which gave the judgment then an application can be made by the defendant in the importing country to resist the enforcement proceedings. Article 29 of the Convention prohibits the review of a foreign judgment as to substance. Therefore, in enforcement proceedings under the Convention, any challenge to the enforcement of a foreign judgment, based on fraud, will not be permitted except where it would be permitted to set aside a judgment of the court of the 'importing' State. For example, in the English courts, an English judgment can be set aside where there is fresh evidence of fraud. Therefore, in the English courts, fresh evidence of fraud would be required to dismiss or stay enforcement proceedings of a foreign judgment in another Contracting State.

Practical procedure for registration and enforcement of judgments in and from the English courts

The procedural rules for registration and enforcement will vary in each Contracting State. However, the registration procedures to be followed are essentially formalities. Nevertheless, it will be necessary to instruct local lawyers in the 'registration State' to deal with these formalities.

As an example, the procedural rules relating to English judgments are set out below.

Registration of an English judgment abroad

Any judgment in the English courts, which is due to be exported to another Contracting State, will have to be certified, in order to be registered in the courts of the importing country, in accordance with the 1982 Act. In High Court cases, the plaintiff's solicitors must apply for a certified copy and they must submit a sworn affidavit to the High Court formally requesting a copy of the judgment to be certified. The application is therefore made *ex parte* and the defendant is not represented. Leave to apply for a certified judgment will then be endorsed on the affidavit. The endorsed affidavit and a sealed copy of the judgment must then be presented again to the High Court in order to obtain the certified judgment. The certificate will be signed by a High Court Master and the sealed certificate and the judgment can then be collected from the High Court a few days later.

This procedure will therefore take a few days and this should be taken into account by the plaintiff's solicitors when calculating the length of time required before a UK judgment can be exported for registration in another Contracting State.

Consideration should be given to applying for ancillary relief when a judgment is exported to another Contracting State for registration. For example, in Ireland, it is possible to enforce a UK judgment by asking the Master in the Irish High Court to make it a condition of the order of registration that the defendant must not reduce its assets within the Irish jurisdiction below the amount of the judgment. In effect, a Mareva injunction is granted freezing the defendant's assets between the period of registration and the expiry of the time period during which the defendant can appeal against the registration of the judgment. The possibility of obtaining similar protective measures should be explored when registering foreign judgments in all other Contracting States.

Registration of a foreign judgment in the English Courts

(1) The application for registration must be made *ex parte*, that is to say without notice to the defendant, supported by an affidavit stating the following:

(a) whether the judgment provides for the payment of a sum or sums of money;
(b) whether interest is recoverable on the judgment in accordance with the law of the State in which the judgment was given and, if so, the rate of interest, the date from which it is recoverable and the date on which it ceases to accrue;
(c) an address within the jurisdiction for service of process on the applicant and the name and the usual or last known address or place of business of the person against whom the judgment was given;
(d) to the best information and belief of the deponent:
   (i) the grounds on which the right to enforce the judgment is vested in the applicant; and
   (ii) as the case may require either that at the date of the application the judgment has not been satisfied or the part or amount in respect of which it remains unsatisfied.
(2) There must be exhibited to the affidavit:
(a) the judgment (or a certified copy) together with documents showing that the judgment has been served and is enforceable;
(b) in the case of a judgment in default of a defence being served by the defendant, then the original or certified copy of the document which establishes the defendant being served with the documents commencing proceedings;
(c) if the applicant is in receipt of some form of financial assistance in the proceedings then the relevant document should be lodged;
(d) a certified English translation must be lodged.

The English court must then give its decision without delay following this procedure. Registration can only be refused by an English court for one of the reasons specified in arts 27 or 28. The court must notify the decision to the applicant without delay and, if enforcement is authorised by the court, then the applicant must draw up the court order. The court will state a period within which an appeal may be made against the order and must notify the applicant and execution cannot take place until that period has expired.

A Notice of Registration may then be served on the judgment debtor by delivering it to him personally or sending it to him at his usual or last known address or place of business.

Appeals and stage of execution

If enforcement is authorised the judgment debtor can appeal against the decision within one month of service of the notice. The period will extend to two months where the judgment debtor is domiciled in a Contracting State other than England or Wales.

An English or Welsh court will stay proceedings where it is notified that an appeal has been lodged against the judgment in the country where the judgment was given (thereby staying the enforcement of the judgment in the judgment State) or where the time for such an appeal has not yet expired.

During the above one month/two months time period specified for an appeal to the High Court in the United Kingdom, no enforcement procedures other than protective measures can take place. The judgment creditor can, in certain circumstances, apply for an order freezing a defendant's assets or restraining any continuing infringement of its intellectual property rights.

An example of a successful appeal against the registration of a foreign judgment was in the recent case in the High Court of *EMI Records Ltd v Modern Music Carl-Ulrich Walterbach GmbH* [1991] 3 WLR 663. In that case an injunction had been obtained on an *ex parte* application to the Land Court in Germany without prior notice or service of documents on the defendant. Judgment was initially registered in the English High Court but the defendant, an English company, appealed and it was held, on appeal, that this was not a judgment within the scope of the Convention and the registration of the judgment of the Land Court of Berlin, which restrained the English company from reproducing and distributing recordings of a pop group, would be set aside.

Nicholas Rose

Belgium

Introduction

Injunction overview

Most of the types of injunctions which can be obtained in the United Kingdom are available in Belgium.

Classification, however, is usually by reference to the type of proceedings leading to the injunction rather than to the type of measure which can be applied for.

Under the Belgian system, injunctions can be sought from different courts, at different levels and under different forms depending on the result sought, the subject matter of the dispute and its circumstances.

Injunctions can be applied for:

(1) Within the framework of proceedings relating to the merits of the case: prior to hearing the merits of the case, the judge may order measures which will assist the provisional settlement of certain matters as well as investigational measures. This type of decision (in French called *jugement d'avant-dire droit*—in Dutch *vonnis alvorens recht te doen*) ensures the protection of interests which would or could be jeopardised by the length of the proceedings until the trial. Both mandatory and prohibitory injunctions can be requested. They always will be interim injunctions, pending the decision regarding the merits of the case.

(2) By applying for it in chambers (*référé—kortgeding*): measures can be ordered by the Judge in Chambers regarding immediate but temporary action on urgent issues. The Judge in Chambers is entitled to give both mandatory and prohibitory injunctions. They will always consist of interim measures since the Judge in Chambers is not entitled to decide on the merits of the rights of the parties. Injunctions granted in chambers usually aim to prevent a wrongdoing from happening although they can also involve investigation measures.

(3) By filing an application in the form of proceedings in chambers (*procédure comme en référé—procedure zoals in kortgeding*) when such is authorised by law. Specific laws provide for actions where the judge acts, under the same procedures as if he is in chambers, to make a judgment on the merits. A *procédure comme en référé* therefore implies a full trial of the case, but a trial in Belgium basically means that the parties will exchange submissions and present their case orally before the judge who will then make his decision.

Within the framework of any court proceedings, the court may also order specific measures with regard to discovery and evidence, for instance ordering a party to produce documents. The court's decision (called *jugement sur incident—vonnis op tussengeschil*) constitutes a final adjudication on the specific *incident* brought up during the court proceedings. Measures of investigation may also be ordered by the president of the court sitting in chambers to deal provisionally with matters of special urgency. This chapter does not examine the various cases where such a *jugement sur incident* can be sought, with the exception of the proceedings regarding the production of documents, see p 65.

Finally, by applying to the judge of seizure (*juge des saisies—beslagrechter*), it is possible to obtain an authorisation to freeze or force the sale of the debtor's assets. These measures are examined at p 64.

Scope of the injunction

Interlocutory judgments

Interlocutory judgments can be made with regard to the same issues as those which can be handled in proceedings in chambers. Obtaining such a judgment, however, is not subject to the requirement of 'urgency' as required when applying for a judgment 'in chambers'.

Case law shows that interlocutory judgments have been made, for example, in order to obtain:

(a) the production of documents;
(b) a provisional prohibition on advertising price reductions or making comparisons of price while awaiting a decision on the legitimacy of advertisement;
(c) a temporary prohibition on making use of a slogan while awaiting a decision as to its compatibility with the Fair Trade Practice Act;
(d) provisional amounts of compensation or fees.

Court decisions in proceedings in chambers

Article 584 of the Judicial Code enumerates a certain number of measures which may be ordered by the presidents of the courts provided the conditions thereto are fulfilled.

The intervention of the Judge in Chambers, however, is not limited to the cases listed by that provision.

Generally speaking, it can be stressed that proceedings in chambers have skyrocketed over the last few years. As a result of the congestion of the usual courts and the consequent slowness of procedures in Belgium, lawyers have shown a noticeable tendency to make use of the *référé*, with the hope of giving their clients a speedier result. Judges have responded by extending the *référé* to matters which by tradition were excluded from its field as well as by enlarging the concept of *référé* itself (see below).

A good example of the extension of the practice of proceedings in chambers is to be found in the *référé-provision—provisie in kortgeding*. Here the judge grants a creditor the payment of a provisional amount. Initially hesitant, case law now appears quite favourable to the *référé-provision*. Numerous decisions allow claims of *référé-provision* in diverse fields. The *référé-provision* is favoured particularly within the framework of disputes relating to compensation for road accidents, labour law and social security.

Generally speaking, injunctions of all kinds can be obtained from the Judge in Chambers in the most varied matters. These include:

Company law The Presidents of the Courts of Commerce often play a major role within the framework of disputes involving company law, and they usually show a noteworthy audacity, efficiency and flexibility. Matters subject to the injunction procedure include:

(a) the prohibition on a shareholders' general meeting from deciding on specific items;
(b) the suspension of decisions of a general meeting, of the board of directors or of the managers;
(c) the appointment of a provisional manager (*administrateur provisoire—voorlopige bewindvoerder*), of an officer *ad hoc* who will call and chair a general meeting, of a *controller ad hoc* entrusted, for example, with the specific task of preventing assets of a company from being transferred abroad;
(d) the prohibition on a transfer of shares; and
(e) the authorisation for the shareholder (*associé*) of a co-operative

company to be assisted by his lawyer during the discussions relating to his expulsion from the company.

Contractual law   The Judge in Chambers shows an increasing tendency to intervene in contractual relations by ordering measures which result in a party being granted the benefit of the rights he alleges, without waiting for a decision of the court which has jurisdiction over the merits. Examples in this area of case law are to be found at any stage of the contractual relationship and include:

(1) formation of contracts

(a) the President of the Court of Commerce of Brussels has temporarily prohibited a group of shareholders from selling their majority holding to persons other than those with whom they had come to an agreement in principle after lengthy negotiations;
(b) the same judge considered himself competent to verify whether the conditions laid down by a car dealer for the acceptance of orders made by an intermediary are in conformity with arts 85 and 86 of the Treaty of Rome;
(c) the courts have prohibited a party from concluding or executing a share transfer agreement until a decision regarding the merits of the case has been reached (the right of the court to order such a measure against the will of one of the parties is disputed as a matter of doctrine);

(2) execution of contractual obligations

(a) the seller of 'goodwill' in a business can be prevented from starting a new competing business in the vicinity of the 'goodwill' sold;
(b) an authorisation can be given to a lessor to recover the equipment which is the subject of a contract of *crédit-bail* which has terminated;
(c) stop orders can be given to a bank within the framework of on-demand guarantees provided, ie, that the call is obviously abusive or fraudulent;
(d) in the absence of any clear obligation, a party has been ordered to complete demolition works, and, if he fails to do so, then he has to pay for the works;

(3) rescission of contracts

(a) a party has been ordered to leave the premises immediately which he is no longer authorised to occupy as a result of the termination of his contract of employment or of the withdrawal of his office;

(b) competition can be prohibited during the period of time provided by contract after its termination, irrespective of the motive of termination;

(c) the consequences of the termination of a distribution agreement of indeterminate duration have been suspended (the jurisdiction of the Judge in Chambers to disregard a decision to terminate a (distribution) contract, which as a rule is an irrevocable and final decision, is again widely disputed as a matter of doctrine).

Administrative law Belgian courts are not entitled to impose prohibitions or suspensions on an administrative authority. However, this will be possible when the administrative deed is so blatantly illegal that it cannot be considered authorised (*voie de fait—daad van geweld*). Another exception allows the Judge in Chambers to intervene conservatorily when, even without amounting to a *voie de fait*, the action of the administration can prejudice subjective rights, the existence of which appear sufficiently likely.

Examples of injunctions ordered in this field are numerous: injunctions obliging an administrative authority to suspend the enforcement of appointments, dismissals, etc whose legality is disputed; imposing on the beneficiary of a building permit a suspension of the execution of the works as a result of an apparent illegality of the permit. Here again the intervention of the Judge in Chambers is constantly increasing. (The law of 15 July 1991 has now also provided for proceedings in chambers before the Council of State (*Conseil d'Etat—Raad Van State*.)

Bill of exchange legislation The courts have, for instance, prohibited the publication of a protested bill of exchange when such would cause irreparable harm.

Employment law In this field, examples of injunctions can be as follows:

(a) an employer has been required to release a sum indisputably owed to an employee (for example, outstanding salary arrears and holiday pay), pending the outcome of the law suit regarding the merits of the case;

(b) an employer has been required to deliver employment documents to the applicant;

(c) the execution of an employment contract has been suspended;

(d) a referendum has to be organised during a strike in order to authorise an employee to ascertain whether his personnel wished to strike.

The intervention of the Judge in Chambers in collective labour conflicts is a rather recent phenomenon. Traditionally, the view was held that the Labour Court was not competent to handle collective disputes which resulted from conflicting interests of social groups and whose solution was negotiated on the basis of political and economic requirements. More and more frequently, the Judge in Chambers is required, and agrees, to make injunctions in order to stop a lock-out, to prohibit specific conditions of strikes or even to prohibit a strike. Most decisions, however, show that courts tend to refrain from intervening in the settlement of the collective dispute itself and to limit their intervention to the settlement of subjective rights which are threatened by behaviour occurring at the occasion of the conflict.

Intellectual property law　Injunctions have been made to order the cessation of counterfeiting acts, the withdrawal of counterfeited products from the market and the sequestration of documents.

Trade mark law　Holders of trade marks often invoke art 13(1) subs 1 and 2 of the Benelux Trade mark Law in order to oppose any use of a similar trade mark, or of a similar sign, in connection with the product for which the trade mark is registered or with similar products. Usually provisional measures are ordered even in circumstances other than where the trade mark or a similar sign is used without valid reasons.

Judgments 'as in chambers'

Specific laws provide for the possibility of obtaining an injunction from the President of the court sitting as in chambers, for example:

(1) Fair trade practices: pursuant to the law of 14 July 1991 it is possible to obtain from the President of the Court of Commerce, acting as in chambers, a court order prohibiting a party from carrying out activities which infringe the provisions of that law. This also enables any seller, whether a trader or not, to obtain the cessation of any act of unfair trade practice made by another seller which causes him damage.

(2) Take over bids: pursuant to the law of 12 March 1989, the Banking Commission (*Commission Bancaire et Financière—Commissie voor het Bank en Financienwezen*) is authorised to seek an injunction from the President of the Court of Commerce acting as in chambers if it considers that the terms and conditions of a planned take over bid do not comply with the Royal Decree dated 8 November 1989. The court may be required to impose on the candidate offeror compliance with those conditions or to prohibit him from gaining any advantage from his infringement.

(3) Employment law: pursuant to the law of 20 September 1948, the President of the Court of Commerce or of the Labour Court, as the case may be, acting as in chambers, is competent to appoint an auditor in companies where the workers' council cannot agree on his appointment.

General principles of civil proceedings

The general principles regulating any civil proceedings are as follows.

(1) Hearings and judgments are public (arts 96 and 97 of the Constitution as well as the European Convention for the Safeguard of Human Rights and Fundamental Freedoms).

(2) The parties dictate the course of the proceedings: since a law suit is intended to obtain the recognition of subjective rights, parties commence, pursue or abandon the proceedings as they deem appropriate. In addition, pursuant to art 1138, 2 of the Judicial Code, the judge may not make decisions on issues which are not submitted to him; this principle is part of Belgian public order.

(3) Proceedings are both written (summons, petition, submissions) and verbal (hearing and pleadings). Parties may agree that proceedings will be conducted exclusively in writing (art 755 of the Judicial Code).

(4) The rights of the defence must be strictly complied with.

(5) Parties must invoke and prove the facts on which their claim or defence is based. The judge, however, may order *ex officio* measures of investigation and even combine them together. The judge may not, however, decide on issues *ultra petita* (ie beyond the limits of the claim and the defence).

(6) As a rule, parties should be diligent in the presentation of their claim and of their defence. Such is not always the case, however, and courts often complain about the lack of diligence, sometimes intentional, of the parties.

In Belgian proceedings, the party who seeks an injunction must have, as in the case of any claimant:

(a) an interest, ie he must derive an effective and personal advantage, either practical or moral, at the time he initiates the proceeding (art 17 of the Judicial Code). That interest must have arisen and be current at the time of commencement of proceedings. However, institution of proceedings in chambers does not require an interest arisen and current and an anticipated dispute suffices;

(b) authority to initiate the proceedings (art 17 of the Judicial Code):

when the claim aims to obtain the recognition of a subjective right and is initiated by the holder of that right, then he will of course, have the authority to initiate proceedings.

In addition, the claimant who seeks an injunction must comply with the specific conditions provided by law (in the Judicial Code or other legal provisions): for example the condition of urgency for proceedings in chambers, and the capacity of a trader being a condition to obtain a stop order under art 95 of the 1991 Fair Trade Practices Act.

Structure of the courts

Summary of the structure of the civil courts

The jurisdiction of the courts is determined on two grounds:

(a) their practical field of activity (*ratione materiae*); and
(b) their geographical area of competence (*ratione loci*).

Jurisdiction based upon the court's practical field of activities

In this area, there are two degrees of jurisdiction in Belgium:

(a) the first degree is the Court of First Instance, the Court of Commerce and the Labour Court as well as the Justice of the Peace;
(b) the second degree is the appropriate Court of Appeal for each of the above, or the Court of First Instance for the decisions made by the Justice of the Peace.

Finally, for extraordinary remedies, there is the Supreme Court, which will not examine the facts of a case and only considers matters of law. The Supreme Court examines the legality of court decisions by second degree jurisdictions and, where applicable, will refer any decisions it revokes to a jurisdiction of second degree for a re-trial.

First degree   Competence to hear law suits in the first degree is granted to:

(1) The Court of First Instance (*tribunal de première instance—rechtbank van eerste aanleg*). This court is granted a general jurisdiction

to deal with all claims except those which fall within the scope of activity of the Court of Appeal and of the Supreme Court.

In addition, the Court of First Instance is granted jurisdiction in specific areas listed in arts 569–572 of the Judicial Code (such as copyright claims above BF 25,000). Specific jurisdiction is granted to some of its judges regarding the protection of young persons (*tribunal de la jeunesse—jeugdrechtbank*).

The Court of First Instance is composed of one or more civil, criminal and juvenile chambers.

(2) The Court of Commerce (*tribunal de commerce—rechtbank van koophandel*) hears all disputes among or against traders and relating to subject matters of a commercial nature provided they do not fall within the general jurisdiction of the Justice of the Peace (arts 573–576 of the Judicial Code as well as art 577).

The Court of Commerce is also granted jurisdiction over specific matters (such as cases relating to bills of exchange and promissory notes, when the amount exceeds BF 50,000, disputes between shareholders, directors and other persons involved in commercial companies).

(3) The Labour Court (*tribunal du travail—arbeidsrechtbank*) handles labour disputes (arts 578–583 of the Judicial Code).

(4) The Presidents of each of the above mentioned courts have jurisdiction to hear cases in chambers (*référé—kortgeding*) and to decide on specific issues on an *ex parte* application (arts 584–589 of the Judicial Code).

The Presidents of the three courts also constitute the *tribunal d'arrondissement* (*arrondissementsrechtbank*), which has jurisdiction to hear the disputes relating to the jurisdiction of the court where the law suit was initially introduced.

(5) The Justice of the Peace (*juge de paix—vrederechter*) has jurisdiction to handle minor law suits (when the amount involved does not exceed BF 50,000), with the exception of those which belong to the special jurisdiction of another court, family matters, real property matters, problems regarding agricultural exploitations, and other issues.

Second degree Appeals lodged against decisions made by the courts in the first degree belong to the jurisdiction of:

(1) the Court of Appeal also includes (as does the Court of First Instance) civil, criminal and juvenile chambers. This Court chiefly hears the appeal of decisions made by the Court of First Instance and of the Court of Commerce (arts 602–606 of the Judicial Code) or by their respective Presidents;

(2) the Labour Court of Appeal (*cour du travail—arbeidshof*) hears disputes relating to decisions made by the Labour Court and its President;

(3) the Court of First Instance is the appeal court for judgments made by the Justice of the Peace; the Court of Commerce is competent to hear appeals in cases which are within its exclusive jurisdiction (art 577 of the Judicial Code).

Pursuant to art 104 of the Constitution, Belgium has five Courts of Appeal: Brussels, which is competent for the province of Brabant; Ghent, for the two provinces of Flanders; Antwerp, for the provinces of Antwerp and Limburg; Liège, for the provinces of Liège, Namur and Luxemburg; Mons, for the province of Hainaut.

Supreme Court   Decisions of the courts of final instance which, in the view of one of the parties, contravene the law or violate procedural requirements, are referred to the Supreme Court (*Cour de Cassation— Hof van Cassatie*) (see also below).

Jurisdiction of the courts based upon geographical limitations

Courts are granted jurisdiction only within the boundaries of the territory they are allocated by law.

Except where international conventions, such as, for example, the Brussels Convention of 1968, provide otherwise or where exclusive jurisdiction is granted to other courts pursuant to the Judicial Code or specific laws (eg art 73 of the law of 28 March 1983 on patents), the claimant is, in Belgian practice, entitled to initiate proceedings, at his choice, before the judge of:

(a) the domicile of the defendant or of one of them;
(b) the place where the obligations in dispute or one of them has arisen or where they are, were or must be carried out;
(c) the domicile elected for the execution of the deed;
(d) the place where the process server has talked to the defendant, if the latter (or, as the case may be, no other defendant) has a domicile in Belgium or abroad.

Foreign nationals may be summoned before the Belgian courts, by writ issued either by a Belgian or by a foreigner in the cases listed in art 635 of the Judicial Code (eg real estate matters; cases where the obligation on which the claim is based has been or must be carried out in Belgium; claims connected with proceedings already pending before a Belgian court, etc) and in any other case where Belgian courts are competent in accordance with international conventions such as the Convention of Brussels of 27 September 1968 on jurisdiction and enforcement of judgments in civil and commercial matters.

Foreigners may be sued before Belgian courts, by Belgians as well as by foreigners, at any time when provisional or protective measures (*mesures provisoires et conservatoires—provisionele en bewarende maatregelen*) are sought. (In accordance with art 24 of the Brussels Convention, this will be the case even where, in accordance with other provisions of that Convention, the courts of another Contracting State have jurisdiction over the substance of the case.)

When injunctions are required in chambers, the case must, as a rule, be initiated before the court which is territorially competent to hear the merits of the case. However, bearing in mind the urgent character of the proceedings in chambers, the case may also be initiated before the court of the place where the measure requested must be enforced or where the urgent circumstances arise.

Supreme Court

Belgium has one single Supreme Court (*Cour de Cassation—Hof van Cassatie*) which has jurisdiction, among other things, over all disputes regarding decisions made by the Courts of Appeal (art 95 of the Constitution).

The Supreme Court includes three different divisions:

- (a) the first division hears appeals to the Supreme Court against decisions in civil and commercial matters;
- (b) the second division, against decisions made in criminal, correctional and police matters;
- (c) the third division, against decisions made in labour matters.

Regional considerations

Belgium is constitutionally structured into:

- (a) three regions (Flanders, Wallonia and Brussels);
- (b) four linguistic regions (the French speaking region, the Dutch speaking region, the German speaking region and the bilingual region of Brussels-capital); and
- (c) nine provinces (Antwerp, Brabant, West Flanders, East Flanders, Hainaut, Liège, Limburg, Luxemburg and Namur).

Each region has been given specific powers either as a region (art 107 quarter Constitution and the special law of institutional reforms dated 8 August 1980) or as a community (art 59 *bis* Constitution and the above-mentioned special law).

Specific legislation is now being issued by the relevant administrative bodies in the matters which fall within the framework of their competence (eg most environmental issues are now regulated at regional level).

However, the organisation of the courts and the procedural rules are still governed by the national Judicial Code, which applies throughout the country. (Each court has, of course, its own idiosyncracies which should be borne in mind.)

One 'regional' consideration will be of importance when conducting proceedings in Belgium, ie the language of the procedure, which usually will depend on the place where the court case can or must be initiated. (The use of languages in judicial proceedings is governed by the law of 15 June 1935, as amended.)

As a rule, the procedure will be conducted in the same language as that of the document instituting the proceedings. However, in the Brussels district (*arrondissement*), where the plaintiff is usually entitled to initiate the procedure either in Dutch or French, the defendant is entitled to require that proceedings be conducted in the other language if he has not mastered the original language.

A court may, at the request of the adversely affected party, order the translation into the relevant language of all documents produced as evidence and drafted in a language other than that of the proceedings.

Tactical considerations

Tactics will be of importance when choosing the type of proceedings one will use to seek an injunction.

Once the type of proceedings is determined, the competent jurisdiction will depend on the Judicial Code and other relevant laws. Practitioners are said to prefer to opt for courts located in Belgian major cities rather than for the more provincial courts, whenever it is possible.

Legal team

As a rule, only duly registered members of the Bar (*avocats—advocaten*) are entitled to plead in front of the courts. There are some exceptions, eg direct family members and the representative of a trade union, who may represent a party in front of the Labour Court provided he or she has a specific power of attorney to that end.

Avocats are entitled to appear before any court, with the exception of the civil chambers of the Supreme Court. Here only a limited number of 16 lawyers, specifically appointed thereto, have right of access.

Pursuant to art 728 of the Judicial Code, however, parties are not obliged to be represented by an *avocat*. They may appear at the hearing in person. The court may prohibit the party from presenting and defending his case, if it appears that passion or inexperience prevents him from doing so properly (art 758 of the Judicial Code). In any event, it is usually inadvisable for a party to present his case himself and the intervention of a lawyer is advisable.

No distinction is made between barristers and solicitors. Traditionally, in Belgium, advice was sought from lawyers 'too late', ie when a court case was already pending or seriously threatening. Belgian lawyers therefore usually could be compared to barristers (or specialist litigators) rather than to solicitors (general legal advisors). The situation has changed, and lawyers are now consulted in their capacity both as legal advisors and litigators. In most firms, therefore, the classical Anglo-Saxon distinction has established itself in practice.

No regional qualifications are required. However, it goes without saying that it is advisable to select a lawyer who is fluent in the language in which the proceedings will be conducted.

The level of specialisation required from the lawyer will depend on the type of case in which an injunction is sought.

Criteria for obtaining interlocutory injunctions

Features

Interlocutory judgments

An interlocutory judgment can be sought, in accordance with art 19 of the Judicial Code, either to obtain a measure of investigation or the provisional protection of a party's rights, pending the final decision.

An application therefore may be filed at any stage of the proceedings and may even be the subject of an independent claim filed with the civil courts prior to any procedure on the merits being started.

Both parties shall be entitled to present their arguments in writing and verbally.

The court shall not examine the merits of the case. It may, of course, make a *prima facie* assessment of the arguments put forward by both parties regarding the merits. Its main concern, however, will be to determine from the general circumstances of the case whether investigatory measures or interim measures are justified and to determine to what extent the measures sought are appropriate.

The court's decision will not prejudice the final outcome of the case and the court is entitled to change its mind as to the parties' rights within the course of the proceedings.

Court decisions in proceedings in chambers

In accordance with art 584 of the Judicial Code, urgent issues may be referred to the President of the Courts having jurisdiction in the first degree, with a view to a provisional settlement.

Proceedings in chambers usually must be initiated by way of a writ of summons. In a case of extreme urgency, they may be started by making an *ex parte* application, in which case the plaintiff only needs to file his application with the court and the defendant is not informed of the proceedings until after the court order is made. If started through an *inter partes* application, the proceedings shall be governed by the same rules as apply in any other proceedings, bearing in mind the specific procedures of proceedings in chambers, where, by definition, time is of the essence (see below).

Whether proceedings are initiated by a writ of summons or by an *ex parte* application, the court shall not decide on the merits of the case and its decision shall not be binding on the judge who will later decide on the merits.

Judgments in proceedings 'as in chambers'

The procedural rules applicable to procedures 'as in chambers' are those applicable to proceedings in chambers, although the decision made within their framework constitutes a judgment on the merits of the case and is said to have *force de chose jugée—kracht van gewijsde*. Institution of those proceedings shall, however, usually be subject to specific conditions or circumstances laid down by the relevant legislation.

The relevant test

Pre-emptive remedies through interlocutory judgment

As stated in art 19, para 2 of the Judicial Code, the judge may order, prior to making his final decision, any previous measure intended to investigate the claim or to settle provisionally the situation between the parties.

No urgency is required. The applicant, however, will need to give evidence that the measure sought is necessary at this stage of the proceedings. The court shall follow the general principles of law and equity.

This provisional judgment is made in order to ensure the protection of interests which could be jeopardised during the proceedings. It can be made either by the judge hearing the merits of the case or, as the case may be, by the Judge in Chambers.

In theory, the court has, in such a case, broader powers than the Judge in Chambers, who is competent only when the situation is urgent. However, practice shows that most of the time, provisional measures are required from the Judge in Chambers, who is usually asked to deal with matters expediently and whose jurisdiction has been widened by the progress of the concept of urgency (see below).

Obtaining an interlocutory judgment, on the basis of art 19 of the Judicial Code, and a decision 'in chambers', on the basis of art 584 of the Judicial Code, follows similar provisions. As a result, the judge may allow a claim as soon as the existence of the right appears sufficiently established in order to justify it (Cass 29.9.1983, RW 1984-1985, 751); no blatant infringement is required. Of course, the more indisputable a right is, the easier it will be to obtain the decision sought.

The court which is requested to make an interlocutory decision is not required to examine first the admissibility of the main claim, since its decision shall not have the effect of a final judgment (Cass 11.4.1949, Arr Verbr 1949, 468).

The interlocutory decision made pursuant to art 19 of the Judicial Code does not prejudice the merits of the case. As a result, the reimbursement of a provisional amount, granted at an interlocutory hearing, could, for example, eventually be ordered if the liability of the defendant is not recognised.

Pre-emptive remedies through proceedings in chambers

Pursuant to art 584 of the Judicial Code, issues which require an urgent and provisional solution can be submitted to the Presidents either of the Court of First Instance, the Commercial Court or the Labour Court, depending on the subject matter of the dispute.

Proceedings in chambers may be initiated independently from any prior, simultaneous or later suit regarding the merits of the case. This applies even when the merits of the case could not be the subject of a judicial trial as a result of an arbitration agreement.

The obtaining of an injunction on the basis of art 584 of the Judicial Code is subject to two major conditions:

(a) the issue must be recognised as urgent by the court;
(b) the solution sought must be provisional and may not prejudice the merits of the case.

In addition, the subject matter of the dispute must fall within the areas of jurisdiction of the court as defined by the Judicial Code.

Urgency   The *juge des référés—kortgedingrechter* is competent only when the issue at stake is urgent at the time he makes his decision (as opposed to the time when the case is filed).

The court must check *ex officio* whether the case it has to hear is urgent or not, ie even if the parties do not require him to do so. The court is granted absolute power to assess such urgency.

In some circumstances, 'urgency' is presumed by law; the judge then is not required to examine whether that condition is fulfilled. (Such as in the case of attachments and measures of execution, or for stop orders on the basis of the law on fair trade practices—where the court acts 'as in chambers'. As far as attachments and measures of execution are concerned, the judge shall examine whether or not there is 'urgency' if the law provides that the claim must be filed by an *ex parte* application.)

The Judicial Code does not contain any definition of the urgency which is required under art 584 or criteria which would help the court to assess the urgent character of the matter.

Traditionally, the matter was considered to be urgent as soon as the slightest delay might result in irreparable damage. Recent case law goes beyond such restrictive interpretation. It accepts, for instance, that there is urgency when damage could result from maintaining the existing applicant's situation or when the delays involved in the proceedings regarding the merits are likely to cause the applicant damage beyond repair, material damage and even commercial troubles or merely serious inconveniences. This grants the Judge in Chambers a wide factual power of assessment and, within fair measure, the widest freedom.

When assessing the degree of urgency, the court will compare the damage the applicant might suffer from the absence of provisional measures to that which the defendant might incur if such a measure is taken. Sometimes the court will also pay attention to the overall economic context surrounding the parties or the general interest. The factors to be considered by the court are as follows.

The court first of all will bear in mind the factual circumstances of the case, plus other criteria such as:

(a) the nature of the claim: in some cases, the courts have considered that the nature of the claim itself implied urgency, for example, the requirement for unimpeded economic activities, latent defects or difficulties relating to deliveries;
(b) the behaviour of the applicant: it is traditionally accepted that the applicant would be deprived of his right to make use of proceedings in chambers (i) if he waited too long before initiating them or (ii) if he created the situation of urgency himself. His claim could nevertheless be acceptable if the delay could be excused for a legitimate reason or if new matters caused the damage to be more serious;
(c) an existing threat: case law and various authors consider that the required measure can no longer be ordered if the claim is out of date because the threat has passed or the damage has already been done.

Depending on the degree of urgency, proceedings in chambers may be initiated either through a writ of summons (*citation—dagvaarding*) or through an *ex parte* application (*requête unilatérale—eenzijdig verzoekschrift*).

An *ex parte* application is only authorised in cases of absolute necessity. It is usually accepted that there is absolute necessity when:

(a) the urgency is exceptional, ie when the danger is so immediate that even the *référé d'hôtel* (ie a hearing at the house of the judge) is excluded. There will be no hearing at all and a decision will be made solely on the basis of the plaintiff's written application;
(b) bearing in mind the measure requested, any other type of hearing would obviously render any order of the court ineffective if the defendant had any warning of the application.

Fulfilment of only one of these conditions would not be sufficient in order to justify an *ex parte* application (Cass 13.6.1975, Pas 1975, I, 984).

The assessment as to whether or not there is absolute necessity depends on factual circumstances, and courts have an absolute discretion in that respect. Practice shows that courts are often less severe than authors when assessing the existence of a situation of absolute necessity.

'Absolute necessity' has been recognised where there are reasons to believe that a party could try to destroy the relevant documents if warned in advance that investigative measures would be carried out (comm Anvers 31.12.1974, JPA 1974, 449) or where, as a result of the defendant living abroad, the usual form proceedings, even expedited, would take too long (comm Anvers 31.5.1974, JPA 1974, 259). In a case of 'absolute necessity' the plaintiff will not serve a writ but will merely file an application with the court.

Regarding intellectual property rights, it is often accepted that there is absolute urgency justifying an *ex parte* application, provided the requested measures do not require, for instance, the cessation of the activities in question.

The decision of the judge in respect of urgency does not have to be confirmed by the Supreme Court. (This does not mean, however, that such decisions made by the Judge in Chambers cannot be revised by the Supreme Court if there is a valid reason for doing so.)

If the court does not recognise that the claim is urgent, it must refuse jurisdiction. There is some dispute as to whether or not, in such a case, the court must transfer the case to a court competent to hear the merits or merely dismiss the claim, a practice which seems to be popular with most courts and authors.

Provisional decision   Article 584 of the Judicial Code authorises the President of the courts which have jurisdiction in the first degree to order *provisional* measures. The same principle is repeated under art 1039 of the Judicial Code, which expressly provides that decisions in chambers do not prejudice the merits of the case.

It was traditionally held that art 584 of the Judicial Code prohibited the Judge in Chambers from considering the merits of the case and that this prohibition was absolute and was part of the Belgian public order (Cass 15.2.1972, Pas 1972, I, 469).

Case law and authors have considerably extended this interpretation of the powers of the Judge in Chambers.

The Judge in Chambers is still not entitled to make decisions on the merits of the case, even provisionally. However, it now seems generally accepted that he may base his decision on the right of a party or on a factual situation, provided that right or situation is obvious or could not seriously be disputed. Sufficient likeliness of a right authorises the court to order an interim measure (Cass 29.9.1983, JT 1984, 330, which refers to the *apparences de droit suffisantes—ogenschijnlijke rechten*; and Supreme Court, 9.9.1982, Pas 1983, I, 48 and 21.3.1985, Pas 1985, I, 908).

As a result, the interim character of the measure sought no longer seems to be a condition for the jurisdiction of the President and even for the admissibility of the claim.

Authors, however, indicate that the degree of certainty of the rights alleged will determine whether or not the court shall be authorised to order more or less stringent decisions:

(a) if the rights alleged are the subject of a serious dispute, the judge shall order protective measures (*mesures conservatoires—bewarende maatregelen*) linked to the equitable adjustment of a waiting period. These measures are intended to avoid rights being irreparably jeopardised or exposed to serious violation. Examples include the appointment of bailees, or temporary managers, an injunction to do or to refrain from doing something, prohibition on disposing of or setting up real sureties, etc;

(b) if there is no serious dispute regarding the rights alleged, the judge shall order, by anticipation, measures of protection or safeguard of unquestionable rights. These measures can include prohibitory injunctions, mandatory injunctions or injunctions to pay a sum of money.

In any event, the Judge in Chambers must take care that the measures he orders do not create damage which would be irreversible and beyond repair (Cass 9.9.1982, Pas 1983, I, 48). If the trial judge (who eventually determines the merits of a case) overturns the decision made in chambers, and if the situation cannot be restored to its original state, damages can be claimed from the party who benefited from the decision in chambers.

The provisional character of the decisions made in chambers means that compliance with the decision, even without reservations, cannot itself prejudice the merits of the case of the party who so complied. Likewise, initiating proceedings in chambers in front of Belgian courts does not prevent the applicant from disputing the jurisdiction of the Belgian courts when it comes to hearing the merits of the case.

The judge who hears the merits of the case is not bound by the decision made in chambers, although he must pay attention to its existence. He remains completely free to assess the case as he deems appropriate.

The decisions in chambers, however, are final in law for the judges who made them, and are often final in fact. But these decisions can still be the subject of an appeal, despite their finality in the Court of First Instance:

(a) the judge making the decision may not withdraw or modify it upon request of the parties, unless new circumstances have arisen. Based on new circumstances, the President judge may withdraw or modify previous measures, even if they were decided by the Court of Appeal, provided no appeal is pending;

(b) a decision made in chambers can have irreversible consequences even if it does not limit the trial judge's discretion to determine the merits of the case. In such a case, as mentioned above, damages can be allocated by the judge who hears the merits of the case in order to compensate for any damage suffered by the defendant as a result of a provisional measure.

Jurisdiction   Proceedings in chambers may be initiated, pursuant to art 584 of the Judicial Code, in front of:

(a) the President of the Court of First Instance, in all matters, unless the subject matter of the dispute does not come under his judicial power, such as fiscal matters.

   He is competent even when another court, or its President, is competent to hear the merits of the case in the main action;

(b) the President of the Commercial Court and of the Labour Court, who are competent in matters which fall within the field of their jurisdiction.

Pre-emptive remedies through proceedings 'as in chambers'

Proceedings 'as in chambers' abide by the same rules as proceedings 'in chambers', with the exception of art 1039 of the Judicial Code. However, court decisions made 'as in chambers' are final judgments on the merits, without prejudice to possible further remedies at law.

Those proceedings are available only where specifically provided for by law and provided the conditions laid down by the relevant law are complied with (for example until the new law regarding fair trade practices entered into force, only a trader or craftsman was entitled to request a stop order based on unfair trade practices).

The plaintiff's cross-undertaking in damages

This concept does not exist under Belgian law. In the event that, as a result of either an interlocutory judgment or of a judgment in chambers, the defendant suffers damage which is considered unjustified by the judge hearing the merits of the case, he will be allocated compensation. The defendant must then recover his losses from the plaintiff. No safeguards protect him.

As a first step in the proceedings (*in limine litis*), a Belgian defendant may request a foreign plaintiff to give a security (*cautio iudicatum solvi*) to cover the costs and damages resulting from the trial. The court determines the amount of the security. The plaintiff can later be released from this obligation, having paid the money into an escrow account, if he proves that his real estate in Belgium is sufficient to cover the amount or if he creates a pledge (arts 851 and 852 of the Judicial Code). Security may not be required from citizens who are released from such an obligation by an international treaty. The obligation to put up a security is, for instance, inapplicable when the plaintiff is an EC citizen.

Alternative to an application for an interlocutory injunction or for an order in chambers

Short debates
In accordance with art 735 of the Judicial Code, cases which require only short debates can be heard at the introductory hearing or postponed to be heard at a predetermined date.

This provision will apply only in circumstances where the claim really is not challenged. Arguments by the parties should not last more than 10 to 15 minutes.

Courts often are reluctant to grant the plaintiff the benefit of that provision in proceedings other than proceedings in chambers. This is partially due to the fact that the law does not contain any definition of the circumstances where this article can be applied. Therefore, the courts often are reluctant to make a decision at the introductory hearing once a party challenges the claim. (A draft law was filed in May 1989 to modify art 735 by itemising cases where short debates could be accepted.) It must be emphasised that art 735 of the Judicial Code can be used within the framework of any court proceeding.

Summary procedure for an 'injunction to pay'
Articles 1338–1344 of the Judicial Code provide a specific procedure applicable to disputes relating to the payment of sums not exceeding BF 50,000, which fall under the jurisdiction of the Justice of the Peace (*procédure sommaire d'injonction de payer—summiere rechtspleging om betaling te bevelen*).

Practice and procedure

General introduction

As a general rule, Belgian civil proceedings are initiated by having an *inter partes* Application (*citation—dagvaarding*) served on the plaintiff by a process server (art 700 of the Judicial Code).

Parties may also initiate proceedings in the Courts of First Degree by appearing voluntarily before the court (*comparution volontaire— vrijwillige verschijning*).

In some cases, the law authorises initiation of the proceedings by an *ex parte* application (*requête unilatérale—eenzijdig verzoekschrift*).

Claims can be lodged within the framework of existing proceedings by filing an incidental claim (*demande incidente—tussenvordering*), such as a counterclaim (*demande reconventionnelle—tegeneis*). Most of these incidental claims may be lodged by way of submissions.

Notice

Interlocutory judgment

As mentioned above, an interlocutory decision may be sought at any time, either during existing proceedings (whether in the first instance or on appeal) or by initiating independent court proceedings.

If the measure is sought during pending court proceedings, the claim shall be instituted through an incidental claim filed by way of submissions (art 807 of the Judicial Code).

If the claim for an interim measure is made the subject of separate court proceedings, the claim shall be filed by an *inter partes* application or a voluntary appearance.

Proceedings in chambers

Proceedings in chambers can be instituted in accordance with the general rules provided by the Judicial Code (see above). *Ex parte* application is expressly authorised in situations of absolute necessity.

Inter partes application

(1) Conditions of form—the *inter partes* application must contain all the information required by arts 43 and 702 of the Judicial Code. Failure to comply with these provisions results in the application being null and void *ex officio*.

The application and possible submissions must set out all the relevant matters relied on by the plaintiff in the dispute. Therefore, the mention in the application of the subject matter of the dispute and of the grounds of the claim is essential. As in any law suit, the judge may not decide *ultra petita* (ie beyond the claim).

(2) Period of time—the period of time for the issuing of an *inter partes* application is two days from the day following that on which the writ is served. This is subject to the extensions provided by art 55 of the Judicial Code in the case where the defendant does not have his domicile (effective or elected) or residence in Belgium.

In the event that the matter requires prompt handling, the President may authorise the issuing of an application, either in court or at his own house (*référé d'hôtel*), even on holidays, within a day and even within an hour (art 1036 of the Judicial Code). Application for an abbreviation of the period of application can, according to some authors, even be made verbally.

(3) Service—the *inter partes* application may not be served on the defendant at night (ie not between 9.00 pm and 6.00 am) nor in a place which is not open to the public, nor on a Saturday, Sunday or holiday (unless there is urgency and it is specifically authorised by the court).

As a rule the application is served on the defendant personally, at any place where he can be found. If this proves impossible, the process server will go to the defendant's domicile or residence. If the defendant is absent, notice can be served on a parent, a relative or any member of his staff on the premises.

If the notice cannot be served in accordance with the above-mentioned rules, the process server will leave a copy of the application in a sealed envelope at the defendant's domicile. He shall also inform the defendant by registered letter sent, at the latest, on the very next working day, confirming that he can take delivery of the writ within the next three months. Service, however, is considered completed upon delivery of the copy to the defendant's domicile or residence.

If it seems obvious that it will be physically impossible to serve notice at the domicile or the residence of the defendant, a copy of the application will be handed to the relevant Public Prosecutor.

Service abroad is considered validly completed by the process server sending the summons by registered letter with return receipt (art 40 of the Judicial Code). Derogatory rules, however, are provided by international conventions, such as the Hague Convention of 15 November 1965. These derogatory provisions have precedence over Belgian rules.

Ex parte application   In a case of absolute necessity, proceedings in chambers may be initiated by an *ex parte* application (art 584 of the Judicial Code).

An *ex parte* application must comply with art 1026 of the Judicial Code and contain the information required by that provision, failing which any order can be declared null and void.

Proceedings as in chambers

Proceedings as in chambers shall be instituted in accordance with the rules applicable to proceedings in chambers.

The question, however, arises whether they can validly be instituted through an *ex parte* application.

There is no unanimity among the courts and authors on this matter. The recent trend has been to refuse it (Pres Comm Brussels, 12.2.1985, JT 1985, 539; Antwerp, 24.6.1986, RW 1986–1987; against: Fettweis A, *Manuel de Procédure civile*, 332, no 448, who advises on having an *inter partes* application served at the same time as the *ex parte* application. The judge will order provisional measures, on the basis of the *ex parte* application, and make a final decision having heard the parties after service of the *inter partes* application).

Investigation of the claim and procedure

Rules applicable to any court proceedings

Inter partes application   When a court case is instituted by an *inter partes* application, the main steps of the procedure are as follows.

Introductory hearing (*audience d'introduction—inleidingszitting*): on the date mentioned in the application, parties must appear before the court where the case is introduced. At that hearing:

(a) cases which only require short debates will be heard (art 735 of the Judicial Code—see above);
(b) more complex cases or cases which require measures of investigation shall be stood over to the general roll (*rôle général—algemene rol*) or sent to another chamber. Most cases are dismissed to the general roll where they remain until either party requests a new hearing date.

If the defendant fails to appear at that hearing, a judgment in default may be entered.

When the case has not been heard at the first hearing date, the parties must exchange documents and submissions.

Documents Parties must provide evidence of all the facts they seek to rely on. The types of proof, their rank and their force are determined by the rules applicable to civil, commercial or labour law, as the case may be.

In support of his arguments and assertions, a party may submit to the court as much evidence as he considers appropriate to ensure the success of his case.

There is no general definition of the standards of proof to be met in civil cases, or of the nature of the type of evidence which may be submitted. It could be a document, picture, object, film, written statement, expert's report, etc. It must be borne in mind, however, that:

(a) information obtained in breach of professional confidentiality will be inadmissible;
(b) personal private letters may not be used as evidence without the agreement of the interested parties (except in matrimonial or family matters).

Great care must be taken when photographs, copies, etc are produced, because of their possible falsification, etc. Further to a regulation made on 8 May 1980, the correspondence exchanged between lawyers is, as a rule, confidential and may only be produced with the approval of the Dean of the Order of which the lawyer is a member. That correspondence, however, is no longer confidential in certain circumstances, ie when the correspondence contains precise proposals which are accepted without reservation on behalf of the other party, or when correspondence expressly qualified as non-confidential contains a unilateral commitment made without prejudice.

The documents are traditionally lodged with the registry of the relevant court, where parties are entitled to consult them but may not remove them. Parties may also pass their files to each other on an amicable basis and without formality. If this is the case the files must be given back within the period of time granted to the party in question to hand in his submissions. (Usually copies are either sent directly from one lawyer to the other or passed on in the lawyers' cloakroom at the Court of Justice.)

In any case, any document which a party intends to produce in court in support of his arguments must be disclosed to the other party before being used at least eight days before the hearing date (except when art 735 of the Judicial Code is used). Failure to comply with this rule will result in the hearing being automatically postponed.

Submissions—are the next step in the process. Pursuant to art 748 of the Judicial Code:

(a) the defendant has one month, as from the moment he has received the documentary evidence of the applicant, in order to draft his submissions;
(b) the applicant has one month in order to reply;
(c) thereafter the defendant has 15 days to reply.

Parties may, however, agree on shorter periods of time or, by failure of agreement, the court can shorten them in accordance with the final paragraph of art 748 of the Judicial Code. In addition, use may be made of all rules usually applicable in any court proceedings for compelling a party to produce his submissions (art 751 of the Judicial Code for instance).

As a rule, all submissions and notes in support of a party's claim must be communicated to the other party at the latest before the closing of the debates, under the penalty of the procedure being adjourned.

Pleadings (verbal defence)—is usually the next step once the exchange of documents and submissions is completed or when a party fails to send his submissions. In either case, a new hearing date may be requested where parties will be entitled to present a verbal defence. Parties shall usually have to indicate how long they need to present that defence. The process of verbal defence means both parties' lawyers will defend their case verbally before the court.

If, by a new hearing fixed on the basis of art 751 of the Judicial Code (see above), a party still has not supplied his submissions, the other party is entitled to request a judgment in default which will effectively be considered as given after trial (*jugement par défaut réputé contradictoire—verstek vonnis dat geacht wordt tegensprekelijk te zijn*).

After the parties have been heard, the closing of the debates is ordered by the court. From that moment on, no submissions may be filed or other investigative measures ordered.

The debates may be re-opened, either *ex officio* or upon request of the parties, if the court considers it appropriate.

As a rule, several hearings take place prior to debates being closed. Usually a hearing is requested with a view to compelling a party to supply his submissions. Hearings can also be requested with a view to settling pre-trial motions relating to the competence of the court, carrying out investigative measures, etc.

After consultation by the court, the judgment is made in public. As a rule, this occurs one month after the closing of the debates or after obtaining the opinion of the Public Prosecutor as the case may be. (In some cases, the Public Prosecutor must be supplied with the file or may request the file in order for him to issue an opinion.)

Ex parte application The judge will investigate the case and may convene the applicant and possible intervening parties in order to ask for explanations. As a rule, no specific period of time is provided between the filing of the application and the invitation notice.

In theory, third parties are entitled to appear voluntarily in the proceedings: in practice this seldom happens.

The decision is made in chambers and is served on the applicant, and on the third parties as the case may be, by the court registrar.

Specific rules applicable to proceedings in chambers

As a rule the procedure is the same as in any court case. However, the specific characteristics of the proceedings in chambers (urgency, provisional decision and need to decide quickly) imply that it will, to a certain extent, have features of its own.

(1) Most of the time, applicants make use of art 735 of the Judicial Code (*débats succincts—korte debatten*)—see above.

(2) The exchange of submissions between the parties is, as a rule, governed by the principles applicable to the conduct of any hearing. Usually one of the parties will apply to expedite the exchange of submissions.

(3) If the President orders or authorises an investigatory measure, it must be carried out in accordance with the usual rules. Again, the President is entitled to shorten the periods of time provided for by the Code for the implementation of these measures.

(4) *Demandes incidentes—tussenvorderingen*, ie any claim made during the course of the proceedings, such as counterclaim, etc may still be initiated within the framework of the proceedings in chambers, provided they are urgent and capable of being assessed provisionally.

(5) As a rule, claims submitted to the Judge in Chambers are not referred to the Public Prosecutor. (In civil matters, the Public Prosecutor may be required, or as the case may be, is entitled, to study court files, and thereafter to issue an opinion.)

(6) The decision made, following an *inter partes* application, is pronounced in open court as in any other court decision. The decision made pursuant to an *ex parte* application is given in chambers (*chambre du conseil—raadkamer*).

Costs and disbursements

Only the court's decisions in the main action regarding the merits of the case can include an order of costs against the losing party (art 1017 of the Judicial Code). Since proceedings in chambers do not relate to the merits of the case, the disbursements relating to that procedure will be reserved, pending a decision regarding the merits of the case.

Costs incurred unnecessarily or which result from the negligence of a party shall be borne by the party who initiated them.

The costs and disbursements, which the losing party must pay, include, pursuant to art 1018 of the Judicial Code:

(a) stamp, registry and registration duties;
(b) the fees of the process server;
(c) the cost of the original copy of the judgment;
(d) the cost of any investigative measure;
(e) the travel expenses of the magistrates, registrars and parties when reimbursement of the travel costs has been ordered by the court;
(f) costs relating to deeds, when incurred exclusively as a result of the trial (eg costs of the application for the purpose of obtaining a shorter period of time);
(g) procedural indemnities (ie the remuneration of the lawyer for practical duties performed as *mandataire ad litem*); and
(h) enforcement costs.

The principle is that the party who initiates the proceedings bears all the costs relating to it, including enforcement costs, until a final judgment orders their reimbursement.

Registration duties levied on the judgment no longer have to be paid in advance by the plaintiff. They are reserved by the court administration and must be paid the party who loses at trial.

The cost of litigation in Belgium is lower than in other EC countries. For example, the costs for the service of a summons amount to a maximum of around BF 15,000 and the procedural indemnity referred to above amounts to a maximum of BF 14,000 at the Appeal level. In proceedings 'in chambers', the procedural indemnity at present amounts to BF 3,600, when the amount in dispute is indeterminate or lower than BF 100,000, and to BF 7,200 when the amount in dispute is higher than BF 100,000.

In Belgium, the fees of the lawyers are borne exclusively by the party they defend and may not be recovered in court from the other party. This is a general principle of Belgian judicial law.

Post-injunction factors

Service of the injunction

Prior to the injunction being served by a process server (or notified by mail, as the case may be), the other parties are deemed to be unaware of the decision and therefore not bound by it.

As a rule, enforcement requires the following.

(1) Prior personal service on the other party of an official copy of the decision (*expédition—expeditie*) bearing a specific wording authorising enforcement (*formule exécutoire—uitvoerend formula*).

Within the framework of proceedings in chambers, the Judge in Chambers is entitled, in cases of absolute necessity, to affix that formula on the *minute* of the decision. (*Minute—minuut*, is the name of the official document which records the judgment. It is kept at the Registrar's office.) The process server shall then serve the *minute* itself on the other party.

Service must be carried out in accordance with the same rules as those applicable to the service of the writ of summons (see above).

(2) The lapsing of the periods of time provided for appealing against the decision (*appel—beroep*) or contesting it (*opposition—verzet* when the judgment is made in default), unless the decision has been made provisionally enforceable irrespective of any remedy at law.

As far as the decisions made pursuant to the proceedings referred to in the present chapter are concerned, the situation is as follows.

(1) A decision ordering an investigation based on art 19 of the Judicial Code is provisionally enforceable, in spite of any appeal or 'opposition' of the judgment (art 1496 of the Judicial Code).

If the measure ordered by the court, pursuant to art 19 of the Judicial Code, relates to the provisional settlement of a situation pending a later decision, doubts arise as to the immediate enforceability of the interim measure based on that provision. As a result, it is prudent to obtain from the court an express authorisation in that respect in accordance with arts 1398 and 1401 of the Judicial Code.

(2) Decisions made 'in chambers' are always provisionally enforceable.

(3) Decisions made 'as in chambers' will be provisionally enforceable when such is stipulated by the law which provides for that type of procedure (eg stop order on the basis of the Fair Trade Practices Act).

The defendant can also accept the decision either expressly or tacitly, ie by waiving his rights to lodge an appeal or opposition against all or part of the provisions of the decision (art 1044 of the Judicial Code).

Decisions in default must be served within one year after they have been made. Otherwise they are considered to have lapsed.

Sanctions

(1) The Belgian Judicial Code as such does not provide for any criminal sanction which could be imposed on the party who is in breach of a court decision.

Criminal sanctions are sometimes provided for by specific laws (eg pursuant to the Fair Trade Practices Act, non-compliance with stop orders is sanctioned by a fine equal to between BF 1,000 and BF 20,000, to be multiplied by 80. The fine is double when there is a relapse within the five years following the Stop order).

(2) By the Law of 31 January 1980, Belgium ratified the Uniform Law relating to the *astreinte—dwangsom* signed in The Hague on 26 November 1973. As a result it is possible to request the court to accompany the injunction with a penalty in the event that the injunction is not complied with, in order to persuade the defendant to comply with the terms of the injunction.

Pursuant to the above, a party may be required to pay a sum of money, as a penalty, if the main portion of the judgment is not complied with. It can be either a single amount or an amount determined per time unit (eg per day of delay in abiding by the decision), or per breach.

The *astreinte* may be ordered in all matters, with the exception of decisions regarding the payment of sums where rules governing seizures apply and in respect of claims regarding the performance of an employment contract. Seizures in this context (*saisie*) include any freezing of assets including goods and money.

Once ordered, the *astreinte* is considered final and may be enforced as soon as the judgment has been served. It is, however, subject to a short statute of limitation (six months after the *astreinte* is incurred).

Otherwise, enforcement of court decisions can be ensured through attachments where applicable.

Variations or discharge of the injunction

As a rule, unless otherwise provided by law, court decisions made in first degree:

(a) may be appealed (*appel—beroep*) by anyone who was a party to the proceedings and suffers a prejudice as a result of that decision. It is important to note that once a decision is appealed, the case is totally removed from the jurisdiction of the first judge (this is called in French the *effet dévolutif de l'appel*);

(b) may be contested (*opposition—verzet*) under the same conditions, when the decision is made by default;

(c) may be opposed in front of the court which made them by anyone who was not involved in the original proceedings (*tierce-opposition— derdenverzet*), for example, a bankrupt may not lodge an appeal against the judgment which pronounces his bankruptcy *ex officio*. He must file third party opposition.

Parties may apply with the judge who made the decision for a modification of decisions made in chambers or of interlocutory decisions based on art 19 of the Judicial Code if there are new circumstances since the date of the decision. As far as decisions in chambers are concerned, a new action will be required to that end. No such modification is possible if the first decision has been appealed or contested.

In very specific circumstances, parties can also apply to the court to rescind its decision.

Specific procedures are provided therefore by the Judicial Code:

(a) the *requête civile—herroeping van het gewijsde* which provides for the rescission of any final judgment for the specific causes provided by the Judicial Code which are based on a factual mistake unknown to the court and discovered after the judgment has been issued;

(b) the *prise à partie—verhaal op de rechter* which provides for the rescission of any decision made fraudulently by a judge;

Judgment in default

When an injunction is granted in default, the party in default is entitled to file *opposition* against it in order to have the case re-tried before the same court. He can also decide to appeal immediately. Where *opposition* is possible, it is usually considered preferable to make use of that remedy. To file an appeal in these circumstances amounts to losing one degree of jurisdiction.

The conditions for contesting a court decision are as follows:

(a) the person who files *opposition* must have been involved in the initial proceeding as a party and the decision must give him a reason to complain ('grief');

(b) the law prohibits the filing of an *opposition*.

As a rule, application for *opposition* must be filed by a writ served by a process server. Alternatively parties can agree to appear voluntarily.

The application must list the reasons for which *opposition* is sought by failure of which the application is null (provided the nullity is invoked *in limine litis*, ie as a first step in the proceeding). The mere allegation that the decision is not grounded is not sufficient.

Opposition must be filed within one month of the judgment being served, on the party in default or otherwise. If the defendant has no domicile or elected residence in Belgium, this one-month period is extended as provided by the Judicial Code. When *opposition* is filed within the framework of proceedings 'in chambers', no such extension is authorised. Likewise, in proceedings 'in chambers', the period of time between service and the hearing is usually two days, instead of the eight days' period provided for usual court proceedings (subject to possible extensions when service is made abroad).

Judgment after the parties have been heard

A party claiming damage suffered as a result of a court decision may apply to have it reversed or modified, by appealing. Most decisions may be appealed, even an interlocutory judgment or a decision in default (in that event *opposition* and appeal may not be pursued at the same time). The appeal application lodged against a final court decision may include an appeal against an interlocutory judgment which was made in the same proceedings and which in normal circumstances could no longer be appealed against.

As in any court proceeding, the party who appeals must have an interest and the capacity to do so (see above). Compliance with these conditions will be examined by the court *ex officio*.

As a rule, appeal must be lodged at the latest one month after the original decision has been served. This period of time may be extended when one of the parties is not domiciled and has no residence in Belgium, unless the appeal relates to a judgment made on an *ex parte* application, in summary proceedings or by the attachment judge.

The period of time between service of the writ of appeal and the first hearing is equal to eight days, or two days if proceedings are conducted in chambers, subject to extensions for service abroad. When an appeal is filed against an injunction made on an *ex parte* application, the application must contain the exact date of the first hearing and must be signed by a lawyer.

The appeal may be lodged, depending on the circumstances, by either:

(a) a writ served by a process server,
(b) on an *ex parte* application,
(c) by registered letter, or
(d) by submissions.

The application must contain specific information, such as the grievances at the judgment which is the subject of the appeal, or it is null and void.

It is important to stress that the appeal judge has jurisdiction over the whole dispute. Once the appeal application is filed, the judge in First Instance completely loses jurisdiction over the whole case.

As a result, if an appeal is lodged against an interlocutory decision based on art 19 of the Judicial Code, the Court of Appeal will usually try the whole case, including the merits (art 1068 of the Judicial Code). Consequently, the parties will lose the possibility of having a case tried before a Court of the First Degree.

As a rule, this will not be the case when a decision made 'in chambers' is appealed, unless the Judge in Chambers made a decision on the merits (in spite of the fact that he is not competent to do so).

Enquiry into damages

If the injunction is discharged, damages can be awarded to a party who proves that he suffered damage as a result of its enforcement.

In order to obtain that reimbursement, it will be necessary to prove that there is damage and that it results from the enforcement of the injunction, in accordance with the rules provided by the Civil Code (art 1382 of the Civil Code).

The amount of the award is determined by the court on the basis of the evidence brought by the claimant.

If a claim is proved vexatious and rash (*procédure téméraire et vexatoire—tergend en roekeloos geding*), the plaintiff may at any time be ordered to pay an indemnity, the amount of which is determined *ex aequo et bono* by the court.

Freezing orders

Belgian law provides for several types of *attachments* (both conservatory and executory).

(1) *Saisie mobilière conservatoire—roerend bewarend beslag*. This is a seizure of movable goods belonging to the debtor which are in his possession.

(2) *Saisie immobilière conservatoire—onroerend bewarend beslag*. This attachment is used for real estate belonging to the debtor.

(3) *Saisie-arrêt conservatoire—bewarend beslag onder derden*. This attachment is made on movable goods belonging to the debtor which are in the possession of third parties (this includes money in bank accounts, claims owed to one's debtor by a third party for instance as a result of services rendered to the latter by the debtor). Orders freezing bank accounts or monies due to be paid to a debtor are very frequent in Belgium.

(4) *Saisie-gagerie—pandbeslag*. This type of seizure is available to the lessor on furniture and other movable property belonging to his lessee.

(5) *Saisie-revendication—beslag tot terugvordering*. This seizure aims to recover the ownership or possession of movable property.

(6) *Saisie conservatoire sur navires et bateaux—bewarend beslag op zeeschepen en binnenschepen*. Conservatory seizure of sea vessels and other ships.

(7) *Saisie en matière de contrefaçon—beslag inzake namaak*. This seizure authorises the holder of a patent or copyright to allow an expert appointed by the court to investigate and describe anything which can establish the alleged infringement. The court also can:

(a) prohibit the defendant from parting with the counterfeited objects;
(b) appoint a custodian;
(c) have the objects sealed; and even
(d) authorise the attachment of the proceeds obtained with the counterfeited objects.

Conservatory attachments are used to block the sale of property belonging to a debtor in order to avoid disposal in a way detrimental to his creditor.

Once served, the judgment on the merits of the case *ex officio* will transform the conservatory seizure into an executory seizure. Such a seizure, however, may be operated as soon as the creditor holds any executory title whatsoever, whether it is the result of a court decision or not.

Any creditor who holds a claim which is certain, due and liquid or at least susceptible to being provisionally assessed is entitled to initiate proceedings aimed at obtaining a conservatory attachment provided the case requires urgency.

Unless exceptions are provided for by law (eg for the *saisie-arrêt conservatoire*), the creditor will need to obtain authorisation from the Judge of Seizures prior to attaching conservatorily the property of his debtor. Proceedings are initiated through an *ex parte* application. The Judge of Seizures shall make his decision within eight days from the filing of the application. This decision must then be served on the debtor.

If the attachment is made on the property of the debtor held by a third party, the deed of attachment must be served on the latter as well. The third party must then inform the creditor of the assets, which are the subject of the attachment, within 15 days from the service of the court order. Failure to make such a statement may result in the third party being held purely and simply to be the debtor of the sum owed to the creditor.

Production of documents

It is not possible to obtain a 'search and seize' order in Belgium, similar to Anton Piller orders in England and Wales. If the plaintiff fears evidence may be destroyed, he can apply to the court for an order that the other party produces the evidence in court. Each party must prove the facts he alleges (art 870 of the Judicial Code; art 1315 of the Civil Code).

Each party, however, has the duty to fully co-operate with the administration. The court may order any party to produce the elements of proof he has in his possession (art 871 of the Judicial Code).

Several investigative measures may be required from the court:

(a) verification of handwriting;
(b) verification of civil documents (*faux civil—valsheidsprocedure*);
(c) hearing of witnesses; measure which can be ordered *ex officio* by the court;
(d) hearing of expert witnesses;
(e) hearing of the parties; this measure can be ordered *ex officio* by the court;
(f) oath; and
(g) viewing of the premises.

In addition, art 877 of the Judicial Code provides the *actio ad exhibendum*:

When there exist serious, precise and concordant [*graves, précises et concordantes—gewichtige, bepaalde en met elkaar overeenstemmende*] presumptions, that one of the parties or a third party possesses a document containing the proof of a pertinent fact, the judge may order that such document or a certified copy thereof be deposited in the file of the proceeding.

If a document is held by a third party, the court will first invite him to file it. The third party then is entitled to issue observations in writing or intervene verbally in the judge's chambers (*chambre du conseil—raadkamer*). Parties may examine and answer them.

Professional secrecy does not necessarily impede the production of a document.

The judgment ordering the production of a document may not be opposed or appealed. It will be served on the parties or on the third party by judicial letter (*pli judiciaire—gerechtelijke brief*). The judgment may provide, upon request of a party, a penalty as a sanction for non-compliance with its provisions.

Failure to comply with the judgment is sanctioned by damages (art 882 of the Judicial Code). The amount of damages is determined by the court on the basis of the prejudice suffered, ie in consideration of the importance of the document. Forced execution is impossible.

Louis Lafili and Nicole Van Crombrugghe

Denmark

Introduction

Types of injunction

Together with seizure or arrest, the injunction (*forbud* or *fogedforbud*) forms part of the system of so-called provisional legal remedies.

The law on the administration of justice, Law No 90 of 11 April 1916—the Administration of Justice Law (Rpl) (as amended), lays down provisions, in chap 57, paras 641–653, governing use of the injunction and the exact procedural rules for its implementation.

There are separate rules on seizures aimed at securing monetary claims, chap 56, paras 627–640, Rpl though it is acknowledged that the injunction has much in common with seizure, and indeed many of the rules applying to seizures are directly applicable to injunctions.

The principal difference between the injunction and the seizure is that a seizure is used to secure a monetary claim (a financial entitlement), whereas an injunction is used to secure observance of an agreed obligation in cases where non-performance of that obligation is not covered by the general provisions of law in terms of punishment and compensation.

The injunction is a judicial process which is conducted and served by the bailiff's court, which, pursuant to para 14, Rpl is a department of the *Byretten* (the City Court), see further details below within Structure of the courts, at p 81.

An injunction can only be introduced against actions which are contrary to the plaintiff's rights, see para 641. The provisions of law in this area are based on the common Scandinavian legal theory which says that an action may only be banned if that action is found to be unlawful after weighing up the various interests involved and after assessing the damages and benefits that would result from the action in question. This principle is based on the premise that the limits on an individual's freedom of action may be transgressed and that a right might be jeopardised. Transgressing the limits of individual freedom of action therefore acquires the characteristics of an objective offence. A transgression or offence may have occurred even though it is not possible to hold any offender responsible.

Conventional jurisprudence cannot be relied on to provide suitable criteria in its literature for determining when there has been an offence which would justify the implementation of an injunction. A brief general description of the areas in which such injunctions are used can hardly serve to clarify matters. The closest one can come to a definition is to say that 'the courts have powers to introduce an injunction to rectify non-compliance with an obligation in so far as this is necessary, in the light of the provisions of the law which apply in a given case, in order to protect the interests of the plaintiff'.

As stated above, an injunction may only be introduced if it contains an order to request that the other party refrain from taking certain positive action, in other words an injunction can only be used to enforce compliance with obligations not (primarily) to perform certain actions.

To a certain extent, however, it is also possible for an injunction to require performance of a certain action, but only in so far as this requirement has a subordinate significance and is linked in an accessory manner to the obligation not to perform certain (other) actions and on which the injunction is actually based, see para 641, Pt 2, and Sanctions, p 92 below.

General principles

The general principles for the introduction of an injunction are laid down in para 642, Rpl, which states:

An injunction can be introduced provided it is confirmed or shown to be likely:

(1) that the actions against which the injunction is being sought are contrary to the plaintiff's rights;
(2) that the defendant will take actions for which the injunction is being sought; and
(3) that this result could not be achieved if the plaintiff were to seek acknowledgment of his rights through normal court procedures.

An injunction may only be introduced if there are special grounds for its introduction, see (2) (Just Cause). It follows then that the introduction of an injunction is not permitted in cases where there are no grounds for believing that the rejection of the plaintiff's request for an injunction would jeopardise the plaintiff's rights. If there is no repeat action, therefore, it shall be a requirement that the conduct or action referred to in the request, either before or during the injunction process, will be grounds for assuming that he (the defendant)—if the injunction is not introduced—will engage in certain specified actions, contrary to the plaintiff's interests, within a legally defined period.

The provisional nature of this legal remedy means that it may only be resorted to as a means of preventing the plaintiff losing his rights through having to go to court in the normal way to obtain a judgment followed by the enforcement process for that judgment, see point (3) above. The plaintiff must therefore be able to show, or demonstrate the likelihood of the fact, that he stands to lose his rights if he is obliged to go through the normal court action procedures.

If it is found that an ordinary civil action could go through before any action were taken which might jeopardise the plaintiff's rights, the injunction will not be granted.

The defendant's ignorance of the plaintiff's right is not sufficient reason for not allowing the injunction. In such a case, however, introduction of the injunction will require that there are grounds for assuming that once he has been made aware of the plaintiff's right, the defendant will nevertheless act in a way which is contrary to the plaintiff's interests.

The provisions also stipulate that an injunction may only be granted if the plaintiff is able to show, or demonstrate the likelihood of the fact, that all the conditions laid down in para 642, points 1–3 have been fulfilled. As a general rule the burden of proof here rests with the plaintiff (see Criteria for obtaining interlocutory injunctions, at p 83 below for further aspects of evidence to be provided).

In para 643, Rpl we read:

(1) An injunction may not be granted in cases where it is acknowledged that the general provisions of law, in terms of punishment and compensation, or a possible assurance from the defendant, would provide the plaintiff with sufficient protection.

(2) The bailiff's court may refuse to serve an injunction if it would cause the defendant damage or inconvenience out of proportion to the interests which the plaintiff is seeking to safeguard by the injunction.

The introduction of an injunction is also excluded if the right for which protection is being sought is already adequately protected by penalty clauses or by the defendant's liability to pay compensation, and possibly by a security deposit to cover damages which the defendant might cause the plaintiff.

According to the position adopted by the legislators (Deliberation No 1107/1987, relating to seizure and injunctions), the threat of a penalty and liability to pay compensation, to only a limited extent, will constitute adequate protection for the plaintiff. This provision is included to underline the subsidiary nature of the injunction in contrast with the seeking of a normal court judgment.

Entitlement to introduce an injunction is further limited by the rule of proportionality in para 643, point 2. The weighing up of interests carried out by the bailiff's court must be based on a thorough assessment of the facts and due consideration of the substantive regulations governing the points at issue between the parties. It is stressed in the legislators' provisions that the rule of proportionality has the nature of an exception provision which may be brought into play in those rare cases where there is a significant discrepancy between the plaintiff's interest in introducing the injunction and its possible harmful effect on the defendant.

The above provisions, which have the effect of excluding the granting of an injunction, are not meant to be exhaustive. Other special factors may also prevent the introduction of an injunction. For example we could refer to the case in the Supreme Court of Justice (UfR 1980/1070) when the court lifted an injunction, already served, in the common interest of a free exchange of ideas. The circumstances of this case were as follows. An artist had produced a poster with the picture of a pig quite similar to the emblem which the plaintiff, Esfood, had registered as a trademark. Over the picture was the caption: 'Danish pigs are healthy'. Underneath, in the same typeface, were the words: 'They are bursting with penicillin'. The majority opinion in the Supreme Court was that the poster did not constitute a sufficient offence for entitling the plaintiff to introduce an injunction against use or distribution of the poster, or for having the poster's text declared null and void.

The justification for this ruling was found in society's interest in the free exchange of ideas, which in some cases may mean that an injunction cannot be served in connection with expressions of opinion, etc, which are in themselves against the interests of the plaintiff. This judgment should not be regarded as grounds for assuming that the Supreme Court has challenged the general principle that false statements—even if they do not affect the honour or clearly recognised rights of a party—are unlawful. The judgment merely serves to show that there can be exceptions to the principle, not only when the person who produced the statement had special reasons or entitlement to do so, but also when society's interest in the free expression of opinion is of greater importance than an individual's interests, and the statement does not exceed the traditional limits for public debate. A counterpart to this judgment is a case handled by the Eastern High Court (UfR 1986/428), in which the defendant invoked this freedom of expression but his claim was not accepted.

The time factor is also taken into account when considering whether an injunction is to be granted against unlawful action. The chances of having a request for an injunction granted are greatest if the injunction application is submitted as early as possible and as soon as the plaintiff becomes aware of the action against which he requires an injunction.

The scope of injunctions

If the conditions are fulfilled, the protection of rights secured by injunctions can apply to both property rights and to personal rights. The main area for the practical use of the injunction is contained in the regulations of the Administration of Justice Law.

In addition to the injunctions allowed under the Administration of Justice Law, other legislation contains a series of different regulations for injunction-related measures for securing compliance with obligations not to commit certain actions. For these injunction-related measures the injunction regulations contained in the Administration of Justice Law are not applied unless specifically stated.

With regard to injunction-related regulations outside the Administration of Justice Law we would refer to paras 78–9 of the Constitutional Provisions for injunctions against certain associations and assemblies, the injunction against the media (the Press Law) in connection with the broadcasting of information, the public injunction against employers in connection with the payment of salaries to employees, where there are arrears in the payment of taxes or maintenance, and the injunction in the Restaurant Business Law, the Animal Protection Law, etc.

The legislation on public planning also contains an injunction of a provisional nature which may be applied in the short term, and which bans alterations to existing buildings or changes in their use, etc. In the legislation for protection of the environment there are also injunction rules against pollution by companies, and in the Law on Marketing Activities the Consumer Ombudsman has powers to grant a provisional injunction against actions which are contrary to chap 1 of the Law which, among other things, contains regulations on marketing practice.

Within the framework of the Administration of Justice Law the injunction is used in a wide range of areas, of which the following should be highlighted.

Rights of access

An injunction may be granted against access (use of a road). A good example is case U1981/326 in which a number of landowners gained acceptance of their position that a private road, belonging to them and to the lessor of a piece of land, could not be used as a means of access to an area leased by a flying club from the lessor, and the injunction against the lessee's use of the road in this way was therefore confirmed.

It is also possible to have an injunction granted against an obstruction to access; see case U1984/389, in which an injunction was served on a landowner, ordering him not to prevent access from a property to a road.

Lease matters

An injunction can be granted against both the lessor (owner) and the tenant in connection with the lease of a property, etc.

Injunction U1985/439 was granted against an owner who had introduced a rule to the effect that parking in a courtyard belonging to the owner was only permitted for the owner's own personal cars, thereby preventing a tenant in a commercial property from using two parking places in the courtyard which were assigned to that commercial property.

An injunction against a tenant may be granted, for instance, in cases where the tenant's use of the leased premises is other than that agreed to in the lease agreement or where the tenant uses the premises in some other irregular fashion, eg not complying with the provisions relating to closing times in premises used for restaurant/recreation activities, see U1938/427.

Employment matters

Boycotts and picketing   A boycott exists when employees, acting in consort, refuse to be employed by a certain employer or at a given working site.

The handling of disputes between employers and employees is assigned to the Labour Court in Copenhagen. The decision of the Labour Court cannot be brought before a higher court or before the ordinary courts.

In the context of Labour Court judgments it is stipulated that a boycott introduced under labour law does not give the right to hinder people who are employed in a company, suppliers to that company, customers and other persons from having free access to and from the company. The so-called picket is not a legally established method of fighting a case. In a judgment delivered by the fifth section of the Eastern High Court, case 188–92/1983, it was ruled that a picket is illegal as a means of defending a case. This raises the question to what extent an employer whose activities are affected by a picket may prevent that picket by the introduction of an injunction. If an injunction is sought in labour disputes, the application must be made, not to the Labour Court, but to the city courts, that is the bailiff's court, whose decisions can be challenged in the higher courts.

This presupposes that the bailiff's court can grant an injunction against an unlawful activity such as a picket. Examples of this from legal practice are limited, the most recent being UfR1938/1989 in which an employer obtained an injunction against a picket set up by a national trade union. With regard to a number of the pickets set up to prevent employers' activities in recent years, no injunctions have been sought by the employers. Instead employers have availed themselves of police assistance, pursuant to para 3 of the Police Regulations, to counter the effects of a picket. It was assumed by those issuing pronouncement No 759/1976 that para 3 of the Police Regulations gave the police general powers to take action against a picket, which is why as a rule the bailiff's court will refuse to grant an injunction in such situations.

In judgment UfR80/294 the Eastern High Court had occasion to take up a position on the implementation of an injunction against an existing picket or boycott. The Injunction Section of the City of Copenhagen gave as its reason for not granting an injunction the fact 'that one cannot through an injunction, cause the defendant to stop an already established boycott or picket, and that an injunction which is only aimed at the defendant cannot serve any purpose, since discussion of the labour conflict cannot be banned in the daily press and via the other media, just as it is not possible in general to prevent the defendant or the members of the company from expressing their views publicly'.

The matter was referred by the employers to the Eastern High Court which expressed the following view: 'It is clearly established here that since spring 1979 the national trade union and the employees have been striving to reach an effectively or potentially more limited agreement.

'Subsequently, and in the light of the contents of the union's communication to the employers on 3 July 1979 concerning the boycott/picket, it is clear that the wish for an agreement was such an important objective of the boycott/picket that the question of its lawfulness is a matter for the Labour Court on the basis of the Labour Court law. The matter will therefore be rejected by the bailiff's court in accordance with point 1 of para 11.'

As can be seen, the Injunction Section of the City of Copenhagen considered the substantive issues relating to the grounds for the injunction, whereas the more important High Court kept to more formal considerations such as the absence of competence on the part of the bailiff's court to deal with the matter.

Publication of names, addresses, etc The publication of the names and addresses of persons who continue to work through a strike (strike-breakers) is against the law. Publication of such details is illegal both from the employees' point of view and from the employer's point of view, see UfR1925/551H. It is also against the law to publish the names of non-unionised workers. Thus an injunction was granted in the case UfR1928/375 against a trade union which, in its members' newsletter, published the names and addresses of the company's employees who were not members of the union, but who had their own personal association.

In conclusion, then, the use of an injunction as a means of preventing unlawful actions, in the context of a labour dispute, must be regarded as rather limited.

The right to privacy/peace
An injunction can be granted against actions which jeopardise a person's privacy or peaceful existence. At the insistence of the deceased's survivors, an injunction was granted, in case UfR1975/1008, against the public showing of a film which showed the life of a drug addict over the last few months before his death, closing with shots of him when dead, despite the fact that the person in question was presumed to have given his consent to those shots being taken.

The right to privacy of name
The right to privacy of name is usually exercised to prevent authors or artists from using a person's legally recognised surname as a synonym or pen-name. The right to a given name can be protected by means of an injunction.

Company names and trade marks
A monopoly on use of a trade mark can be secured in Denmark partly through registration and partly through use.

By a law dated 14 May 1991, concerning trade marks and standardisation marks, Denmark adapted its legislation to EEC Directive No 89/104 of 21 December 1988. As far as the former law is concerned, the most important modification, with a view to coming into line with the EEC Directive, was the requirement of actual use of the trade mark, which also applies to registered trade marks.

In practice there are often problems in terms of the extent to which company names or trade marks resemble one another. It is possible for the injured party to seek to protect his rights through the introduction of an injunction.

In judgment UfR1983/824 a pharmaceutical company had registered the trade mark '*SOR-BITS*' and '*SORBITS*' under product categories 5 and 30, but for more than 16 years had only used the trade marks on chewing-gum and not on other products belonging to the relevant product categories. In the light of these circumstances it was found that in both cases the protection of the trade marks should be limited so that an injunction would not be able to have the effect of preventing the marketing of a slimming product under the name 'Sobit', which belonged to quite a different category of product from the plaintiff's chewing-gum. The judgment is based on an assessment of how likely it is that the defendant would damage the plaintiff's rights.

In cases covered by the decree of the European Economic Community dated 1 December 1986, No 3842/86, concerning measures aimed at introducing an injunction against products made under counterfeit trade marks, the bailiff's court is the competent authority, see art 3 of the decree, para 653, point 1.

In case UfR1990/102 the release of goods at the request of Hugo Boss AG was suspended for three months in accordance with art 3, point 3, para 2, because there were found to be good grounds for fearing that there were plans to introduce products with counterfeit trade marks into Denmark, even though there was no information on the recipients, etc.

Copyright, patents, chips and other exclusive rights

Copyright or intellectual property rights relating to literary or artistic works, including computer programs, may be protected by means of an injunction. It is assumed that an injunction can be introduced even if access to the sanctions provided by law, in the form of fines and the payment of compensation, has ceased to apply on the grounds of passivity.

The use of an injunction to seek protection for intangible rights is of great importance because the sanctions provided under Danish law have a somewhat limited effect and importance. In comparison with international yardsticks the compensation ordered in the event of an infringement of intangible property rights is a fairly modest amount. Hardly ever does the owner of the infringed rights get 'full' compensation for the infringement. It is very important therefore to bring a stop to the infringement as quickly as possible by means of an injunction.

As stated below the granting of an injunction is usually dependent on the plaintiff providing a security, see para 644, points 1 and 2, Rpl. In practice when a claim has to do with intangible rights, be it in the form of the infringement of a copyright or of patent rights, the security required is a relatively high amount.

In certain cases a defendant can have an injunction lifted by providing a security himself and in so far as this security gives the plaintiff adequate protection, see para 643, point 1, Rpl. In practice this rarely occurs, and indeed is never the case where there has been an infringement of intangible rights.

Experience shows that there is a long time between submission of a patent application to the patent authorities and the granting of that patent, just as only a limited number of patent applications are accepted.

It is assumed in the literature on this subject that an injunction for protection of rights in the form of registered titles, eg patent rights, can only be granted and implemented once acceptance of the patent has been notified. However the possibility of granting an injunction before a patent is granted is a vexed question. Until this matter is clarified by the Supreme Court it is best to assume that only a granted patent may be protected by means of an injunction. On the other hand it would be quite justifiable and appropriate to assume that an injunction may be granted in all cases as from the point at which an application is submitted to the authorities. From that point on an injunction will give effective protection against misuse of the information which comes into the hands of the authorities when the patent application is submitted, even if protection exists in the form of provisions governing compensation.

It is assumed in legal practice, see UfR1964/628H, that the defendant, whose damaging activities are stopped by the injunction, will be given a reasonable time, depending on the circumstances, in which to bring his activities to an end, and this is supported by the proportionality rule mentioned earlier.

There are not yet any judgments concerning the infringement of exclusive rights to chips, but it is assumed that any infringement of such rights could be protected by an injunction, even if the infringement gave entitlement to compensation and the imposition of a fine.

Competition clauses

A clause in contracts designed to restrict any unfair advantages being obtained by a competitor can be enforced by means of an injunction. However, an employer cannot use an injunction to prevent an employee who has failed to take up his position or who, without giving notice, has left his position, from taking up other employment, because an injunction cannot be used to enforce a positive action, see Types of injunction, at p 67 above.

An employer, licence holder or joint contractor may as a rule take out an injunction when an employee, or another joint contractor, is acting contrary to a valid competition clause by taking up a position with a competitor, or is engaging in independent competitive activities of his own, or using the knowledge he has acquired contrary to what was agreed between the parties. If an employment contract contains a contractual penalty in the event of a competition clause not being observed, this will not as a rule be assumed to mean that the employer cannot seek an injunction, even if the contractual penalty is imposed (if a fine is paid).

There are special limitations under Danish law in terms of contractual freedom in the area of competition clauses. The rules governing this are to be found in the Salaried Employees Law and in the Contract Law.

As an example, see case No UfR1983/157H. In that case, a sales engineer with the main agent of a German company which, among other things, produced oil filters, gave an undertaking that for two years following his leaving that position he would neither approach, nor accept overtures from, the main agent's principal; there were also provisions for a corresponding contractual penalty and a provision to the effect that the competition clause could be supplemented by an injunction. When the principal terminated the agency in question, the employee resigned of his own free will and set up a company with the principal for the sale of the latter's products which enjoyed by far the greater part of the market in Denmark. The original main agent, who now sold filters of another make, sought an injunction against its former employee's activities which were being carried out within two years of his having left that employment. Since the former main agent's scope for enforcing the clause was not regarded as adequately protected by the contractual penalty clause, the Supreme Court confirmed the injunction granted by the bailiff's court, and it also ruled that there were no grounds for the lapsing of the contractual penalty.

Moreover it is assumed that in certain cases it is the responsibility of former employees to refrain from unfair competition, even in cases where those concerned have not committed themselves to an actual competition clause.

Competition and marketing related matters

Pursuant to para 16, point 1 of the Marketing Law, the Consumer Ombudsman has powers to grant an injunction against action which is contrary to the rules of good marketing practice.

If there is a likely risk that the purpose of an injunction would be missed or forfeited while waiting for a court judgment, the Consumer Ombudsman has powers, in his own right, to grant a provisional injunction. However there is little experience of this in legal practice.

Moreover any private individual who feels that his rights under the Marketing Law's rules on good marketing practice or the provisions for protection of professional secrets are in jeopardy, may seek an injunction from the bailiff's court.

Here is an example from case law:

An engineer who had been employed by a company which produced a special product, began to produce a similar product immediately after leaving that employment. It was later found that this product had a slight difference with respect to the product made by the aforesaid company. The engineer tried to sell his product to the company's customers who accounted for 90 per cent of the total market in Denmark. It was assumed that the engineer had made unauthorised use of professional secrets he had learned during his employment with the company, and he was charged with acting against the provisions of the Marketing Law. The company's application for the granting of an injunction against the former employee's attempts to sell his products to its own customers within a period of one year was upheld (UfR1983/ 105).

Also worth referring to is case UfR1975/1049 in which an employee who resigned from his position in July, and who was employed to manage the development of radio communication equipment for ships, started immediately to produce similar equipment himself. Within a month and a half of leaving his position the former employee was sending out sales letters and brochures, offering delivery around four months later. On the basis of an assessment of the period of time required for development of such equipment, and in the light of the similarities between the equipment offered by the two parties, it was found that the former employee had taken advantage of the knowledge gained during his employment. It was decided that the employee had made use of this confidential information and had infringed the Competition Law as it then was (now the Marketing Law), and a fine/penalty was imposed on him. The former employee was also ordered to pay compensation for the losses he had caused the company by misappropriating an unauthorised competitive advantage. At the start of the case the company obtained an injunction against the former employee, preventing him from producing, selling or offering, as a package, radio communication equipment for ships with certain technical specifications. The injunction was granted in November 1971 and was later lifted in October 1975 by the Supreme Court because, as stated in the Supreme Court's introductory remarks: 'in essence the infringement of rights was characterised by the fact that the employee had gained a temporal/ temporary advantage in the development of the equipment, but that now after several years there are no grounds—in contrast with other manufacturers—for banning production of the equipment containing the alleged points of similarity with the company's equipment'.

Company law matters

A director of a company may seek an injunction against the management's actions if these are at variance with the decisions of the majority of the directors.

On 20 December 1990 the bailiff's court of Lyngby received an application from two members of a board of directors, including the chairman, for an injunction against three of the company's five managers because they had decided, as part of a rationalisation programme, to close down production of the company's products at a certain factory, which involved the sacking of 35 employees. Of the board's total of six members, three were against the programme and the other three were in favour of it. The company was owned by two groups of shareholders in the ratio of 50:50, and the board of directors was made up of three members to represent each group. In accordance with its articles of association the company could be bound by the directors as a whole, or by one director together with the chairman of the board and the vice chairman. The plaintiff's claim was worded as follows: 'In their capacity as directors of NN A/S the defendants must be required to refrain from closing down the company's production plants, including the moving of production from V to S, and to refrain from dismissing the following company employees: . . . [the names of 35 employees] unless a valid management decision is taken to this effect in the company.'

The ruling of the bailiff's court was worded as follows:

It is felt by this court that the decision to close down production at the factory in V, accompanied by the complete dismissal of its 35 employees—both in terms of Company Law para 54, and in terms of the shareholders agreement and the agreement on the management structure of the company—is of such great importance that it comes under the competence of the board of directors. It was also found that for a long time the working relationship between the shareholders in terms of management of the company had been characterised by very serious inconsistencies/instances of incompatibility and that over the last few years operation of the company had had negative results. The fact that a deadlock had been reached in the relationship between the shareholders and between the directors over matters of considerable importance for the company cannot be used as a reason for changing the rules on competences. It was found that there had been a vote on the proposal put forward by the chairman of the board of directors in October 1990, in which all the directors took part, and that following the voting procedure there was an equal division of votes. According to normal voting rules this would result in the proposal becoming of no effect.

Accordingly it was the court's decision that the defendants (the majority of the managers) were not entitled to carry out the rationalisation programme.

It was also found to be the case that in view of the evidence that, not only after the board of directors meeting of October 1990, but also after the defendants had been notified of the application for an injunction submitted to the bailiff's court, the defendants had continued with their rationalisation programme, it was likely that the defendants would continue those actions against which the injunction was sought and that therefore the conditions of para 642, point 2, Rpl could be regarded as applying.

Concerning the claim for an injunction against the closing down and relocation of production activities, it was found that around 75 per cent of the production which had hitherto been carried out in the factory in V had been closed down and transferred to the factory in S. Since that relocation had already taken place it was found that the injunction application could not apply to the production activities which had already been relocated since it would not be a case of requiring the defendants not to perform a given action, see para 641, point 1, of Rpl. An injunction could only therefore apply to that part of production activities which were still being carried out at the factory in V.

With regard to the request for an injunction against the combined dismissal of 35 employees it was ruled that director NN lacked the competence to dismiss these employees in October 1990.

On the basis of the evidence obtained it was found that the chairman of the board's communications of September and October 1990, with respect to the company's employees, demonstrated that he had gone beyond his area of competence, and it was therefore ruled that the dismissal was of no legal effect, both in terms of the company and of the employees. The court stated in its judgment:

Since the employees have not resigned it is possible for an injunction to be sought against the defendants' dismissal of the employees *en masse* or dismissal of the relevant employees. There are, then, grounds for granting the injunction request, but since the plaintiffs have failed to provide full evidence of their rights, it is required that the injunction be conditional upon the plaintiff providing a security in the sum of 5 million Danish Kroner, to cover the damages and inconveniences which could be caused to the company by the injunction.

As will be seen from the above quotation from the judgment of the bailiff's court, the court stressed the extent to which the actions against which the injunction was being sought had already been performed, in which case an injunction could not be granted. In addition, the provision of a security, required for the granting of the injunction, involved a third party, in this case the company itself, whose interests could have been affected by the injunction security.

What has been demonstrated in this section is the type of cases in which primarily private persons can invoke the remedy of an injunction. The examples given are in no way meant to be exhaustive, nor should they be taken as laying down general limits for an application for an injunction.

Structure of the courts

The courts

In accordance with para 1, Rpl the ordinary courts deal with all legal matters which are not—due to their special nature—matters that must be referred to some other court or authority.

The ordinary courts, in this context, are the city courts (of which there are 82 in total—1 for each judiciai district), the High Courts (the Eastern and the Western High Courts) and the Supreme Court.

All city courts are operated as one-man courts (ie there is only one judge), whereas the High Courts and the Supreme Court have a panel of judges. In the High Courts there is a panel of three judges, and in the Supreme Court a panel of at least five.

In the ordinary courts the judges normally preside over all types of cases, irrespective of their nature, and reach their judgments without the involvement of lay assessors or of fellow judges with special expertise. Dividing up cases into areas of specialisation, according to their subject matter, among different departments in the large city courts and High Courts is only practised to a very limited extent, and is based solely on an internal division, and not on a legally based one.

The term 'ordinary court' also includes the Maritime and Commercial Court of Copenhagen which deals with maritime and commercial cases in the greater Copenhagen area, which comprises 13 judicial districts in the immediate vicinity of Copenhagen.

The Western High Court's area of operations is to the west of the Little Belt, in other words, primarily Jutland, whereas the Eastern High Court's area of operations is to the east of the Little Belt, including Funen, Zealand and surrounding islands.

As a general rule the judgments of the city courts may be appealed against at the High Courts, and the primary (first instance) judgments of the High Courts and the judgments of the Maritime and Commercial Court in Copenhagen may be appealed against in the Supreme Court.

The allocation of cases to the various ordinary courts, in terms of which court has competence, depends partly on the rules of substantial competence, paras 224–232, Rpl, and partly on the rules of geographic competence, paras 235–248, Rpl.

As a general rule the city courts deal with all civil actions of the first instance: however, cases involving the examination of decisions taken by a ministry or by another authority which has final administrative competence, cases of principle or of a special substantive matter, or cases involving a sum of money in excess of 500,000 Danish Kroner, may be dealt with, either on request or directly, by the High Courts of First Instance.

The geographic competence of the city courts and of the High Courts is defined by geographic areas, and the dividing-up of cases among them is based on the geographic affiliation of the parties or of the object of the legal action. The main criterion is the defendant's place of residence, see para 235, Rpl. If the defendant has no recognised place of residence, the place where he is staying will be the deciding factor. The domicile of companies will be the place where they have their main office/headquarters, or where this is not clear, the place where a member of the board of directors or of the management has his place of residence.

The enforcement of judgments pronounced by a court is the responsibility of the bailiff's courts which come under the auspices of the city courts. There is thus a bailiff's court in each of the 82 city courts.

In addition to being responsible for the enforcement of judgments, the bailiff's courts are also responsible for the implementation of provisional remedies of seizures and injunctions.

An application for an injunction is submitted to the bailiff's court in the judicial district, see para 646, Rpl, where the defendant has his place of residence. If the defendant has no place of residence in Denmark, the application can be submitted to the bailiff's court in the place where the defendant is staying, happens to be, or has some activities, or where the action against which the injunction is being sought is being carried out, compare the principles contained in para 487. Since the competence of the bailiff's court is determined by the legal provisions on place of residence, there are seldom grounds for tactical considerations with regard to the competent bailiff's court.

Legal team

In Denmark only solicitors are authorised to conduct court cases. The title of solicitor may only be used by a person qualified to act in that capacity. All solicitors may appear in the city courts, and thus in the bailiff's courts. Most solicitors are also entitled to appear in the High Courts, and to a lesser extent in the Supreme Court: solicitors need a special qualification to be entitled to appear in the Supreme Court.

There has not in the past been a tradition of specialisation to any great extent among Danish solicitors. In addition it has also been the case that solicitors have been subject to relatively strict regulations about advertising their services and any areas of specialisation they might have. However there is now a tendency towards a relaxation of these provisions. The *List of Law Firms In Europe* by John Pritchard (London, 1991), contains a summary of law firms in Denmark with an indication of the respective firms' main areas of activity.

Criteria for obtaining interlocutory injunctions

Evidence

The provision of evidence in Danish legal cases normally takes place orally and in the immediate presence of the court which is to pass judgment. This basic principle also applies in matters relating to the granting of injunctions. Danish law does not acknowledge sworn statements as a basis for evidence and the rules relating to the taking of an oath were cancelled by law in 1961.

Before a party or a witness makes a statement in court, the judge stresses the need for the parties or witnesses to tell the truth, and in the case of the witnesses the obligation to make a statement. False statements are punishable either by a penalty or imprisonment.

The extent of the evidence which may be obtained during the handling of an injunction case is not directly regulated by the Administration of Justice Law. Section 647 of the Administration of Justice Law states that the bailiff's court may cut short the production of evidence the nature and extent of which falls outside the framework of the injunction case, in just the same way as the bailiff's court also has the right to dismiss evidence which is clearly of no relevance to the case under examination, or the purpose of which is simply to delay the judgment.

By the amendment of the Administration of Justice Law on 1 January 1989, provision was made for extending the powers of the plaintiff to provide evidence in an injunction case, both in terms of the existence of the right and in terms of the infringement of that right. These powers to provide evidence are particularly relevant in matters involving the infringement of intangible rights. This extension of powers to provide evidence, under the aforesaid amendment, should be seen in the context of the simultaneous sharpening of the requirements relating to evidence which in the first instance are required to protect the defendant from any adverse effects, and in respect of which the defendant cannot later receive adequate compensation for an unjustified injunction.

As stated above, an injunction can only be granted if the plaintiff is able to show, or demonstrate the likelihood, that the actual conditions governing implementation of an injunction apply. The burden of proof therefore rests with the plaintiff, which is in accordance with the general principles of Danish law. As can be seen from the foregoing, the bailiff's court does not reach any final decision on the merits of the case, since such a judgment is dependent on an actual court examination in the subsequent court proceedings, compare Notice, p 87, below.

The relevant test

The principle behind the provisional remedy—the injunction—is that this measure can be introduced before the court has reached its final judgment to substantiate the plaintiff's claim. An injunction may be applied for irrespective of whether the bailiff's court is provided with evidence that the actions to be restrained are contrary to the plaintiff's rights, but simply where the plaintiff is able to prove, or demonstrate the probable existence of his right. If, on the basis of his own presentation of the facts, the plaintiff has no right to require the defendant to refrain from the actions against which the injunction is being sought, the bailiff's court will reject the injunction application, see para 642, No 1. As a general principle the bailiff's court shall give a ruling on any matters of dispute as to the general interpretation of the legal rules; however actual exercising of given rights (where the evidence is not clear) will not involve comprehensive evidence, but simply the substantiating or demonstration of the likelihood of the plaintiff's right.

As stated earlier, it is not possible to bring an injunction against actions which are a violation of the plaintiff's right if that right is already adequately safeguarded by the regulations governing criminal liability or the defendant's liability to pay compensation for damages to the plaintiff, and for which the defendant may have provided a security, see para 643, point 1.

Nor does the plaintiff have the right in such cases to seek a ruling whereby the defendant is required to refrain from these actions, regardless of their unlawfulness. Where the general sanctions of the Danish legal system provide adequate legal protection, there are no grounds for supplementing them with special, individually formulated injunctions against specific unlawful actions.

The following case, UfR1977/578, will illustrate this. The circumstances were as follows. Under the law on the transportation of goods, permits are issued to individual shipping companies for operating in certain geographical areas. A haulage contractor, who was in possession of one of these permits, sought an injunction against a competitor who was engaging in competing haulage activities without a permit. Since the transport law contained penalty clauses, which gave the plaintiff the right to request that the competing haulage contractor be fined, it was decided that the plaintiff already had adequate protection, and that the injunction the latter was seeking could not be granted.

However, the main problem in the most frequently occurring injunction cases involving intangible rights is not usually whether the penalty clause provisions found in the law on copyrights, patents and trade marks, etc, can be regarded as providing adequate protection in the event of an infringement, but whether the defendant, by his actions, has infringed, or will infringe, the plaintiff's rights. Effective protection of the plaintiff's intangible rights requires that a speedy stop to any misuse, unlawful use or plagiarism of the plaintiff's rights can be implemented. It is often not possible, in a case whose final judgment may not be pronounced for several years, to redress any damages in the form of compensation.

The granting of an injunction is not generally limited by whether the plaintiff is able to claim compensation from the defendant if it is determined in the proceedings, or in any other way, that the defendant, through his action, has infringed the plaintiff's rights. The general rules on compensation do not provide the plaintiff with adequate protection in cases where the possibility or expectation of having to pay compensation is not regarded as sufficient motivation for preventing the defendant from acting in a certain way, or where the pronouncement of a judgment to pay compensation at a later time would not adequately compensate the plaintiff for his loss, or where the defendant may be assumed to lack the resources with which to pay the aforesaid compensation.

The rules to the effect that the defendant can apply for an injunction to be lifted by providing a security are not actually used in practice.

Cross-undertaking in damages

If the bailiff's court decides that an injunction may only be granted if the plaintiff provides a security deposit for possible damages and inconveniences which the injunction could cause the defendant, pursuant to para 644, point 1, the bailiff's court will also determine the nature and size of that security, see para 644, point 2.

If the bailiff's court requires such a security deposit, it will first grant the injunction requested and state that the latter will only take effect when the security deposit required has been established, see para 644, point 3.

The nature of the security is normally either a cash deposit paid to the court, or the setting up of an irrevocable bank guarantee.

The size of the security is a matter for the bailiff's court to decide. The decision on the size of the security rests on the bailiff's court's assessment of the likelihood of the defendant sustaining a justifiable loss in the event that the proceedings find that the injunction was imposed without justification. It is outside the scope of this chapter to discuss in depth the rules governing compensation which are taken into account when making this assessment.

In the afore-mentioned bailiff's court judgment of December 1990, see p 79, an injunction was granted on the basis of a security of 5 million Danish Kroner. The defendant made a statement to the effect that if the injunction were to be granted, it could only be granted on the basis of a security of at least 210 million Danish Kroner. This difference indicates the uncertainty and randomness that characterise the Danish bailiff's court's decisions in the area of security deposits. In general terms it can be said that, measured against international yardsticks, the securities required in Denmark are very modest, particularly in light of the sums involved, which must be seen in the context of Danish law and the Danish courts' reluctance to order 'full compensation' for a loss suffered.

Alternative to an application

The length of time involved between submission of the plaintiff's request and the eventual granting of an injunction obviously varies from case to case.

It can generally be stated that the Danish bailiff's courts act quickly when an application for an injunction is received in order to provide the appropriate remedy. Depending on the extent of the evidence involved or required, a realistic time-scale would be to expect the granting of an injunction within 4 to 30 days of the application being received.

This is in contrast with the normal average period for handling a case in the courts, in cases where the plaintiff does not need to secure his rights through an injunction, but simply through an ordinary court action. The normal time for handling cases in the city courts varies from district to district and from case to case, but an average handling period of 6 to 18 months is characteristic.

There is not really any direct legislative alternative to a request for an injunction, apart from bringing an ordinary legal action.

The courts cannot decide that a case is to be given priority treatment or accelerated in any way, since the processing and preparation of an action starts with the parties involved. The Danish courts are inclined to allow the other party a reasonably long, and often a particularly long, period of time in which to formulate their defence, and only intervene if the court gains the impression that the party's preparations are taking an inordinately long time; but even in such cases the scope of the court to take positive action is limited in practice.

Practice and procedure

Notice

Ex parte

Section 646, point 2 of the Administration of Justice Law refers to a number of procedural rules within that Law, both in first instance cases and in injunction cases, which are applicable in cases involving injunctions.

In accordance with para 491, Pt 1, point 1, the bailiff's court determines the time and place for a hearing. The basic rule is that the hearing is held in the office of the bailiff's court, that is to say at the court. The bailiff's court will advise the applicant where and when the matter is to be heard. This notice to the applicant will be given in the way which the bailiff's court deems most appropriate, and may be by telephone. If the plaintiff fails to appear at the hearing fixed by the bailiff's court, the application will be rejected.

The rules governing the summoning—or ordering to attend—of the defendant (see para 493, Pts 1 and 2, and para 494, Pts 1 and 4), are applicable in injunction cases. However, the bailiff's court may dispense with informing the defendant of the injunction application in special circumstances. Dispensing with informing the defendant will occur in cases where there is an urgent need for the injunction to be granted. If these circumstances do not apply to the defendant, it will be a condition for the granting of the injunction that the available materials—the application, attachments, etc—can substantiate, or demonstrate the likelihood of the fact that the prerequisites for granting an injunction are met. If the applicant is unable to meet the burden of proof requirements, he can agree to the case being heard *inter partes* and for the serving of a summons on the defendant, together with a copy of the application and any attachments thereto.

This possibility of dispensing with informing the defendant is only exercised on rare occasions, and only in cases where it is feared that the possibility for having the injunction granted in any other way would be greatly reduced, for example in cases where the defendant might immediately take defensive action and where this action could render any injunction ineffective.

Inter partes

The main rule in terms of the handling of injunction applications is that the defendant is summoned to appear, and as a rule will appear or be represented, at the bailiff's court hearing.

With regard to the general procedural rules refer to p 89 below. If the defendant is summoned in accordance with the relevant legal provisions, but fails to appear at the hearing without good cause, the plaintiff's application for the injunction will be granted, see para 646, Pt 2, and para 354, Pt 3.

The bailiff's court will determine the time and place for the hearing at its sole discretion. If the plaintiff has special reasons for wanting the matter speeded up, the bailiff's court is required to take this into account and will do all it can to comply with the plaintiff's wishes in terms of timing. The hearing will normally be held during the bailiff's court's normal office hours—between 9.00am and 4.00pm, Mondays to Fridays. If it is essential that the hearing be held outside normal office hours, the bailiff's court will be required to comply with a request to this end.

If the plaintiff is not required to make a statement as a party during the proceedings, it is not essential that he be present and the application may be submitted by the plaintiff's solicitor.

Generally

An application for granting an injunction must be submitted in writing to the bailiff's court in the judicial district where the defendant has his domicile, see para 646, point 1. The purpose in using the general venue regulations for civil cases in preference to the special venue regulations relating to enforcement, see para 487, is to ensure that in the widest possible sense the defendant is represented throughout the injunction proceedings. The venue regulations mean that it is possible to ensure that the injunction case and the subsequent ordinary action/proceedings are dealt with by the same court, unless—because of the size of the sum involved—the matter comes under the competence of the High Court or—because of its special nature—the case comes under the competence of the Maritime and Commercial Court in Copenhagen as the Court of First Instance. This relationship between the competence of the bailiff's court and the ordinary court, on geographic grounds, can also have the effect of avoiding unnecessary court costs in larger, more complicated matters, in those cases where the ordinary action can be dealt with by the same judge in both the bailiff's court and the ordinary court.

In those cases where the defendant is not a national, the injunction proceedings may be dealt with by the bailiff's court in the judicial district where the action against which the injunction is being sought was carried out.

The bailiff's court will take the necessary steps to ensure that it is competent to deal with the plaintiff's request. If the defendant attends a hearing or if he is involved in an injunction matter and does not challenge the competence of the bailiff's court in question, that bailiff's court will be regarded as having competence.

Procedure and rules

The formal requirements with regard to the procedures for an injunction application are the same as those applying to a summons in a civil action to a Court of First Instance. In summary these requirements are as follows:

The application must contain:

(a) the parties' names and addresses, including a postal address in Denmark to which the plaintiff's communications can be sent;
(b) identification of the bailiff's court which will hear the injunction application;
(c) the plaintiff's claim;
(d) a short summary of the facts on which the claim is based, that is to say the documents and evidence that are to be produced; and
(e) a list of the documents and other evidence to which the plaintiff intends to make reference during the hearing.

The application must be submitted in quadruplicate with duplicates of attachments. The application must be accompanied by payment of the court fee which is currently (July 1991) 300 Kroner, plus a supplement of 400 Kroner if the proceedings are to be conducted outside the court's own offices.

Determination of whether an injunction application provides a suitable basis for proceeding with the case will be subject to the same rules as those applying to civil cases. If the bailiff's court considers the application inappropriate it may reject the application. The plaintiff will normally be given a period of time in which to rectify any deficiencies in the application.

In larger, more complicated cases the defendant will normally be provided with a written statement containing the plaintiff's claim and the documents and evidence will be sent to the defendant before the hearing.

If the bailiff's court decides to grant the injunction application and thereby acknowledges the plaintiff's claim, the injunction will take effect once notice thereof is served, or if the injunction is made subject to the establishment of a security deposit, as from the time the latter is established.

An injunction must be followed by an ordinary court action in the courts of first instance, in which the court has to decide whether the injunction granted by the bailiff's court was legal, see the provisions of paras 634 and 648.

The period in which an action must be brought is two weeks from the date on which the injunction is granted. If this period expires on a Saturday or a Sunday, on a public holiday or any other day on which the court is normally closed, eg Constitution Day, the summons for the legal action must be in the hands of the court before closing time on the last working day before the aforesaid two-week period expires. If the summons for the legal action is submitted late the defendant or summonsed party may call for the injunction to be lifted. The summons will be served to the defendant's (summoned party's) domicile in accordance with the provisions contained in paras 235–248. If the sum involved in the action has a value in excess of 500,000 Danish Kroner, it may be submitted direct to one of the High Courts, see para 227, Pt 1, point 2, or if the subject matter warrants it, it may be submitted to the Maritime and Commercial Court in Copenhagen, in which connection see para 9, Pt 2, and Pt 3.

If there is already an action relating to the same infringement, the new action must be submitted to the same court and dealt with alongside the matter already submitted.

It is the ordinary court which will determine whether the injunction was legally well founded. During the legal proceedings connected with the ordinary action brought by the plaintiff, the defendant may submit any objections he has against the legality of the injunction, see also below, The defendant's ability to vary or discharge, p 94.

Costs

The applicable principle under Danish law is that the party which loses a case is liable to pay the other party's legal or court costs, unless the court finds that there are special grounds for departing from this general principle, see paras 311–329.

In the light of the provisional nature of the injunction case, the bailiff's court does not issue instructions for the defendant to pay the plaintiff's costs in connection with the granting of the injunction. The determination of these costs is deferred to the court responsible for dealing with the corresponding legal action and which will award costs to the plaintiff or claimant if it upholds the latter's case.

On the other hand the bailiff's court will award costs to the defendant, at the latter's request, in the event that the plaintiff withdraws his application or if the bailiff's court is unable to admit the plaintiff's application for an injunction, see para 647, Pt 2. In this case the bailiff's court will award costs on the basis of the financial value of the case and time factors involved.

It is usual for the 'winning party' not to get full reimbursement of costs for the services of his solicitor in connection with the award and assessment of costs. The court will fix the amount of costs at the same time as making the award.

When the bailiff's court reaches its decision on the award of costs, these must normally be paid to the opposite party within 14 days of the decision being notified. A decision on costs may be requested by either party, see below at p 94.

Post-injunction factors

Service of the injunction

Either when submitting a written statement, answer, or when defending itself orally at a hearing, the defendant must give an address in Denmark to which all communications, including the summons, are to be sent/delivered, see para 349.

The court's judgment will be reached as soon as possible after the corresponding proceedings have been completed. If, when the matter is accepted or admitted by the court, the parties are not informed when the judgment is to be pronounced, the parties must request that the proceedings be conducted in accordance with para 644, Pt 3, and para 219, Pt 3. This request may be made in an ordinary letter or in the form of telephone instructions. If the parties have been informed when the judgment is to be pronounced, the period for appeal and enforcement of that judgment will run from the date of its pronouncement.

If the defendant is represented by a solicitor, all communications and summons may be sent to the solicitor, whatever their nature in the proceedings, and they will be regarded as having been sent to the defendant himself, see para 161. If notification of the pronouncement of a judgment is given by telephone to the parties' solicitors, the date of the pronouncement will be regarded as having been communicated, whether or not the parties themselves are informed thereof.

The bailiff's court may grant the defendant a shorter period in which to prepare its response to the injunction, but in such cases this must be clearly stated in the notification. It is normal for an injunction to take effect immediately, as soon as it is granted, so that an infringement of the injunction's provisions from that moment will be subject to the relevant sanctions, see below and p 95.

Sanctions

When an injunction is deliberately infringed, the defendant may be subject to a fine or to imprisonment, in which connection he will be ordered to pay compensation, see para 651. This provision also applies to anyone who intentionally assists the defendant in infringing the injunction.

The criminal proceeding involved here is a so-called private criminal case in which the right to take proceedings rests with the plaintiff, see para 725.

The defendant may only be punished if he could have known that his action was contrary to the injunction, see para 1, the Penal Code. An infringement of the injunction is also punishable, provided the injunction is not lifted, whether or not the injunction is confirmed in the subsequent ordinary action, due to the banned activity having no legal justification. Where a criminal case is brought, pursuant to para 651, therefore, this will be subject to the judgment in the ordinary action, depending on the circumstances. However, a criminal case must be brought, even if an ordinary action is not commenced, if it would otherwise be the case that a well grounded injunction would lose its effect, eg where an injunction is directed at a blatant plagiarism of a product. In case UfR1984/356H the Supreme Court decided not to defer a criminal case in anticipation of an ordinary action because the judgment in the criminal case was seen as a necessary condition to enforce the injunction.

In the Maritime and Commercial Court judgment UfR1974/287 the owner of a business which traded in a brand of whisky in bottles whose appearance and labels were easily mistakable for an existing well-known brand, and against whose activities an injunction was granted, was ordered to pay a fine of 5,000 Danish Kroner for infringing the injunction, in addition to paying compensation.

If an infringement is due to an excusable misunderstanding, the defendant cannot be punished. It is the deliberate infringement of the injunction which is punishable pursuant to para 651; thus a penalty may be imposed irrespective of whether the actions in question are lawful under substantive law.

Normally the plaintiff's claim for compensation will be dealt with in the ordinary proceedings, so no decision will be taken on the matter of compensation as a general rule before a judgment has been pronounced in the main action. However, in special cases, a judgment can be pronounced on a claim for compensation, where there is a flagrant infringement of an injunction, at the same time as the criminal case is dealt with; see UfR1974/287 above. A condition for being awarded compensation is that the plaintiff is able to show that he has suffered a loss which is covered by the general compensation regulations under Danish law.

At the request of the plaintiff the bailiff's court is also under an obligation to assist with the upholding of the injunction, see para 645, including preventing the infringement of an injunction and invalidating any action taken contrary to the terms of the injunction. In order to fulfil these obligations the bailiff's court may enlist the necessary police assistance.

The legal remedies implemented to prevent actions that would infringe the injunction must be contained in the injunction granted, otherwise the bailiff's court's assistance in this respect would involve having to hear the injunction proceedings again.

The actions being referred to may take the form of physical actions which in themselves are suitable for preventing infringement activities. If the injunction imposes accessory obligations or actions on the defendant, the bailiff's court may order that the necessary enforcement action be taken on the plaintiff's behalf.

Furthermore, in accordance with para 645, Pt 2, the bailiff's court can order the seizure of objects if they have been used or are being used in violation of the injunction, or if there are good grounds for assuming that those objects will be used in this way.

Seized objects will be impounded by the bailiff's court and retained at the cost of the plaintiff. The bailiff's court may make seizure subject to the plaintiff providing security for costs, or subject to an increase of an existing security provided in connection with the injunction, in order to cover the defendant's potential right to compensation if the plaintiff subsequently loses the main action.

The defendant's ability to vary or discharge

The defendant is at liberty to submit a claim and supporting documents in the main proceedings in order to show that the injunction was granted without justification. In accordance with para 650, the judgment of the bailiff's court can be appealed against in the High Court which has jurisdiction over the bailiff's court in question. The judgment pronounced by the High Court in the context of such an appeal cannot normally be taken further by appealing to the Supreme Court, though where there are special grounds, the Minister of Justice may authorise this.

The period during which appeals may be lodged is four weeks as from the date on which the judgment is pronounced, provided that the parties are made aware of this, or as from the date on which the parties receive such notification, see Service of the injunction, p 92.

The bailiff's court's decisions in terms of granting the injunction and in terms of the provision of a security, may be appealed against either individually or together. An appeal can be lodged if an injunction is granted or rejected.

An appeal is normally in writing and is submitted to the bailiff's court which issued the judgment in question.

An appeal that has been lodged cannot suspend the injunction, which means that if an injunction has been granted and it is appealed against, the defendant must nevertheless comply with the terms of that injunction. It also means that arrangements must go ahead for the corresponding main action, irrespective of whether an appeal is lodged.

In an appeal the parties are able to submit claims which have not already been submitted to the bailiff's court. However, this does not apply to appeals in cases where the bailiff's court has granted an injunction, see para 587, Pt 4. An appeal is normally processed in writing, but within para 587, Pt 6, there is the possibility of an oral hearing if, depending on the nature of the case, it is found that the circumstances warrant this. If both parties apply for oral proceedings, this will normally be granted.

The submission of an appeal does not mean that the plaintiff can dispense with bringing an ordinary legal action.

Enquiry into damages

A person who has been granted an injunction on the basis of a claim which, as a result of the outcome of the main proceedings is found to be invalid, and as a result of which the injunction is discharged, must pay the defendant compensation for losses and damage, see paras 648 and 639. Compensation for financial damage is only awarded if the defendant can show that he has suffered such damage.

If not awarded in the context of the main action, the defendant's claim for compensation must be made in a separate action. The matter must be submitted within three months of the injunction expiring or being lifted at the defendant's request. Where an injunction has been discharged, any security deposit set up by the plaintiff will be released to the plaintiff once the three months has passed and the defendant has not submitted a separate action.

Worth mentioning are the following examples from Danish case law.

An unlawful injunction against the construction of a planned summer-house which was held up for about one year, entitled the defendant to compensation for lost rents and increased building costs as well as the costs incurred in boarding up and then re-opening the site, etc. No compensation was given for non-economic damage. The court awarded compensation based on the details provided by the defendant (UfR1975/408).

In the Maritime and Commercial Court judgment No UfR1982/650, the court ruled that:

... since the injunction went further than the circumstances of the case warranted, the injunction in its existing form is unlawful. In view of the foregoing there are no grounds for assuming that the defendant has been caused loss by the short duration of the far-reaching, albeit in other respects, well founded, injunction, and the plaintiff is therefore not regarded as liable for paying the defendant compensation on the basis of the latter's claim.

Seizures

Seizure to secure a money claim

By art 627 of the Code of Civil Procedure the court may order seizure to secure a claim if (1) execution cannot be ordered in respect of the claim; and (2) it is assumed that the possibility of obtaining payment subsequently would otherwise be substantially reduced. The present wording was introduced by an amendment of 7 December 1988, which came into force on 1 January 1989.

Conditions for the making of an order

The Civil Procedure Committee stated, in Report 1107/1987 regarding the rules concerning seizure and injunctions, that normally seizure may not be ordered unless there is an actual ground for assuming that by his dispositions the debtor will jeopardise the creditor's capacity to obtain payment.

The creditor must therefore present to the court concrete facts regarding the personal or financial position of the debtor which enable it to hold that seizure should be ordered to prevent the creditor's ability to obtain subsequent payment being reduced. An exhaustive list of such facts cannot be given, but as examples the committee mentioned cases where the debtor intends to take up permanent residence abroad, realises his assets to an unusual extent, makes unusual business arrangements or states openly that he intends to prevent the creditor from obtaining payment. These constitute grounds for making an order under art 627(2).

Proof

Unlike the provisions regarding injunctions (see art 642 and p 68, above) it is not required that the creditor should prove to the court that he has a claim against the debtor. Thus the court does not conduct any thorough scrutiny of the basis of the creditor's application, as it does in the case of an injunction. The rule is that seizure is ordered at the request of the creditor (if he furnishes security, where required) unless the debtor proves, within the limits of the adduction of evidence permitted before the court of execution (*Fogedretten*) (see art 501(2)–(4)), that the claim does not exist. On the other hand, the creditor must prove that the formal conditions for the making of an order are fulfilled (see art 627).

Security

Seizure may be ordered subject to a condition that the creditor furnishes security, the nature and amount of which are determined by the court (art 629(2)).

In determining the amount of security, the court may take into account, in addition to the amount of the creditor's claim, for example, the nature of the assets against which the order is made and their value.

The security will normally take the form of funds lodged with the court, an irrevocable bank guarantee for an unlimited period, the lodging of securities, etc.

Procedure

The application for a seizure order must be submitted in writing to the execution court in the place in which the debtor has his permanent address or, in the absence thereof, the place in which the assets against which the order is sought are situated. The application must contain particulars of the concrete facts upon which the creditor relies and other information required for treatment of the case. It must be accompanied by any documents upon which the creditor relies.

An order may be made solely against a portion of the debtor's assets which, in the opinion of the court, is required to cover the claim together with accrued and estimated interest and the probable costs of the seizure proceedings and the proceedings concerning the claim (see art 632).

An order may not be made if it must be assumed that the claim does not exist (see art 628). This will be the case, for example, where the debtor can show that he has a counterclaim against the creditor which amounts to or exceeds the creditor's claim.

An order may be made against aircraft, foreign ships and ships' cargoes belonging to foreign States solely in accordance with the relevant provisions in other legislation (see Statute 198 of 15 May 1950 regarding ships owned by foreign States, etc). Applications for the seizure of a vessel and an injunction prohibiting its departure to secure a claim under maritime law are treated in accordance with the provisions of chap 12(a) of the Maritime Code.

Seizure may be averted by the debtor or the order rescinded if he furnishes security sufficient, in the opinion of the court, to cover the creditor's claim, together with accrued and estimated interest and the probable costs of the seizure proceedings and the proceedings regarding the claim. Seizure may of course be averted if the debtor pays the claim.

An order may be made solely against assets owned by the debtor and thus cannot be made against assets owned by a third party. An order may be made against an asset of the debtor even though a third party has a limited right over it (eg a mortgage or pledge), but solely subject to that right. Moreover, an order may be made solely against assets against which execution may subsequently be levied. This prevents an order from being made against assets which, in accordance with art 509, must be regarded as necessary for the maintenance of a modest home and a modest standard of living for the debtor and his household or against assets with a value not exceeding 3,000 Danish Kroner which are necessary for the occupation, education or training of the debtor or his household.

Effect of seizure

The order deprives the debtor of the right to exercise disposal *de facto* or *de jure* over the asset seized that would be incompatible with seizure. Consequently, from the time when the order is made he cannot move, consume or destroy the asset or conclude legal transactions concerning the asset.

If the order relates to a claim of the debtor against a third party, the debtor is not entitled to receive the claim.

Provided that the necessary safety measures are adopted, the order is protected against the debtor's business purchasers in good faith and thus it is not protected against the debtor's other creditors. Consequently, execution levied by another creditor will prevail over the seizure order, but does not discharge it. It merely gives way to execution in the order of priority or satisfaction.

It is beyond the scope of this chapter to discuss the order of priority or several seizure orders in respect of the same asset, including priority regarding compulsory sale by auction in competition with other creditors.

In order to obtain protection against the debtor's business purchasers in good faith the creditor who has obtained a seizure order must take the necessary safety measures in accordance with Danish law, for example, in the case of real property the debtor should register the seizure order. With regard to other measures, reference may be made to the relevant provisions of the law of property.

Institution of proceedings

The creditor must institute proceedings in respect of the claim in question within seven days of the date on which the order is made, unless this requirement is waived by the debtor during or after the seizure proceedings. During the main proceedings the creditor must also submit a separate declaration confirming the seizure as lawful.

The main proceedings must be brought in the court which has jurisdiction in accordance with arts 235 *et seq* of the Code of Civil Procedure. Normally this will be the place of residence of the debtor (defendant) (see arts 235 and 238), but in certain cases it may be one of the alternative places mentioned in arts 242–246.

It should be observed in particular that if the debtor is not domiciled in a Member State of the EC and the asset against which the seizure order has been made is situated in Denmark, the proceedings may be brought in the court having jurisdiction in the place in which it is situated (see art 246(3)).

If the proceedings in respect of the claim in question must be instituted in a foreign court, they must be brought within two weeks of the issue of the order. Within the same period proceedings must also be instituted in Denmark to confirm the legality of the seizure (see art 634(4)).

If main proceedings are pending in a foreign court whose decision will be binding in Denmark, the proceedings for the ratification of the seizure must be suspended until that decision is made (see art 634(5)).

The rules regarding the institution of the main proceedings and confirmation of the order apply also to cases where seizure is averted because the debtor furnishes security.

In the ratification proceedings the court determines whether the seizure was lawful. The debtor may raise any objections regarding the legality of the order.

The order may be rescinded by the execution court if the creditor fails to institute ratification proceedings or the main proceedings within the period specified in art 634 or if either of these proceedings are dismissed by the court.

Extinction of seizure

The order is extinguished if the debtor becomes insolvent (see s 31(3) of the Insolvency Statute). At the same time the creditor's obligation to institute the main proceedings also lapses (art 635). This also applies if the debtor dies and his estate is taken into public administration without liability for the debts imposed on the heirs.

Search and seize orders

It is not possible to resort to search and seize orders in Denmark. If a party in a legal action requires the production (submission) of a document or other material which is in the possession of the other party, for the purpose of providing evidence, he can require that his opponent make that material available. If the other party refuses to do so, this will have what is referred to as a damaging effect on the interested party.

It is also punishable to destroy evidence when one is aware that the other party has submitted a request for it to be produced.

If the documents or objects belong to the plaintiff or claimant, as a result of his right of ownership thereof, he can request that they be returned to his possession and where necessary seek the bailiff's court's assistance to this end. However this is outside the scope of this description of an application of the injunction.

Jakob Poulsen

France

Introduction

The different types of procedure

The Code of Civil Procedure provides for various contentious or non-contentious measures which make it possible to obtain a range of immediate judicial measures, particularly in matters of urgency.

Law No 91–650 of 9 July 1991, which comes into effect on 1 August 1992, provides for the appointment of a single judge of enforcement with powers to issue protective orders. This will be the President of the *Tribunal de Grande Instance*, who will have the right to appoint a substitute.

Thus the new law provides for concentration of enforcement procedures, in contrast with the present system under which a disputed matter is divided up between various jurisdictions depending on the subject and the level of the dispute.

A decree of implementation is awaited which will state the ways in which this law will be applied. This will be followed by injunction orders authorising a variety of measures.

In non-contentious measures, several applications may be made, to either the President of the *Tribunal de Grande Instance*, the President of the *Tribunal d'Instance*, or the President of the *Tribunal de Commerce* (Commercial Court).

In contentious matters, the summary procedure (*référé*) before the President of the *Tribunal d'Instance*, of the *Tribunal de Grande Instance* or of the Commercial Court, or even the *Conseil des Prud'Hommes*, also makes it possible to obtain a variety of immediate measures quickly.

Finally, a hybrid measure, the order to pay (*l'injonction de payer*), allows a payment order to be obtained quickly.

At the outset, the procedure is non-contentious and leads to an injunction order against which the debtor may file a counter-claim. The procedure then becomes contentious.

An application for an order to pay may be presented to the President of the *Tribunal d'Instance* or to the President of the Commercial Court.

In France, the *Tribunal de Grande Instance* and the *Tribunal d'Instance* have jurisdiction in civil matters, the *Tribunal d'Instance* having jurisdiction in cases involving sums under FF 30,000 (art R 321-1 of the Code of Judicial Organisation).

The *Tribunal d'Instance* also has jurisdiction (*ratione materiale*) in cases relating to matters such as rents or agricultural leases.

As regards the Commercial Court, this court has jurisdiction in all commercial matters between traders (*commerçants*) or in matters relating to commercial transactions.

Examples of the scope of the procedures

In France, it is necessary to distinguish between non-contentious measures and contentious measures obtained by summary procedure.

Non-contentious measures

These are authorised by orders on application given in the absence of the other party. The principal measures which the court may order on application are:

(1) Applications for a certified report, whereby one party obtains the appointment of a court bailiff (*huissier*) responsible for reporting various established facts; for example, conditions relating to the occupation of premises by a tenant or to the sale of a product by a distributor.

(2) Applications for seizure of an imitation, in matters of registered designs, trade marks and patents, based on different laws relating specifically to each subject.

The latter type of measure leads to an order authorising the holder of a trade mark, registered design or patent to have a court bailiff enter the premises of a third party in order to gather evidence of infringement of a registered design, trade mark or patent.

This will be followed by the trial on the merits, but the preventive measure outlined above is an effective means, in the case of infringement, of gathering evidence of an infringement before the other party disposes of it.

(3) Applications for attachment give the applicant authority, in the absence of a legal document, to obtain leave from the court of the place where the debtor is domiciled, to attach sums owed by a third party to the debtor.

It is then necessary to bring an action substantiating the validity of the attachment before the *Tribunal d'Instance* or the *Tribunal de Grande Instance*, depending on the sum involved in the dispute.

(4) An application for a seizure by way of security, which prevents the disposal of movable assets before a decision has been taken on the merits of the case. The new law of 9 July 1991 gives competence for this to the judge of enforcement.

(5) As regards applications for registration of a charge, these make it possible, in commercial matters, to register a charge on a business belonging to a debtor, for the amount of the debt.

It is also necessary to bring a principal action, once the security has been submitted to the court, ruling on the substance of the case.

(6) Similarly, it is possible, as a preventive measure, to obtain leave to register a mortgage on a debtor's property, provided that an action is brought immediately afterwards.

Contentious measures

Straightforward and simple measures can be obtained immediately by a summary procedure.

In contrast to the procedure for orders given on an application by the plaintiff in the absence of the defendant, this is a contentious procedure. The opposing party is therefore present and asserts his rights.

Immediate protective measures may be ordered. Examples are as follows.

(1) In matters of employment law: unpaid wages, the return of the certificate of employment or other simple measures may be obtained.

(2) In civil or commercial matters: an expert may be appointed and sums awarded on a provisional basis if there is an acknowledgement of indebtedness or accepted bills, or in a case where order forms have been sent followed by deliveries of the goods and unsuccessful reminders for payment.

(3) In matters of trade marks and patents, the new law of 4 January 1991 provides for the option of referral to the *Juge des Référés* in order to obtain, on a provisional basis and subject to periodic penalty payments (*astreintes*), the discontinuation of acts alleged to be an infringement of a trade mark or patent, or to make the continuation of those acts subject to the giving of guarantees aiming to ensure that the owner of the trade mark or patent is indemnified (art 20 of the law of 4 January 1991).

(4) In company law, it is possible to have a receiver appointed by summary procedure, who will be responsible for administering the company's affairs in the event of disputes between the members, or fault on the part of those managing the company's affairs.

Similarly, it is also possible to obtain a minority expert, appointed at the request of the minority members under art 226 of the law of 24 July 1966.

General principles

In contrast to English law, orders on the plaintiff's application or by summary procedure may be obtained independently of any substantive action and any right to damages, or even if loss is suffered.

In general, the aim of these actions is to gather evidence or to put an end to the harm being caused.

Generally it is better to act quickly where there is a strategic advantage to be had in terms of establishing the facts of an infringement. Certain time limits are imposed for the commencement of a substantive action, after a non-contentious measure; it is therefore necessary to bring an action within a week in attachment proceedings, and within two weeks after the seizure of a trade mark imitation.

Conversely, certain rules have to be observed:

Application proceedings

(1) In application proceedings, the court places the greatest value on the utility of the measure.

(2) It is compulsory for certain documents to be submitted, depending on the type of application:

(a) therefore, evidence of ownership of a trade mark or patent or of the creation of a registered design must be furnished in matters of industrial property;

(b) in the case of a dispute relating to rented premises, the lease must be produced;

(c) in the case of an application for seizure of an imitation, or an attachment, and in the case of an application for registration of a charge, it is necessary to prove the principle of the debt, and even its amount, as precisely as possible.

(3) Article 48 of the Old Code of Civil Procedure (OCCP) requires the criteria of 'urgency and danger' (*l'urgence et péril*) in order to authorise a seizure of goods or registration of a charge.

(4) Nevertheless, all orders on an application have only provisional effect, by virtue of art 493 of the New Code of Civil Procedure (NCCP).

This means that they may be retracted in summary proceedings brought at a later stage by the defendant, putting forward his own evidence and documents.

(5) Article 497 of the NCCP provides expressly for the retraction of any order.

Summary procedure

(1) In a summary procedure, the court may immediately order the necessary measures, in accordance with art 484 of the NCCP, supplementing its judgment with periodic penalty payments where appropriate.

(2) In addition, there must be no serious dispute as to the existence of the liability of the defendant.

(3) Thus, the payment of an interim award of damages may be ordered in commercial matters, or compelling the performance of an obligation, even in the case of an obligation to do something, under art 873(2) of the NCCP.

(4) In general, the *Juge des Référés* has authority:

(a) if there are no serious grounds for contention, to order any measure justified by the existence of a dispute;

(b) in a case of difficulty in enforcing a legal document (heard in the Court of the President of the *Tribunal de Grande Instance*);

(c) in order to prevent imminent damage or to stop a nuisance which is clearly illegal (heard by the President of the *Tribunal de Grande Instance*, the *Tribunal d'Instance*, the Commercial Court or the [*Conseil*] *des Prud'Hommes*).

(5) In the same way as in orders made on application, injunction orders obtained by summary procedure are effective only on a provisional basis.

(6) They may be revoked in the substantive proceedings or by means of appeal.

(7) If circumstances change, and the *Juge des Référés* is justified in doing so, he may adopt a different solution at a later date, rescinding his earlier order.

Structure of the courts

In French law, the courts which have authority to order interim measures vary depending on the parties to the case, the type of measures requested, or the sum at issue in the dispute.

However, the new law of 9 July 1991 referred to above, No 91–650, places together—under the Judge of Enforcement—a number of measures whereby he has exclusive competence for the following:

(a) first and foremost in the area of protective measures and disputes involving the implementation of obligations;

(b) claims for compensation relating to the enforcement or non-enforcement of measures of execution.

Jurisdiction depending on the parties to the case or the sum at issue in the dispute

(1) If both parties are traders, the Commercial Court has jurisdiction; the same applies if the defendant is a trader.

If the applicant is not a trader, however, he is free to choose the competent court: either civil or commercial.

The Commercial Court is empowered to authorise a seizure of goods or registration of a charge and may award provisional damages under art 873(2) of the NCCP. There are also Commercial Courts with territorial jurisdiction and there are several in each *département*.

(2) On the other hand, if the parties are not traders and the dispute is therefore civil, the competent court will be the *Tribunal d'Instance* for disputes involving sums under FF 30,000 and the *Tribunal de Grande Instance* for other disputes.

(3) If the dispute concerns a matter of employment law, the competent court is the *Conseil des Prud'Hommes*.

(4) Measures such as the appointment of a court bailiff in order to draw up a report will in general be ordered as a result of an application to the competent *Tribunal de Grande Instance*.

(5) It is also possible to bring summary procedures before the *Conseil des Prud'Hommes*.

The *Tribunal de Grande Instance*, like the *Tribunal d'Instance* and the *Conseil des Prud'Hommes*, is represented in each *département* (district). There are frequently several *Tribunaux de Grande Instance, Tribunaux d'Instance* and *Conseil des Prud'Hommes*, however, in each *département*.

Jurisdiction depending on the type of measures requested

There is, in fact, exclusive jurisdiction, conferred upon the President of the *Tribunal de Grande Instance* in respect of the following measures:

(1) In application proceedings for an attachment, for example, authorising the freezing of a bank account or a distraint order on funds held by third parties.

(2) In application proceedings for mortgage registration.

(3) In summary procedures, in cases of difficulty in enforcing a legal document (either a court order or title deeds).

Means of recourse

(1) In application proceedings, if the defendant is not satisfied, he may initiate a summary procedure to have the court revoke its order. Recourse to appeal is also available, but such proceedings must be instituted within 15 days of the adjudication of the order.

In summary procedures, recourse to appeal is available before the Court of Appeal (*Cour d'Appel*): this is the second step in the hierarchy of the courts.

An application to the judge to revoke his order is quicker, less expensive and more advantageous because this judge already knows the case. If the court has been misled in any way by the plaintiff the same judge is likely to be more severe on the plaintiff and to revoke his earlier order. In contrast, the appeal procedure is slower, more expensive and any non-disclosure by the plaintiff at the hearing of his application, for example, is likely to have less impact in the Appeal Court.

(2) In the case of a mistake of law, there is a Supreme Court, the Court of Cassation (*Cour de Cassation*), which pronounces judgment only on matters of law and no longer examines the facts. This court has a number of competent divisions, depending on the subject matter of the dispute.

While there is a Court of Appeal for each *département*, there is only one Supreme Court in France, which sits in Paris.

Tactical considerations

The President of the *Tribunal de Grande Instance*, the President of the Commercial Court and the President of the *Tribunal d'Instance* have overlapping areas of jurisdiction.

Hence each is empowered to authorise a seizure of goods or the payment of a sum into court by a summary procedure.

Subject to the rules governing jurisdiction and competence and the status of the plaintiff (commercial entity or otherwise), it may sometimes be more judicious to make an application to one court rather than another.

It will all depend on the type of dispute in question and on the nature of the judges in each court.

Authorised representatives

In France it is necessary to distinguish between the *postulation* and the *plaidoirie*. There are some lawyers who are able to *postuler* (follow the procedure) and those who can only *plaider* (plead).

Only lawyers (*avocats*) who are members of the bar at the competent Court of Appeal may represent clients before the *Tribunal de Grande Instance* and are therefore entitled to make applications in these courts. These lawyers are able to *postuler*.

On the other hand, all lawyers registered in France can plead anywhere in France and may act in cases involving summary procedures before the *Tribunal d'Instance, Tribunal de Commerce* and the *Conseil des Prud'Hommes*. There is no need in these courts for a lawyer who can postulate. Indeed, even the parties themselves may do so, as the attendance of a lawyer is not compulsory in a Court of First Instance.

The attendance of a lawyer is not compulsory before the *Tribunal d'Instance*, the *Conseil des Prud'Hommes* or the Commercial Court.

Nevertheless, this type of pre-trial procedure is delicate, and in practice really requires the services of a lawyer or a specialised authorised representative.

Up until January 1992, there were advocates, juridical counsellors and commercial companies who could collect debts through the process of the courts. However, after January 1992, only advocates may practise in the courts and there are no longer any juridical counsellors or debt collection companies.

Criteria for obtaining interlocutory injunctions

Characteristics

All forms of evidence are accepted in summary procedures, including evidence from witnesses and cross-examinations. In application proceedings, however, the judge pronounces judgment on the basis of the written documents submitted to him. It is important to point out that, in both application and summary proceedings, it is possible to submit statements by witnesses to the judge. These statements must, however, respect certain prescribed legal forms (art 2000 of the NCCP).

The judge, in ordering a summary procedure measure or any interim measure, must not settle the substance of the dispute. Nevertheless, it is possible, if there is no serious dispute, for the *Juge des Référés* to order an interim payment of damages or to impose a ban which may have serious consequences. These measures are only provisional, and a trial on the merits is required in order to confirm them.

Rules

However, there are no common general rules in summary procedures and application proceedings. The following points should be noted.

(1) 'Urgency and danger' are necessary criteria in obtaining an order for seizure of goods, registration of a charge or a mortgage.

(2) To obtain a seizure of goods in matters of trade marks or registered designs, it is necessary to prove the ownership of the trade mark or design and, where appropriate, to submit the imitation to the judge.

(3) In summary procedures there must be no serious dispute as to the obligation in question or else the request for the interim measure is likely to fail.

Security

In French law if an interim measure has been ordered, the applicant will be liable for the expenses incurred and any damage suffered by a third party.

Nevertheless, it is rare for the applicant to have to deposit a security or a sum of money, but in summary procedures in particular, the judge may order the deposit of a sum of money.

So far as giving security is concerned; under French law it no longer makes a difference whether the applicant is French, an EEC national or a national of any other third country.

Expedited trial

Where measures are ordered in summary procedures or application proceedings, French law also provides for the possibility of an expedited substantive action in matters of urgency.

After obtaining leave from the President of the court, the applicant brings an expedited action and a fixed hearing date will be announced in the near future. This will be a full trial of the merits of the action.

This fixed-day procedure is available before the *Tribunal de Grande Instance*, the *Tribunal d'Instance*, the Commercial Court and the Court of Appeal.

It is not available, however, before the *Conseil des Prud'Hommes*, which decides on matters of employment law and, in general, the procedure there is very long, because the tribunal is heavily burdened and lacking in resources.

Finally, the procedure will necessarily be short before all the courts if the counsel for the defence does not submit a defence.

Practice and procedure

General points

Procedures 'on application'

As in English law, it is possible to obtain measures *ex parte* in the absence of the defendant: this is the case with *all* orders given on application.

It is not necessary for the defendant to be dishonest. However, this type of measure is taken usually in matters of urgency and danger where evidence must be preserved or funds must be frozen. It will always be possible for the defendant to initiate a summary procedure to have the order retracted. As the defendant is not represented, it is necessary to exercise special care when making such applications, and to make full disclosure to the court of all the relevant facts.

Contentious procedures

In summary procedures, both parties are present. The defendant will be summoned to the hearing by a writ served by a court bailiff and the writ of summons will set out the evidence and documents relied on by the plaintiff. The writ contains the date and place of the hearing. All documents are exchanged between the parties, either between them personally or between their lawyers.

It is possible in exceptional cases to obtain a hearing at a late time of day, or even, if it is really essential, on a public holiday or at the weekend.

In both non-contentious and contentious procedures

All documents in support of the application must be submitted to the judge hearing applications or the *Juge des Référés*.

There are no general rules as to what documents must be lodged with the court, but each area of subject-matter has specific rules. For example, to obtain leave for seizure of an imitation in matters of trade mark infringement, it is essential to submit the trade mark filing certificate.

Alternatively, to obtain an interim payment of damages in a summary procedure, it is necessary to submit accepted bills or an acknowledgement of indebtedness, or formal evidence of the debt. Witness statements may be submitted in both types of procedures and a lawyer at the Court of Appeal (an *avocat*) must make the application.

Before those courts which do not require the attendance of a lawyer, however, the application may be made by the plaintiff himself, or by an authorised representative such as a legal representative. This is so before the *Tribunal d'Instance*, the *Conseil des Prud'Hommes* and the Commercial Court.

Procedures

There are no general rules governing the submission of documents prior to the hearing, apart from the following:

(a) all non-contentious applications must be accompanied by a list of documents;
(b) in contentious proceedings, the documents must be exchanged between the lawyers before the hearing, by virtue of the rule on disclosure of evidence and observance of the adversarial nature of the proceedings.

In either non-contentious or contentious procedures, it is not necessary to fix a time limit for Counsel's pleadings in advance. Pleadings will set out the facts relied on in a party's case but they are very short in all injunction proceedings.

In the event of a particularly delicate summary procedure, it is possible to apply to the *Juge des Référés* for a hearing in chambers. The judge will then have more time to devote to the case, as he will be able to set aside the necessary time for it. Where the judge hears summary procedures in open court, on the other hand, he will deal with a number of cases (in general, around forty, perhaps even more) in the same day in a general list, and there may be insufficient time to hear a complex 'summary procedure' case.

Costs

As regards the payment of the costs, it is customary in France for the costs to be borne by the unsuccessful party.

In non-contentious proceedings, however, they are borne in principle by the applicant, at least on a provisional basis, because the application will be followed by substantive proceedings.

The court ruling on the merits in the substantive proceedings will therefore adjudicate upon the costs associated with any interim measures in such proceedings. In summary procedures, the costs are also frequently reserved pending the outcome of the main proceedings.

At the conclusion of the main proceedings, the unsuccessful party normally pays the full amount of the costs, unless the judge decides otherwise—for example—costs shared equally, or two-thirds to one-third, etc. In the event of dispute as to the amount of the costs, the costs are verified by the court which pronounced judgment, and which will settle all issues relating to the costs.

Post-order factors

Service of the order

The order is served by a court bailiff. In certain matters, however, notably matters of employment law, the order is served by the Clerk of the Court.

If the order is not served personally, the order can be served on the Town Hall (*mairie*) or on a third party accepting the order, or even to the public prosecutor's office if the counsel for the defence no longer has a known address. The law permits these different types of service provided that the court bailiff gives an account in his report of the steps taken in attempting to serve the order personally.

Injunction orders obtained by summary procedure, and on application, are enforceable notwithstanding an appeal.

To enforce an order, the court bailiff draws up a special writ and then he will enforce the order wherever necessary if it is appropriate to do so.

Sanctions

If the defendant does not comply with the order of his own volition, it will be enforced by a court bailiff.

In civil or commercial disputes, the judge may order that it be enforced by means of a periodic penalty payment. French law does not provide the option of committal, in either civil or commercial matters, as does English law. The court bailiff may enforce the order by means of distraint or seizure of goods followed by a compulsory sale ordered by the court if there are provisional orders to pay certain sums of money.

Means of recourse

The defendant may, of course, in submitting his defence, apply to the judge who has given the order in non-contentious proceedings for a discharge of that order.

He will therefore act by means of summary procedure and must serve a writ of summons.

In the case of an injunction order obtained by summary procedure, the defendant may come back before the same judge if the circumstances have changed or, possibly, appeal against the order to the Court of Appeal.

The new law of 9 July 1991 provides that the decisions of a Judge of Enforcement, particularly in terms of a seizure for security, may be appealed against before a Court of Appeal which must give its judgment in a short space of time. The appeal is not suspensive. However, the First Chairman of the Court of Appeal can make an order that enforcement of the measure should be stayed.

Redress in the event of a discharge or annulment of the order

If the order is retracted or annulled, the defendant may obtain damages from the plaintiff, but he will have to prove any financial disadvantage suffered by him.

This type of redress may be obtained with greater certainty in the course of substantive proceedings if an application is made by the defendant and it can be expedited.

Nevertheless art 22 of the new law of 9 July 1991 reaffirms in this context that 'the creditor has a choice of measures whereby he can ensure that his credit is preserved. The execution of these measures cannot exceed what is found to be necessary for obtaining payment of the obligation'.

This same Article makes express provision for the judge to withdraw his order, 'to order the lifting of any ineffective or abusive measure and to order the creditor to pay damages in the event of unjustified attachment or seizure'.

Thus the Judge of Enforcement/Execution appointed under the new law has powers to impose penalties in connection with all abuses of such measures.

Freezing orders

By means of attachment or seizure of goods, the judge hearing injunction applications may order both the freezing of all the defendant's bank accounts and the seizure of his movable property.

Moreover, the registration of mortgages on buildings, or possibly registration of a charge on a business, may also be ordered by the competent courts.

Several courts may have jurisdiction if the defendant's property is located in more than one *département*.

Such a measure will in fact require exceptional circumstances and, in a monetary claim, the certainty of important debts (accepted but unpaid bills of exchange or an acknowledgement of indebtedness or a summons that has not been responded to or unpaid cheques). In intellectual property cases, it is also possible to obtain this type of 'seizure' order thus freezing the defendant's assets.

In addition, the following judges have jurisdiction to order:

(a) a charge on business: the President of the Commercial Court,
(b) the seizure of movable property, depending on its value: the judge of the *Tribunal d'Instance* or the President of the *Tribunal de Grande Instance*,
(c) the registration of mortgages on buildings: the President of the *Tribunal de Grande Instance*.

As soon as notice of attachment is served, the bank, in its capacity as a seized third party (*tiers saisi*), will be obliged to declare the sum of the assets in its possession, and will be unable to part with the funds (on penalty of owing the debt itself to the applicant).

Nevertheless, this type of measure, leading to the freezing of all the assets of a debtor, remains fairly exceptional, and, in any case, calls for formal evidence of the credits in question.

Search and seize orders

There is no overall procedure authorising the seizure of documents by the plaintiffs as there is in English law—the procedure known as Anton Piller orders.

However, in matters of intellectual property infringement, on application by the plaintiff the court bailiff may examine the relevant invoices and seize drawings, emblems, diagrams or other items of evidence.

Summary

Non-contentious applications can result in a wide variety of interim measures being obtained, ranging from the appointing of a court bailiff authorised to enter the premises of a third party for the purpose of drawing up a report, to the attachment of bank accounts or movable property, or the registration of mortgages or charges on property.

In matters of industrial property, the seizure of an imitation can lead to the discovery of evidence and, possibly, a ban on the sale of imitations of products by the defendant, or a ban on the use of the infringing trade mark.

By summary procedure, urgent measures of all types may be obtained, this time in a contentious framework, whether it is an obligation to do something or the release of control over money or an eviction or an order to pay interim damages.

In all cases, these measures are provisional, and substantial proceedings must be issued at a later stage.

Philippe Bessis

Glossary

Tribunal de Grande Instance   Court of First Instance. The normal Court of First Instance (except for the small claims dealt with in the *Tribunal d'Instance*). It is also a Court of First Instance in criminal matters.

Tribunal d'Instance   district court. The lowest court in the hierarchy and the only court in France to sit with a single judge. It has geographical jurisdiction corresponding to the *arrondissement* (subdivision of a *département*) and hears cases where the sums in dispute are under FF 30,000.

Tribunal de Commerce   Commercial Court. Hears all disputes relating to commercial transactions and bankruptcy. Consists of three lay judges who have all been in commerce themselves.

Conseil des Prud'Hommes   industrial conciliation tribunal. Handles employment disputes exclusively.

Juge des Référés   a judge sitting in chambers to deal provisionally with matters of special urgency.

Astreinte   periodic penalty payment. A daily (or weekly, monthly, etc) fine for delay in performance of a contract or in payment of debts. Primarily a means of bringing pressure on a recalcitrant debtor.

Département   A district.

Cour de Cassation   The Supreme Court.

Germany

Introduction

Summary procedure and provisional protection

Any legal proceedings in the civil courts require a certain period of time, from the preparation of the case through the institution of proceedings to the delivery of a decision. It is inevitable that during this period rights may be damaged and the damage may be irreparable or cannot be remedied by a subsequent judgment. Measures are therefore provided by the German legal system in all types of proceedings and in all courts whereby a threatened infringement of a right may temporarily be prevented, often with a drastic reduction in the normal periods allowed for the completion of steps. In many cases this is the only way to ensure that a legitimate right of a plaintiff can still be enforced after a final decision has been obtained.

The procedures for obtaining provisional protection before the civil courts are laid down in arts 916–945 of the Code of Civil Procedure. There are two types of proceedings, seizure and an application for a provisional injunction. They are intended not to satisfy the creditor but to safeguard his claim or the legal relationship. In both procedures a decision of a dispute is sought and not enforcement, however, provisional protection is granted on the basis of a summary (ie accelerated and simplified) procedure. The main features of this summary procedure are the fact that neither an oral hearing (arts 921 and 937(2)) is mandatory nor complete proof is required, but merely satisfactory proof of the claim alleged (art 920(2)). (Unless otherwise indicated, articles cited refer to the Code of Civil Procedure.)

The purpose of seizure is to ensure that it will be possible to enforce execution against movable or immovable property in respect of a debt or a claim that can be converted into a debt (art 916(1)). The purpose of a temporary injunction, on the other hand, is to safeguard a personal right (art 935) or provisionally to resolve a disputed legal relationship (art 940) or, in certain exceptional cases, provisionally to satisfy a claim. Seizure and the provisional injunction are therefore mutually exclusive in relation to the same claim. The two procedures must therefore be treated separately.

Seizure

The purpose of seizure is to safeguard a debt or a claim that can be converted into a debt. It is irrelevant that the claim is deferred or conditional, unless, in the latter case, the possibility of the fulfilment of the condition is so remote that no value can be attributed to the claim at present (art 916(2)).

Seizure may be ordered before and during the main proceedings relating to the claim, but not after a final judgment has been obtained in those proceedings. The creditor may choose between an order against the assets (art 917) or an order against the person of the debtor (art 918). The vast majority of applications made relate to assets.

Seizure of assets

Seizure may not be ordered unless there is a special reason. Under art 917 such a reason exists if enforcement of the creditor's claim is frustrated or made substantially more difficult if the seizure is not ordered. Concern is justified if a deterioration in the debtor's financial position is threatened.

The reason for the deterioration is irrelevant. An order may be made even if, by virtue of lawful behaviour, the subsequent enforcement of a claim seems to be jeopardised. In particular, an order may be made if the debtor adopts measures intended to prevent creditors from attacking his assets, eg frequent changes of address or the squandering, charging or alienation of assets.

The order may be made against all of the movable and immovable assets of the debtor, including his bank accounts.

Order against the person of the debtor

This order may take the form of detention of the debtor or other restrictions on his freedom, eg seizure of his passport or the obligation to report at a police station, at the discretion of the court (art 933). In view of the considerable restriction of personal freedom, an order may not be made unless an order against his assets would not suffice to safeguard the creditor's claim.

An order may therefore be made, for example, if the debtor has various assets known to the creditor but it is feared that he may dispose of them before a seizure order against them could be executed.

As with an order against assets, there must be a ground for making an order against the debtor's person; ie execution against the debtor's assets must appear to be jeopardised.

In the case of both types of order, it is irrelevant whether the debtor is a national or a foreigner.

The provisional injunction

The purpose of a provisional injunction is to safeguard a right to obtain specific performance (art 935), or provisionally to determine a disputed legal relationship (art 940) or, in certain exceptional cases, provisionally to satisfy a claim.

As in the case of seizure, it is irrelevant whether the applicant's claim is deferred or conditional (arts 916(2) and 936).

As in the case of seizure, an order may be made before or during the main proceedings regarding the claim in question, but it cannot be made or enforced if final judgment has been delivered.

Preservation order

A preservation order may be made to safeguard a right if the applicant fears that the enforcement of his rights could be frustrated or made substantially more difficult by a change in the existing situation (art 935).

As in the case of seizure, the most important factor is the plaintiff's individual right and its protection. Subjective fear of jeopardisation of the right is insufficient to justify an order. There must be an objective danger that enforcement of the right could be frustrated or made more difficult. The scope of the order is limited by its purpose, it must not extend beyond provisional safeguarding of the right in jeopardy.

Determination order

Unlike the preservation order this is not mainly intended to protect the existence of a right but to regulate a temporary situation with regard to a legal relationship in dispute. However, it may not be made unless it appears to be necessary, in particular in the case of long-term legal relationships, to avert substantial detriment or to prevent imminent violence or for other reasons (art 940).

The legal relationship in question need not relate to a pecuniary matter. It may be any type of legal relationship between two parties, eg marriage or the exercise of the right to have the care of children.

The resolution of the temporary problem must be necessary. This must be proved by the applicant. It is necessary solely if it is required to avert substantial detriment. Consequently, it is not necessary if, although a breach of the applicant's rights has occurred, repetition of the breach is not feared, eg because the respondent has undertaken to refrain from committing a further breach. Moreover, there is no necessity for protection if the same result can be achieved in normal proceedings and also generally if the applicant can obtain adequate protection of his rights in some other way.

Performance order

It is a basic principle of the rules governing provisional protection that provisional judicial measures must not anticipate the outcome of the main proceedings and lead to the satisfaction of the creditor. A definitive decision is reserved to the main proceedings and the execution of the final judgment.

Nevertheless, in addition to the preservation order under art 935 and the determination order under art 940, the courts have developed a so-called 'performance order', which is granted where provisional satisfaction of the applicant's claim is indispensable. In order to avert substantial detriment to the plaintiff, a performance order may be ordered when other measures, such as seizure or a preservation or determination order, do not seem to be adequate.

The most common instance of such an order is that for the payment of a sum of money. Such orders are made in particular where the applicant is dependent on the immediate receipt of the money in order to deal with an emergency. Other examples of performance orders are those for the delivery of a chattel, the prohibition of an act or the making of a declaration of intention which is a legal statement issued by a person intended to have legal effect, such as a waiver of claims, or consent to a proposal, or acceptance of an offer etc.

Fields in which provisional protection is applied

There are procedures for obtaining provisional protection not only in the field of ordinary civil law but also in many other fields where there is the same need to prevent rights from being damaged by the passage of time. Provisional protection in the field of ordinary civil law and in certain other fields of civil law which are of importance in international legal transactions is discussed in detail below. The other fields will merely be listed here.

(1) Criminal law: protection in the event of arrest (arts 112, 116 and 117 of the Code of Criminal Procedure), the appointment of a lawyer to represent the defendant (art 140), protection in the event of a search

of a dwelling (second sentence of art 98(2)) and protection in the event of confiscation of a motor-vehicle or driving licence (arts 111 e and 98(2)).

(2) Protection in the tax courts: application to suspend enforcement of decisions of the tax authority (art 361 of the Tax Code; art 69 of the Tax Courts Code) and a provisional order in proceedings in the tax courts (art 114 of the Tax Courts Code).

(3) Protection in the administrative courts: suspension of execution of an administrative decision against which an appeal has been brought (art 80 of the Administrative Courts Code) and a provisional order in proceedings relating to personal rights (art 123(1) ACC) and in proceedings to challenge the validity of delegated legislation under art 47(8) ACC.

(4) Protection in the social courts: suspension of execution of an administrative decision (art 97 of the Social Courts Statute) and a provisional order in proceedings in the social courts (arts 57 and 199 of the Social Courts Statute, art 116(6) of the AFG (the *Arbeitsförderungegesetz*—the Law for the Promotion of Labour) and art 19(4) of the Constitution and a decision of the Federal Constitutional Court of 19 October 1977: BVerfGE 46, 166).

(5) Provisional orders in bankruptcy proceedings: provisional orders made by the Bankruptcy Court to safeguard the debtor's assets (art 106 of the Bankruptcy Code).

(6) Protection in proceedings under the General Business Terms Statute: a provisional injunction may be obtained under s 13(1) of this Statute with regard to the use of invalid general business conditions in cases of urgency and enforced after an unsuccessful prior warning.

(7) Protection in proceedings regarding ownership of a dwelling: provisional order under s 44(8) of the Ownership of Dwellings Statute.

Further details of the following fields of civil law must now be discussed:

Competition law
One of the main areas in which the procedure to obtain provisional protection is used is competition law. An application is usually made for a provisional order, rather than for seizure.

In this area orders are usually made under the Unfair Competition Statute and the legislation governing industrial and intellectual property. Swift changes in relationships with customers and suppliers, the drastic effect of the unlawful behaviour of one competitor on the market and profit prospects of another competitor, the importance of the reputation of a manufacturer and his products and the importance of the credit of a business all necessitate speedy protection in order to prevent great or even irreparable harm.

Provisional orders are rare in patent infringement cases. An order may be made only if the infringement is obvious. Proceedings under s 41 of the Patents Statute or s 11(a) of the Registered Designs Statute, whereby a compulsory licence can be obtained by means of the procedure for a provisional order, are also rare. Finally, a provisional injunction may also be obtained under s 97(1) of the Copyright Statute.

In normal competition law cases the order usually made is a prohibitory injunction. Most of these cases are definitively decided in the summary proceedings. They are all disputes which, on the one hand, must be resolved as quickly as possible and, on the other hand, relate to situations which exist only for a limited period of time and have a closely defined set of torts, for example unfair advertising, the copying of products etc.

The respondent must normally be advised before proceedings are instituted to obtain a provisional injunction, so that the plaintiff can avoid paying costs if the respondent admits the claim immediately. In response to the warning the respondent can admit the applicant's claim by making a declaration that he will desist. In that event there is no danger of repetition and therefore no ground for granting an injunction. If the respondent does not submit to the warning or ignores it, there is a danger of repetition and a ground for the institution of proceedings for an injunction.

Labour law

The provisions of the Code of Civil Procedure regarding provisional orders apply also in the field of labour law. Although in this field the provisional order does not have the importance attributed to it in the field of competition law, certain groups of cases have emerged with regard to summary proceedings in the labour courts.

Provisional orders can be made in proceedings in the labour courts under s 85(2) of the Labour Courts Statute regarding matters of co-determination. A payment order can also be made against an employer in respect of outstanding remuneration.

The question of whether an employee in breach of contract can be compelled by means of a provisional order to return to his job or at least be prohibited from taking other employment is the subject of intense controversy.

An employee's right to be reinstated after dismissal can be enforced by means of a provisional order, provided that a definitive decision has not been delivered in the main proceedings regarding the legality of the dismissal.

Finally, a provisional order may be obtained granting holidays and requiring the delivery of employment documents.

Press law

In this field there are two areas in particular where a party may have cause to apply for provisional protection, ie defamation and the right of reply.

There is a right to obtain an injunction to prevent an unlawful attack on a protected legal position not only in respect of allegations of fact but also with regard to defamatory expressions of opinion, unless the defendant has a legitimate interest in expressing or repeating his opinion. A provisional injunction can be obtained in such cases.

In order to obtain an order there must be a danger of the commission or repetition of an infringement of rights and, usually, a fruitless prior warning to the defendant. As in all summary proceedings, the order must be required urgently. If the application is successful the court prohibits the newspaper or periodical from publishing the statement in question.

Under the press legislation of each *Land* (one of the Federal States of the Federal Republic) any person who is affected by a statement of fact published in the press has a right of reply. It applies solely to statements of fact and not to expressions of opinion or value judgments.

The reply is submitted to the newspaper by the person concerned. If publication is refused, it may be ordered by means of summary proceedings. As in all other cases, the applicant must prove urgency, which is initially presumed. However, if the applicant delays in presenting his reply to the newspaper and consequently does not submit his application to the court until some weeks later, there may no longer be any urgency as, due to the passage of time, the reply can no longer have any effect on the reader, because he can no longer remember the statement in question. A delay of five or six weeks would probably be harmful in this respect.

Company law

Provisional protection in this field relates mainly to the activities of the directors of the company. Obviously, the reason for this is that the organs of the company act on behalf of the company in relation to third parties with binding effect and any agreements concluded cannot be rescinded, even by paying compensation to the third party.

Accordingly, a provisional order may be obtained provisionally withdrawing the power to represent and manage the partnership or corporation and transferring it to another person, who need not be a partner or shareholder. In addition to the complete withdrawal of the power of representation, there is also the possibility of obtaining an order compelling a person who has the power to act alone to act jointly with another director or agent.

Provisional orders are also often obtained to prohibit the implementation of void or voidable decisions of shareholders, in particular to prohibit the registration of such decisions in the commercial register. Such orders may have a drastic effect on the fate of the corporation or partnership, eg when the implementation of mergers or the admission of further shareholders or partners is prohibited.

However, orders made by the courts must not encroach upon the freedom of the shareholders or partners to adopt decisions. The current view of the courts is that applications for an order to compel the shareholders or partners to adopt a particular voting behaviour must be rejected.

Execution

There is a need for provisional protection also in the field of execution of judgments under the Code of Civil Procedure.

Provisional suspension of execution can be obtained under art 707 if the debtor has instituted proceedings to quash the title; for example by restoration of the *status quo* or a re-trial, an appeal against a seizure order or other provisional orders or against declarations of enforceability in respect of arbitration awards or settlements concluded in arbitration proceedings; or has instituted proceedings to quash a settlement concluded in court.

Under art 719 execution may be provisionally suspended if an appeal is lodged against a judgment which has been declared provisionally enforceable.

Finally, other examples of provisional protection in relation to execution are: suspension on the grounds of unfair hardship under art 765a, suspension upon the institution of proceedings to avert execution under art 767 and the institution of proceedings to impugn the legality of an execution clause under art 768.

There is also suspension of execution with regard to seizure and provisional orders and this is discussed in greater detail below.

Structure of the courts

Introduction

The system of courts in the German Federal Republic consists of six separate hierarchies and a number of special courts restricted to specific fields. The six separate hierarchies are the constitutional courts, the ordinary courts (civil and criminal cases), the administrative courts, the tax courts, the labour courts and the social courts.

An important feature of the German judicial system is its hierarchical arrangement. Apart from the constitutional courts, which are both courts of first and final instance, upper courts scrutinise the decisions of lower courts. Another important feature is that the courts are adapted to correspond with the federal structure of the republic. In accordance with ancient tradition the constitution of the Federal Republic kept the courts of first instance and the courts of the first appellate level mainly as courts of the *Länder* and installed federal courts solely as supreme courts. However, the courts of the *Länder* are *Land* courts solely in so far as it is left to the governments of the *Länder* to appoint the judges, to bear the expenditure and to administer the budget of the courts. The courts of the *Länder* are nevertheless federal courts organised on a national basis in the sense that their procedural law and the substantive law applied by them is determined almost exclusively by federal law. Thus the Federal Republic has an integrated system of courts at various levels, consisting of courts installed by the *Länder* and by the Federation and divided into various branches based on the fields of substantive law.

The civil courts

The so-called 'ordinary courts' have jurisdiction in both civil and criminal matters. The jurisdiction of the civil courts covers both contentious and non-contentious matters. However, they are not the only courts which determine civil disputes. For example, the labour courts hear all kinds of civil disputes, provided they relate to a contract of employment.

The ordinary courts are arranged hierarchically. In general, upper courts hear appeals against decisions of lower courts. Apart from this structural interdependence, each court is completely independent.

The four levels of the ordinary civil courts are the *Amtsgerichte*, the *Landgerichte*, the *Oberlandesgerichte* and the Federal Supreme Court.

The lowest level is the *Amtsgericht*. This has jurisdiction in general civil disputes where the value of the matter in dispute does not exceed DM 16,000. It also has jurisdiction in non-contentious matters, insolvency proceedings and matters relating to public registers. Disputes are determined by a single professional judge. The larger *Amtsgericht* are divided into sections to which the various cases are allocated. The geographical area covered by an *Amtsgericht* is usually that of a large town or a *Landkreis* (a county).

The next level is the *Landgericht*. Its jurisdiction usually covers the area of several *Amtsgerichte*. It hears appeals against decisions of the *Amtsgerichte*. However, its more important function is that of a Court of First Instance in civil cases in which the value of the matter in dispute exceeds DM 6,000.

Each chamber of a *Landgericht* consists of three professional judges. At the request of a party a commercial case may be allocated to a commercial chamber, consisting of a professional judge and two businessmen, sitting as associate judges.

Appeals against decisions of the *Landgericht* at first instance are heard by the *Oberlandesgericht*. There is no appeal against decisions of the *Landgericht* in appeals against decisions of *Amtsgerichte*. Appeals in the *Oberlandesgericht* in civil cases are heard by three professional judges. Its jurisdiction covers several *Landgerichte*.

The highest court in civil matters is the Federal Supreme Court in Karlsruhe. It hears appeals against decisions of the *Oberlandesgerichte* solely on points of law. It must accept the findings of fact of the lower courts. Each senate of the Supreme Court consists of five professional judges.

Jurisdiction

The jurisdiction of a German civil court consists of three separate elements: local jurisdiction, jurisdiction with regard to the subject-matter and functional jurisdiction. A German court has jurisdiction only when all three elements are present.

The categories of jurisdiction *in rem*, jurisdiction *in personam* and jurisdiction *quasi in rem* play no part in German law. Where and on whom the writ was served are irrelevant, provided that it was served in accordance with the statutory provisions. Similarly, with a few exceptions, it is irrelevant whether a particular physical object or property is situated in a particular geographical area. Apart from questions of extraterritoriality, all natural and legal persons are subject to the jurisdiction of the German courts, provided that the three elements of jurisdiction are present in relation to a particular dispute. Subject matter and functional jurisdiction may usually be determined without any problems. The local jurisdiction of the courts is determined by 25 provisions of the Code of Civil Procedure, most of which are, however, irrelevant with regard to the summary procedure. The special rules of local jurisdiction applicable to seizure proceedings and proceedings to obtain a provisional order will be discussed below.

The applicable law

German law has long consisted of a uniform legal system in which there is neither scope nor necessity for any special rules of equity. This follows from the fact that German law was never at any period as rigid as

English law was at one stage, thus leading to the formation of a special system of equity rules.

Similarly, German law had not accepted the exclusive position of the courts in the development of the law, as was the case in the Anglo-American legal system, where it led to the development of case law. Of course, through their decisions, the German courts exert very considerable influence over current interpretation of legislation. However, the influence of legal theory on legal practice has remained substantial.

The sources of German law are legislation and custom. Apart from certain unimportant exceptions, civil law is federal law. The procedure of the courts in civil matters (including the summary procedure) is governed by the uniform federal Code of Civil Procedure and the Court Structure Statute. This means in principle that all the civil courts must, on the basis of identical procedural and substantive law provisions, governing decide on applications for seizure or a provisional order.

Even though the applicable law is identical, it does not mean that identical decisions are delivered in similar disputes. The interpretation of the law by particular judges is of considerable importance with regard to the content of their decisions and particular local features of the decisions of particular courts are also of importance. Such local peculiarities have developed over decades and are commonly found, in fact, in the area of provisional protection. They are outside the scope of this chapter and are not of general interest. Local lawyers will be aware of the peculiarities of their local courts. It is part of their task to explain them fully to their clients.

Two typical peculiarities found in the summary procedure should be mentioned: as an example some courts have made it a rule not to grant a seizure order or a provisional order without a prior oral hearing, arranged at short notice. In contrast courts in other *Länder* habitually deal with summary applications without an oral hearing. Similarly, the question of whether it is necessary to warn the respondent so that the plaintiff can avoid having the entire costs of the proceedings imposed upon him by the respondent acknowledging the applicant's right to obtain an order, is treated variously by the courts. Some regard it as scarcely ever necessary. Others consider that it is not necessary if the applicant is entitled to assume that the respondent will ignore the warning (without any detrimental effect on costs).

Thus it has been seen that summary applications are treated and determined uniformly by the German civil courts in accordance with the provisions of the Code of Civil Procedure but that regional differences arise in practice in the application of these uniform provisions.

Representation by a lawyer

An application for a seizure order or a provisional order may be presented to the registry of the relevant *Amtsgericht* or *Landgericht* (art 920(3) of the Code of Civil Procedure) without using a lawyer, even in the case of the *Landgericht*.

If the proceedings are continued thereafter, the general rules apply. Representation by a lawyer is compulsory in the *Landgericht*, but not in the *Amtsgericht* (art 78(1)). Thus if the *Landgericht* does not immediately grant an order, but orders an oral hearing, the applicant and the respondent must be represented by lawyers.

However, regardless of the statutory requirements it is advisable to consult a lawyer before commencing the proceedings and before drafting the application so as not to weaken one's own position by avoidable errors and to reduce the chances of succeeding.

Representation in the *Amtsgerichte* may be undertaken by any lawyer authorised to practise in Germany. Representation in the *Landgerichte* may be undertaken solely by a lawyer admitted to the bar of the *Landgericht* in question. In view of the large number of firms of lawyers the selection of a lawyer is difficult. Useful information can be obtained from the lawyers' bodies associated with each *Landgericht* or from international lists of lawyers. It may be assumed that there are lawyers who can converse and correspond in English in the area of each *Landgericht*.

Criteria for obtaining interlocutory injunctions

The urgency of obtaining a decision in summary proceedings is a condition for all orders. In addition to the claim as such, there must also be grounds for making the order, which must be specified and proved by the applicant.

Grounds for seizure

According to art 917 of the Code of Civil Procedure, it is sufficient ground, with regard to seizure of an asset, that if the order is not made, the execution of a judgment would be frustrated or made substantially more difficult. This means that a deterioration in the debtor's financial position must be imminent. This will not be the case if the deterioration has already irrevocably occurred or has long subsisted. If in such cases there is no danger of further deterioration the creditor will be compelled to pursue the main proceedings and to execute the judgment obtained.

However, if the debtor squanders, charges or extensively alienates his remaining assets or there are signs that he intends to do so, a danger will exist for the purposes of seizure. This applies in particular where there is a danger that assets may be transferred abroad.

Another ground for a seizure order is a deliberate breach of contract to the detriment of the creditor, in particular where the debtor commits a criminal offence by damaging the creditor's property. Finally, in the course of proceedings the fact that the debtor defends himself with statements that are proved to be false may be a ground for making a seizure order.

The unconditional ground mentioned in art 917(2), ie imminent execution abroad, is also very important. It is an adequate ground for making an order if the judgment sought in the main proceedings will have to be executed abroad. The fact that at the date of the application for a seizure order the debtor has assets in Germany is not an obstacle to the making of an order if it is feared that the German assets may be transferred abroad. If this danger does not exist, imminent execution abroad will not be a ground for making an order.

Grounds for Provisional orders

As in the case of seizure in addition to the plaintiff's claim based on Substantive law, there must also be grounds for making it. The grounds depend on the type of order sought, as described above at p 119.

Preservation order By art 935 there must be an objective danger (and not merely subjective fear) that the enforcement of the applicant's rights may be frustrated or made substantially more difficult by a change in the existing situation. Thus the existence of the right itself must be jeopardised and not, as in the case of seizure, execution. Consequently, an order may be made under art 935 even where the debtor is solvent.

Determination order An order may be made solely if it appears to be necessary to avert substantial detriment or to prevent imminent violence. Here again the criterion is objective. Subjective fears are irrelevant. Consequently, there is no adequate ground if the applicant can obtain assistance by some other means, and so the provisional order is not necessary. Similarly, there is no necessity for an urgent order if the applicant has tolerated the alleged infringement of his rights for a lengthy period without taking action; he thus shows that he himself does not attribute any particular urgency to the application for an order.

Performance order   Unlike the other two types of order, the requirement in this case is not the urgent need to safeguard rights but the urgent enforcement of the right itself. Here there is urgency, therefore, only if the performance must be fulfilled within such a short time that it appears to be impossible to obtain an enforceable order in normal proceedings. In the case of a performance order for the payment of a sum of money, such urgency will exist only if the money is urgently required, for example, for food and clothing, to maintain health or to avert substantial damage.

Practice and procedure

General principles

Unlike normal proceedings the procedure to obtain a seizure order or a provisional order is a summary procedure. The main difference is that an oral hearing may not be necessary in the summary procedure and the application may therefore be determined without the respondent being heard. The defendant only receives notice of the summary proceedings when he is served with the order. Moreover, the standard of proof is reduced (art 920(2)). The standard of proof required in normal proceedings is probability bordering on certainty. The lower degree of proof (known as *Glaubhaftmachung*), which is sufficient in summary proceedings, is preponderant probability. In addition, the formal requirements prescribed for the production of evidence in normal proceedings need not be observed; for example, the sworn statement of a party to the proceedings will suffice.

On the other hand, proof is made more difficult in that the taking of evidence which cannot take place immediately is not permitted (art 294(2)). This means, for example, that the oral hearing cannot be adjourned in order to receive the testimony of witnesses who are not present.

If the applicant fails to prove his right to an order or the existence of a ground for making the order, the court may nevertheless grant an order if the applicant furnishes security in respect of the possible detriment to which the respondent is exposed if the decision is enforced (art 921(2)). The principle is similar to a cross undertaking in damages in English law but it is only applied in certain cases where the plaintiff fails to establish his case satisfactorily. This will also apply if the procedural preliminary matters conferring jurisdiction were not proved, but not if the applicant's statement of the facts is inconclusive.

Seizure

It is left entirely to the discretion of the court to decide whether to deal with the application with or without an oral hearing (art 921(1)). There is no appeal against this decision.

In proceedings without an oral hearing the court issues its decision in the form of an order. If the application is rejected the court must give the reasons for its decision. The decision is notified solely to the applicant. If the application is rejected he can appeal to the *Landgericht* or the *Oberlandesgericht*, as the case may be.

If the seizure order is granted the applicant is notified. He must then serve it on the respondent (unlike the normal procedure, where judgments are served by the court) (art 922(2)). The respondent may lodge an appeal against the order, but this does not impede its execution. The appeal lies to the court which made the order. It may be brought at any time, even before service of the order, while the order subsists. If the respondent does appeal the court must hold an oral hearing which is conducted in accordance with the rules applicable to normal proceedings. However, the reduced standard of proof allowed is maintained. The court may then confirm the order, wholly or partly, amend it or revoke it; it may also order security to be furnished by the applicant before further execution. An appeal may be brought against its decision, but there is no right of appeal to the Supreme Court (art 545(2)).

If the court orders an oral hearing to deal with the application the procedure is that of normal proceedings, except that the reduced standard of proof applies. There is a right of appeal against the decision—which is issued in the form of a judgment—but not to the Supreme Court.

Provisional orders

Upon an application for a provisional order an oral hearing must normally be held. Only in urgent cases can the court deal with the application without an oral hearing in accordance with art 937(2).

Therefore, if the respondent anticipates an application for a provisional order, he will take the opportunity to lodge a so-called protective brief as precautionary defence against it with the appropriate court. The purpose of this is to induce the court to dismiss the application or at least to hold an oral hearing before it reaches a decision.

The comments made above with regard to seizure apply to applications without an oral hearing. The decision is issued in the form of an order against which there is a right of appeal to the same court. A further appeal to the court above may be brought against the decision on the appeal, but there is no right of appeal to the Supreme Court.

If the court orders an oral hearing to deal with the application the procedure is that of normal proceedings, except that the reduced standard of proof applies. As in the case of seizure orders there is a right of appeal against the judgment granting or rejecting the application, but no right of appeal to the Supreme Court.

The decision of the court (seizure and provisional order)

Seizure   The court must reject the application if it is inadmissible or unfounded. If it is admissible and justified the court issues the seizure order. The order must state whether it relates to the assets or person of the debtor.

As a rule, seizure is ordered in respect of the entire assets of the debtor. The selection of assets takes place upon execution of the order.

The grounds and the amount of the claim to be secured must be specified in the order, together with the amount which the debtor may deposit to prevent execution or to found an application for the revocation of the seizure order (arts 928 and 933).

Provisional orders   Inadmissible or unfounded applications must be rejected, with or without an oral hearing. If an application is admissible and justified the court makes the order, the content of which is determined by the court itself at its absolute discretion. This represents a considerable divergence from the principle of *ne ultra petita* (art 308(1) of the Code of Civil Procedure) namely, that the court should not decide more than is applied for by the applicant. However, the court must observe the limits of the application submitted and must not make an order (apart from cases of a performance order) which would result in the satisfaction of the creditor's claim, instead of the safeguarding of his rights.

Costs   The court includes in the order its decision regarding the costs of the proceedings.

The amounts of costs depend on the value of the matter in dispute and are calculated in accordance with the tables set out in the Court Costs Statute and the Federal Lawyers' Fees Regulations.

The governing principle is that the unsuccessful party must bear all the costs of the proceedings including any court fees. If both parties are partly successful (eg if part of the application is rejected), they must bear the costs in proportion to their success or failure.

As a rough guide it may be assumed that if the value of the matter in dispute exceeds DM 1,000,000, at first instance, after evidence has been taken, the lawyers' fees of one party would amount to about 1 per cent and the court fees to about 0.75 per cent of the value of the amount in dispute. If no evidence is heard the lawyers' fees would be reduced by about a third. If the value of the matter in dispute is less than DM 1,000,000, the lawyers' and court fees would be relatively higher than those percentages. Except for insignificant incidental expenses, the costs can be calculated precisely in advance.

Revocation of seizure order and provisional order

Apart from revocation or amendment upon an appeal, as mentioned above, decisions in summary proceedings may be quashed in the following special cases:

If the main proceedings have not already been instituted, under art 926(1) the court may, at the request of the respondent, order the applicant to commence them within a certain period. If he fails to do so, the court, at the request of the respondent, must revoke the seizure order or provisional order made (art 926(2)).

The respondent may also ask that the order should be revoked if the circumstances upon which it was based have altered substantially (art 927(1)). The alteration may relate to the applicant's underlying claim to the grounds upon which the order was made or the fact that security has been furnished. For example, it may be that after the seizure order was issued the respondent acquired further assets in Germany that cannot be transferred abroad and execution of a judgment in the main proceedings therefore seems to be secured.

The respondent must present an application to the relevant court which will reach its decision after an oral hearing. There is a right of appeal against the decision, but not to the Supreme Court. The decision does not take effect until it has become definitively enforceable.

Execution of a seizure order and provisional order

The applicant's rights are not immediately safeguarded upon the pronouncement of the decision of the court. This does not take place until the order is executed. In principle, the provisions regarding the enforcement of judgments apply to orders obtained in summary proceedings, subject to any contrary provisions in arts 929–934.

Insertion of enforceability provision into the order

Seizure orders and provisional orders are enforceable immediately upon their pronouncement, without any further decision. Insertion of a provision expressly granting enforceability in the order is not usually necessary. However, it should be affixed if the order is to be enforced abroad in a State which is a party to the European Convention regarding the Jurisdiction of Courts and Enforcement of Decisions of Courts in Civil and Commercial Matters.

Time limit for enforcement

By art 929(2) seizure orders and provisional orders must be enforced within one month of pronouncement of the decision or service thereof on the applicant. This period may not be extended. After its expiration, any execution under the order is unlawful, unless it was commenced within the time limit.

In the case of a prohibitory order or a mandatory order the time limit is observed if it is served on the respondent by the applicant within the month; *ex officio* service of the judgment by the court does not constitute execution of the injunction for the purposes of art 929(2). The party itself has to serve the injunction in order to be able to enforce it.

In the case of performance orders (in particular for the payment of sums of money) with regard to single payments, the period of a month applies. With regard to a series of payments (eg monthly payments), service of the order by the applicant on the respondent is required for execution and execution must commence within one month in relation to each of the payments: the order must be served once, within one month before the first payment.

A seizure order or a provisional order may be executed even before service. However, service must be effected within one week thereafter (and within the time limit of one month allowed for execution).

Seizure orders and provisional orders are executed against movable property by distraint in accordance with the general rules. The assets seized may not be sold for the benefit of the applicant.

A seizure order is executed against immovable property by the registration of a mortgage charge in respect of the claim secured.

A seizure order against the person of the debtor is executed either by arrest under arts 904–913 or by some other restriction of his personal freedom, eg an obligation to report regularly at a police station, house arrest or confiscation of his passport. The court which makes the order must specify the form of execution in the order.

Sanctions for non-compliance with prohibitory orders include fines of up to DM 500,000 or imprisonment of up to six months. Sanctions can be imposed repeatedly if a sanction fails to force the defendant to comply with the injunction.

Damages

The liability of a party who has obtained a seizure order or a provisional order to pay damages is governed by art 945, which applies to both types of order.

This provision is based on the principle that a provisional or seizure order obtained by means of the summary procedure is executed at the risk of the applicant. Article 945 provides that, regardless of fault, the applicant must pay damages to the respondent:

(1) If the order proves, in the light of the facts at the date of its issue, to have been unjustified *ab initio*, for example because a condition was not fulfilled; if, however, the right claimed existed at the date of issue of the order, the creditor is not liable for damages, even if the claim is destroyed retrospectively; therefore, if urgency existed at the time of the application but no longer exists, the injunction can be discharged without any liability by the plaintiff to pay damages. Similarly, a change in circumstances later will not mean the plaintiff has any obligation to pay damages. However, if the plaintiff ultimately loses the normal proceedings this will mean that the provisional order was unjustified and the plaintiff will be liable to pay damages to the defendant.

(2) If the order is quashed as a result of failure to observe the time limit laid down in art 926(2) or the time limit for completion of the justification proceedings laid down in art 942(3).

A further condition of liability is that the applicant must have executed the order or that the debtor furnished security or satisfied the claim in order to avert or cancel execution and has thereby suffered damage.

The scope of liability is determined in accordance with the general rules and covers direct and indirect damage and any consequential damage that is not too remote.

The action for damages must be brought in separate proceedings, in the ordinary courts.

Dr Klaus Gerstenmaier

Greece

Introduction

In Greece there are two categories of judicial judgments which can be described as injunctions (other than an injunction in a final judgment):

(a) provisionally executable judgments;
(b) interlocutory injunctions.

Provisionally executable judgments are definite judgments (not final judgments), which, contrary to the general rule that 'only final judgments can be executed', can be declared by the judge issuing the same as executable judgments.

The declaration by a court of a judgment as provisionally executable is either obligatory or simply possible.

According to art 910 of the Code of Civil Proceedings the declaration of a definite judgment as provisionally executable is obligatory in the case of:

(a) return of a leasehold property;
(b) a claim based on a bill of exchange, or a bank cheque;
(c) a claim based on delay in payment of salaries for a period of three months before bringing the action and subsequently.

According to art 908, the declaration of a definite judgment as an enforceable one is at least simply possible in any case, if the court takes the view that there are exceptional reasons or that the delay of execution might cause serious damage to the winning party.

The Code of Civil Procedure sets out some cases in which the provisional execution of a definite judgment is possible:

(a) in the case of maintenance, alimony, etc;
(b) if the definite judgment is based upon the acknowledgement of the claim by the debtor or upon judicial admission on a public document or upon any acknowledged private document;
(c) in the case of a claim based on rights of intellectual property;
(d) in the case of a provisional award of a claim or in the case of claims based on labour disputes;
(e) in the case of disputes relating to possession of property;
(f) in the case of claims based not on nominal deeds.

These are only examples, and the court can always declare a definite judgment as a provisionally executable one.

The court also has a discretion not to declare the judgment as a provisionally executable one, even if the above conditions apply, if the execution would cause irreparable damage to the losing party (art 908, para 2).

The court may also ask the applicant to lodge security in the form of a guarantee which should protect the defendant in the event of the injunction being discharged at trial (art 911).

According to art 909, the declaration of a definite judgment as a provisionally executable one is not possible if:

(a) the Greek State or Local Government Authorities are the losing parties;
(b) the legal consequences should apply only in the case of a final judgment;
(c) payment of legal fees is demanded;
(d) the case concerns personal relations between parents and children.

If the provisionally executable definite judgment is revoked or reformed by a final judgment, the winning party has the right to demand:

(a) the re-establishment of the previous situation; and
(b) compensation for damages caused by the enforcing party if it knew or negligently ignored the existence of an acknowledged right recognised by the final judgment (arts 914 and 940).

Interlocutory injunctions

An interlocutory injunction is a type of legal protection consisting of regulatory measures connected to a private right expected to be acknowledged in the context of the main trial of the merits of the case.

The connection to a private right is the main feature of injunctions which are intended to protect a right against a risk to it (ie a probable insolvency of the debtor) or to regulate provisionally a right because of an urgent need (ie for money from the debtor pending final judgment).

In some cases the plaintiff is obliged to bring a principal action otherwise the injunction issued may be revoked. Such injunctions are: (i) temporary seizure, (ii) provisional award of a claim and (iii) judicial pledge. These will be looked at in detail below.

Structure of the courts

The local magistrates' courts (*Eirinodika*) and the courts of the first instance (*Protodikeia*) consisting either of one or more judges are generally the civil courts of first instance. The courts of appeal (*Efeteia*) are second instance courts.

According to art 683 injunctions may be ordered by the courts of first instance consisting of one judge and the secretary of the court. If the principal case is going to be heard before the magistrates' courts, then the injunction must be ordered by these courts. If the principal case is pending before a Court of First Instance consisting of more than one judge, then the injunction must be heard before the same court.

The proceedings of interlocutory injunctions should be issued either according to the rule of the general jurisdiction (according to the place of residence of the defendant) or according to other special rules of jurisdiction (ie the place where immovables are located, the place of registrations of ships, etc).

For interlocutory injunctions there are parallel jurisdiction rules relating to the court being nearest to the place of execution. In other words, the plaintiff has the right to choose the most convenient jurisdiction in each case between the general jurisdiction of the courts and the place of execution of the injunction (art 683, para 2).

Agreements to arbitrate interlocutory applications for an injunction are invalid, even if the principal case is to be resolved by arbitration (art 685).

Legal team
All lawyers in Greece are members of the same profession: there is no split profession as in the UK with solicitors and barristers. However, the following points should be noted.

(1) Lawyers are members of the Bar in the city or region in which they practise. A lawyer from Athens cannot appear in the courts of another city on his own. He will need to have the presence and assistance of a local lawyer which would legalise his presence in the local courts.

(2) After five years' qualification a lawyer can appear not only in the lower courts but also in the Court of Appeal in his city/area.

(3) After a further three years a lawyer can then appear before the Supreme Court.

Criteria for obtaining interlocutory injunctions

Application

The application is effected through the filing of a legal document (writ) with the secretary of the court where a report of filing must be completed. The application may also be submitted orally before the Court of First Instance which is dealing with the principal case (if the principal case has already been commenced by the plaintiff).

The application must contain the requested measure, the facts supporting the rights of the plaintiff, the urgency and/or the imminent danger to the plaintiff's business and the size of the debt or the pecuniary value of the owed object. In case of an extreme emergency or imminent and immediate danger the court may examine the relevant application even in the absence of the defendant. If both the plaintiff and the defendant appear voluntarily before the magistrate or in the Court of First Instance, the judge is obliged to hold an immediate hearing of the case (art 686–688).

Participation

The writ must be signed only by the applicant (plaintiff) and in the case that the applicant cannot appear before the court his authorised lawyer can replace him. In an injunction hearing, third parties have the right to intervene even orally before the appropriate court.

An application for an interlocutory injunction against a foreign state is inadmissible if the relevant prior permission of the Minister of Justice is not attached to the writ (art 689).

Provisional order

The court may deem it necessary to issue a provisional order which may remain valid up to the issue of an injunction at the end of the full hearing. Such a provisional order must be written under the text of the application or registered in the court's records and it must contain the measures to be taken for ensuring that the plaintiff's rights will not be harmed up to the issue of the injunction (art 631, para 2).

Hearing

The hearing may take place even at the residence of the judge or at any other suitable place, on Sundays or even on holidays for the quick judication of the case (art 686, para 3). The hearing is carried out orally, perhaps even without the defendant submitting a written statement of case if there is an imminent danger to the plaintiff or real urgency (art 687). In urgent cases the court may consist only of the judge without the presence of the secretary of the court (art 690).

The absence of the plaintiff or the defendant has no consequence, because in the case of applications for injunctions the judge has absolute evidential freedom. The presentation of evidence during the hearing is obligatory and even the probability of truth is sufficient; the court also has the right to obtain (*ex officio*) all useful evidence to assist the court in exercising its discretion (art 691, para 1).

Effect of judgments in interlocutory injunction applications

General remarks

The judgment which orders an interlocutory injunction must select the appropriate measure among those provided in arts 704–738: art 732 introduces an exception to this rule providing that any suitable measure is permitted in the case of a 'provisional settlement'.

In the judgment, reference to the right which has to be protected by the interlocutory injunction must be made (art 691, para 3). The court orders the appropriate injunction and is not obliged to order the one requested by the applicant (art 692, para 1). It can also order more than one injunction if necessary. The injunction(s) are not supposed to satisfy completely the principal claims but only to temporarily preserve the *status quo*. Injunctions should not restrict or abolish the rights of third parties, especially if the right to be preserved is a conditional one or limited in time (art 692). The court which orders the injunctions is entitled *ex officio* to obligate the plaintiff to provide a surety (art 694, para 1). If the injunction is ordered before the institution of proceedings relating to the principal case, the injunction judge may also determine a period— not less than thirty days—within which the principal action must be instituted (art 693, para 1).

Variations and discharges of injunctions

Ipso jure removal of an injunction

An injunction is *ipso jure* removed if:

(a) the suretyship ordered has not been deposited by the plaintiff within the period ordered (art 694, para 2);
(b) the period ordered in the judgment for instituting the main action has expired (art 693, para 2).

Recall (discharge) or reform (variation) of an injunction
An injunction may be recalled or reformed by the court:

(a) *Compulsorily* (art 698)
   (i) in the case of the issue of a judgment against the plaintiff in the principal case and if such a judgment becomes a final one;
   (ii) in the case of a judgment in the principal case entitling the plaintiff to compulsory execution, so that the injunction is no longer required;
   (iii) in the case of a settlement in the principal case;
   (iv) in the case of a lapse of 30 days from the cancellation or termination of the principal proceedings for any reason.
   The application for recalling or reforming an injunction should be submitted by anyone with a legitimate interest to the court of the principal case and in the absence of such a court, to the court which ordered the injunction.
(b) *Potentially*—The application for recalling or reforming an injunction should be submitted to the court which issued the injunction by anyone having a legitimate interest. After the first hearing in the principal case, the court involved is exclusively competent for recalling or reforming the injunction (arts 696–707). The reformation or recall of an injunction must be ordered in the case of new evidence justifying such an action; the *reformatio in peius* (a reform increasing the

obligations of the defendant under the terms of the injunction) is also possible if the measures taken do not suffice to preserve the rights of the plaintiff.

Legal consequences of injunctions

Injunctions are provisionally valid and do not affect the judgment in the principal case (art 695); the provisional validity of the injunction is simply taken into account *ex officio* by the court deciding on the merits in the principal case.

As a result of the above rule, no remedies are provided against interlocutory injunctions (the only exceptions being the possibility of an appeal against the judgment of a magistrates' court ordering an injunction on a matter relating to possession according to art 734 and the possibility of discharge or variation of the injunction, see p 142 above).

Execution of an injunction

An injunction is not a formal judicial title for execution; it is merely an order which preserves the rights of the parties in a particular case (this is the real meaning of art 700 defining the execution of an injunction). No execution of an injunction can take place before deposition of suretyship, provided that the injunction was ordered under the condition of suretyship by the plaintiff (art 701). According to art 702 disputes relating to the execution of injunctions are to be judged before the court which ordered the injunction or, in urgent cases, before the court of the place of execution.

The execution of an injunction can also be restricted following the filing of a petition by anyone with a legitimate interest in specific items of property if the court finds for another adequate means for preserving the right of the plaintiff (art 702, para 3).

If the claim of the main case is finally rejected, the plaintiff is obliged to indemnify the defendant for the damage caused by the execution of the injunction only if he (the plaintiff) knew, or was negligent in ignoring, the weakness in his own claims (art 703).

Particular injunctions in the Code of Civil Proceedings

Suretyship

The court may order suretyship from the defendant as the most appropriate injunction for preserving the rights of the plaintiff.

If the court ordered any other injunction in order to secure a pecuniary claim or a claim convertible in money, the court is obliged to replace any such injunction with suretyship if a successful petition is made by anyone holding a legitimate interest (arts 704, 705).

Note of mortgage

A note of mortgage is the registration of a mortgage (charge) pending the final judgment being given in the principal case. It is an interlocutory injunction and can be ordered by the court of the place where the immovable assets are located.

The court orders the registration of a note of mortgage if the defendant is the possessor of the immovable asset which is susceptible to alienation (art 692, para 5). A note of mortgage is registered also on the title of the immovable asset (art 1259). If the immovable asset has already been seized, the registration of a note of mortgage is still possible. The judgment must define the sum of money secured by the note of mortgage (art 706, para 2).

A note of mortgage on a ship is not permitted without the prior consent of the shipowner (art 195 of the Code of the Private Maritime Law). The registration of a note of mortgage takes place when an application is filed by any holder of a legitimate interest followed by a copy of the relevant judgment. Furthermore, an order for payment in a final judgment entitles a note of mortgage to be registered (according to art 724, para 1 of the Code of Civil Proceedings, the issue of an injunction is not necessary in such a case).

The registration of a note of mortgage has the following consequences:

(a) suspension of the time limits in the statute of limitation (art 1280);
(b) right of preference for the plaintiff: if the note is converted to a formal mortgage the latter is considered as being registered on the date of the registration of the note (art 1278).

A note should be converted to a mortgage within 90 days from the issue of a final judgment on the principal case (art 1323), otherwise such a note is deleted. The deletion of the note of mortgage can also take place through the recall of the judgment ordering it or, for the same reasons, the deletion of a formal mortgage will follow the revocation (on appeal) of a final judgment.

Judicial sequestration

The court may order the judicial sequestration—as an injunction—on movable assets, immovable assets, any other items (such as documents) or an enterprise. The relevant judgment must: define exactly the objects to be put under judicial sequestration (special reference to ships and airplanes is made in art 720 of the Code of Civil Proceedings; nominate the custodian and order the delivery to the latter or simply order the public deposition of the objects. Not only can the plaintiff be nominated as custodian, but he can also be the possessor of the asset; in case of a judicial sequestration of an enterprise, it is the creditor who will be nominated as custodian or someone else if there are serious reasons justifying it (art 729).

A judicial sequestration can be ordered, as an injunction, if there is a dispute concerning a property right, possession or any other dispute about documents or other items. Sequestration must be possible according to both the substantial and the procedural law. The court may also order the sequestration of commercial or trading books, or samples of products (art 725).

The judgment ordering the sequestration is immediately executable without any service of the same (art 726, para 4). If such sequestration concerns ships or airplanes, a notice must be given to the harbour- or airport-master, who should prohibit the sail or the departure of the ship or the airplane concerned and to the authorities keeping the public records relating to such prohibitions.

Every judicial sequestration will impose a prohibition on any disposition. This is a similar procedure to temporary seizure (art 727).

Provisional award of claims

According to art 728 the provisional award of the following claims can be ordered as injunctions by the courts:

(a) maintenance provided by the law, by a contract or by a will;
(b) delayed pensions;
(c) delayed ordinary or extraordinary wages of any type or payments including allowances due because of an employment arrangement or expenses incurred during the course of an employment arrangement;
(d) compensation due because of the termination of an employment contract, or an accident at work or expenses incurred as a result of such an accident;

(e) in the case of the death of a person, compensation in favour of those persons to whom the deceased was legally obligated to provide maintenance at the time of his death;

(f) indemnification in the case of partial or total loss of working capacity because of an accident or a disease, as well as for the relevant medical expenses incurred;

(g) in any other case compatible with the substantial law or necessary for the maintenance of the person entitled (beneficiary) or due to the nature of the specific right involved.

In the case of a final or irrevocable judgment providing for periodic payments of a specific sum of money, if there is a change in circumstances, the court may order, as an injunction, either the provisional suspension of the payment or an increase or reduction of the sum of money; the general rules relating to injunctions will apply (ie urgency or imminent danger, etc).

The provisional award of a claim for periodic payments will involve monthly payments: in such a case the court cannot require the plaintiff to provide suretyship as in the case of other injunctions.

The temporary seizure of, or the cessation of payment of, the provisionally awarded sum of money is not permitted. The claimant is obliged to bring the main action within 30 days from the date of the injunction otherwise such an injunction has, *ipso jure*, no validity.

The service of the judgment is essential for the execution of the provisional award. (This is an exception to the general rule in relation to injunctions that 'no service is needed for the execution of injunctions' according to art 700, para 2.)

Provisional measures to maintain the status quo

As an injunction the court is entitled to order any act or to restrain any specific act by the defendant as well as order every suitable measure, which secures or preserves the rights of the plaintiff or the situation which exists between the parties (arts 731 and 732). For example, the exclusion of a shareholder of a limited company, the provisional securing of a dangerous and unstable neighbouring building, provisional entitlement to call a general meeting of a company (art 96, para 2), nomination of a provisional manager or a liquidator of a company, etc. Further, the Code of Civil Proceedings provides for provisional measures by means of an injunction in the following cases.

(1) The suspension of the execution of an invalid resolution of a general meeting of a corporation or an association ordered by the magistrates' court (art 736).

(2) In cases relating to the possession of movable or immovable assets (art 734) a copy of the application including the place and time of the hearing must be served upon the defendant (an exception to the general rule relating to injunctions). The magistrates' court may order any appropriate measure, for example, permission for, or prohibition against, acts of repossession with or without suretyship. An appeal before a three member Court of First Instance is possible against such a judgment of the magistrates' court within 10 days from its service. Such an appeal does not suspend the execution of the judgment of the magistrates' court (the only exception is the general provision relating to the suspension of execution (art 912)).

The judge of the magistrates' court hears such cases only if the secretary of the court is present (art 734). For the execution of the provisional measure service of the relevant judgment is necessary (which constitutes another exception to the general rule that 'no service is needed for the execution of injunctions').

Temporary seizure

In the case of a temporary seizure it is necessary for the judgment to define the sum of money for which the seizure is ordered (art 708). The seizable items of the debtor should not necessarily be stated in the injunction except in cases of temporary seizures of ships or airplanes where the seizable ship or airplane must be exactly defined (art 709).

Certain items cannot be seized under the general provisions relating to execution and other perishable items, such as flowers and fruits, cannot be subject to temporary seizure (art 710). If the items seized may be damaged or if their safe-keeping is expensive in relation to their value, the court may also order their public sale (art 717). The consideration is seized and publicly deposited (art 719).

The proceedings relating to temporary seizure vary depending on the kind of property to be seized.

Temporary seizure of movable assets of the debtor

The temporary seizure has to be executed on the basis of an injunction without any prior service of the same. A copy or a summary of the report of seizure must be served upon the defendant within eight days from the seizure, if he was not present during it. The same copy must be served upon the magistrates' court of the place where the seizure took place so that such report is registered in a special judicial record (art 711). The seized items remain in the possession of the person nominated by the court. The court which ordered the temporary seizure or the court before which the principal case has been brought or the magistrates' court in urgent cases, and upon an application being made by anyone who has a legitimate interest, may nominate another person or order any suitable measure for better protection of the item seized.

Neither the plaintiff, nor any of his employees, can be appointed custodian if the debtor does not consent to that (art 717). If money, or other items which can be deposited, are seized, the court bailiff removes and deposits the same with a public authority, except in the case where the debtor is either the State, or a body corporate under public law, or a bank, in which case the seized items remain in the possession of the debtor (art 716).

Temporary seizure of claims or movable assets in the hands of a third party

This kind of temporary seizure takes place under the following conditions:

(a) service of the injunction upon the third party together with an order to it not to pay the debtor his claim or not to deliver the movable asset(s) to him;
(b) service of the seizure upon the defendant within eight days; if such a service does not take place, the seizure is null and void (art 712).

The seized items remain in the hands of the third party which will be a custodian of the property; in the case of a sum of money or of depositable items, the third party is obliged to deposit such items in public immediately after the seizure. If the third party is the State itself or a body corporate under the public law, or a bank, then there is no such obligation (art 716, para 3). As in the case of a temporary seizure of movable assets in the hands of the debtor, the court may nominate another person as custodian (art 717).

Temporary seizure of immovable assets (immovables)

The seizure of immovables, or exercising a right over any immovable, should be made by serving notice of the injunction on the defendant and on the appropriate public authority (Land Registry). The notice must define the immovable or the real right over the property being seized and the sum of money for which the seizure takes place. The appropriate authority registers the seizure immediately in the record of seizures according to the provisions relating to ordinary seizures (art 714). The possessor of an immovable is by law the custodian (art 700, para 1 in connection with art 996, para 1). The legal consequences of the seizure of immovables will be from the date of service of the judgment upon the debtor. However, in the case of any third party acting in good faith the seizure is valid from the date of its registration in the record of seizures (art 715, para 3).

Temporary seizure to protect special property rights

Temporary seizure may also concern special property rights such as intellectual property rights including rights in inventions, patents, etc. Infringing items may be seized and held in a secure place pending the trial of the action.

Temporary seizure of a ship or an airplane

Such a temporary seizure is possible, only if the ship or airplane is exactly defined in the injunction. In this kind of seizure the relevant injunction must be served upon the debtor of the third party and also upon the public authority keeping the register of ships, or the record in which the airplane is registered, within eight days. The ship, airplane or the 'seized real property' must be clearly defined in the relevant order. The public authority registers the temporary seizure and thereafter the provisions relating to the ordinary seizure apply (art 713). The sail of the ship or the departure of the airplane seized is prohibited and the harbour- or airport-master will be responsible for complying with the order. However, the competent court has the right to permit the sail of the ship or the take-off of the airplane on the application of anyone with a legitimate interest (art 720). The same custodianship rules will apply as in the case of the temporary seizure of assets in the hands of a debtor or a third party. Any sale is prohibited from the time the notice is served upon the defendant. However, in the case of third parties acting in good faith it will be from the time of registration of the temporary seizure in the relevant register of ships or airplanes (art 715, para 3).

The main consequence of the temporary seizure procedure is the prohibition on the sale of the item seized (art 715, para 1). Within 30 days from the service of the seizure document upon the debtor, the creditor has to institute proceedings relating to the principal claim (if there is no such pending claim) or else the seizure is *ipso jure* recalled.

Additionally, any ordinary seizure or any other temporary seizure can be exercised at a later date on a temporary seized item (art 721), but no other seizure is permitted in the case of an ordinary seized item.

The temporary seizure may be converted *ipso jure* to an ordinary seizure if the claim in the principal case is accepted by the court and the consequent judgment is executable, or if all remedies available to the defendant, such as opposition and appeal, against the order of payment have been rejected or exhausted, or if the period for such actions has expired.

Costs and alternatives to interlocutory injunction applications

Costs

Any injunction will also deal with the judicial costs. The general rules are set out in arts 173–193. If costs are not predetermined by the law, the judge must define the same in writing on the application of the plaintiff.

The principle: 'the losing party pays all costs' can be applied also in injunction cases. If the application for an injunction was unnecessary then the relevant costs are to be carried by the plaintiff.

The costs may also be totally or partially imposed upon the winning party if:

(a) this party is found to be in breach of the duty of being truthful to the court;
(b) this party did not contribute to the economic conduct of the trial;
(c) this party was responsible for the invalidation of a part of the proceedings or of a hearing.

In general, each losing party has to pay those costs which are defined by the judge as being necessary for the hearing of the case and especially:

(a) the stamp duties relating to every party of the proceedings;
(b) the payment—according to official tables or estimations—of lawyers and other judicial officers;
(c) the costs and fees—according to official tables—of witnesses and experts;
(d) the justified travel and correspondence costs and also the costs paid for the presentation of evidence.

In so far as the execution of the order relating to costs is concerned, this takes place at least 24 hours after the service of a copy of the judgment upon the defendant (art 700, para 4).

Alternatives to the application for an interlocutory injunction

There are certain other proceedings which may be preferred instead of the interlocutory injunction, because they guarantee an executable judgment in a shorter period. Although the protection given under an injunction is the fastest available, sometimes, under certain conditions, it would be better to pursue other proceedings in order to obtain a definite judgment. The application for an injunction does not exclude such proceedings, therefore an injunction and another special proceeding can be pursued at the same time. Such other proceedings are looked at below.

The issue of an order of payment (arts 623–644)

This applies if the claim of the plaintiff, concerning money or provision of an instrument of credit, is proved by a public or private document and is not subject to any condition. An order of payment cannot be issued if it has to be served upon persons living abroad or of an unknown address.

The magistrates' courts and the courts of first instance have jurisdiction to make an order of payment depending on their general competence (determined by the size of the claimed sum of money).

The application for an order of payment has to include details as to the claim, the exact sum of money due and interest, and attach the relevant evidence. The judge decides as soon as possible on the issue of the order of payment. The debtor can object against the order of payment within 15 days from its service upon him; the objection normally does not suspend execution. However, the court which issued the order of payment may suspend execution on hearing the application of the debtor if he follows the interlocutory procedure.

If such an objection is not lodged by the debtor within 15 days as of the date of the service of the order of payment on him the plaintiff may again serve the order of payment upon the debtor who can object within 10 days from the date of the new service without any order for the suspension of the execution being made. If the ten-day period expires without any objection being filed, then the order of payment acquires the validity of a *res judicata* (final judgment).

Disputes based on letters of credit (arts 635–646)

This proceeding concerns disputes based on cheques, bills of exchange, promissory or credit notes, bonds, warrants, store documents and generally any sort of promise of credit.

The claim must contain a special statement seeking the use of the proceedings provided for in art 635 and the letters of credit concerned must be produced before the first hearing.

The summons relating to the hearing should be served upon the defendant at least three days before the hearing (if his residence is in the seat of the court), or eight days (if his residence is outside the seat of the court) or 60 days before the hearing (if his residence is abroad or he has no known address). The judge is obliged to arrange the date of the hearing in such a way that these periods of time are observed.

The judge of the magistrates' court or of the Court of First Instance which is competent for this special proceeding declares at the end of the first hearing the admission or rejection of the claim; in the claim of admission, the plaintiff may be obliged to offer suretyship. If the case needs a special investigation, the judge admits or rejects the claim and arranges for a special hearing, which must take place within 30 days from the service of the definite judgment upon the other party (if the claim has been admitted) or within 60 days, if such a party resides abroad or has no known address. In this case the execution of the definite judgment may be suspended on hearing an application of the defendant pursuing a procedure similar to the one leading to the issue of an interlocutory injunction.

Other disputes

In relation to certain other types of disputes, the magistrates' court or Court of First Instance can exercise expedited procedures and deal with the dispute quickly.

The judge should try to reconcile the parties and the entire case should be concluded, if possible, at one hearing. All sorts of evidence (even if not fulfilling the strict conditions imposed by the law) can be taken into account by the court, which must issue an equitable and rapid definite judgment.

This proceeding applies in the case of:

(a) disputes relating to fees or costs for services provided (arts 677–681);
(b) disputes relating to car damages and car insurance contracts (art 681A);
(c) disputes concerning the maintenance and custody of a child (art 681B); and
(d) disputes relating to the recovery of possession and title in leasehold property (arts 647–661).

Summary

The aim of interlocutory injunctions, described in detail in the Code of Civil Proceedings, is to secure the rights of plaintiffs as quickly as possible in the most appropriate way.

The court issuing an injunction has an absolute discretion to order the most suitable injunction and to order injunctions simultaneously and in addition to those applied for by the plaintiff.

Due to this rule any sort of measure is justified as an injunction. The temporary seizure and the provisional order have a very wide range of applications. The only difficulty for lawyers is to consider the facts and determine the most appropriate interlocutory injunction(s) which will secure or preserve the rights of their client in the best possible way.

Yanos Gramatidis

Ireland

Introduction

Type of injunctions

It is proposed during the course of this chapter to deal with those types of injunction which might most readily be sought in Ireland by practitioners in other European countries. In general these can be categorised as follows:

(1) *Prohibitory injunctions:* as the name suggests these prohibit or restrain a defendant from doing a specific act or carrying out certain actions.

(2) *Mandatory injunctions:* these require a defendant to actually perform some activity.

(3) *Quia Timet injunctions:* these are applied for in advance of the loss or damage taking place but in the firm belief that detrimental consequences are inevitable if a party is not restrained or directed in some way.

(4) *Mareva injunctions:* these are applied for where the dissipation of certain assets is feared in advance of the trial of the substantive issue.

(5) *Anton Piller injunctions:* these are a form of 'search and seizure' orders granted where an applicant sustains to the court's satisfaction its genuine belief that documents will be removed if not taken into custody.

The nature of the injunction being sought can be further categorised by the timing and procedures applicable to the application for such injunction:

(1) *Interim injunction:* this is sought by way of *ex parte* application, without notice to the defendants but will generally subsist only until such time as the interlocutory hearing takes place.

(2) *Interlocutory injunction:* this is the most common form of injunction and is sought at the initial stages of the proceedings and will generally subsist, unless varied, until the trial of the action.

(3) *Perpetual injunction:* this will generally be sought at the trial of the action.

Scope of injunctions

The use of interlocutory injunctions is far-reaching and extensive and can obviously cover a wide range of issues. Some of the more common examples might be identified in the following list.

(1) Directing the removal of trespassers from lands which are to be developed.

(2) Preventing unlawful picketing of a premises.

(3) Restraining the enforced removal from a position of engagement or board of directors of a member of that board where improper consideration has been given to his/her defence to the charges alleged.

(4) Seeking compliance with certain contractual commitments particularly in the context of sole supplier or distribution agreements.

(5) To restrain the publication of a newspaper article that might be potentially defamatory or damaging in some other way.

General principles

Since the application for an interlocutory injunction necessarily involves a court exercising its discretion, there are certain principles which apply, as in any application for equitable remedies.

(1) An interlocutory injunction will not generally be granted where it can be shown that damages are an adequate remedy for the applicant.

(2) By their nature, interlocutory injunctions are an emergency remedy. Accordingly they are unlikely to be granted in circumstances where the applicant is shown to have delayed unnecessarily and the court will weigh up the extent to which this may have prejudiced the defendant.

(3) The court will consider the balance of convenience between the parties to be affected bearing in mind that this will be of a temporary nature since the ultimate trial of the case will take place at some stage in the future.

(4) The strength of the plaintiff's case will also be considered. Whilst it is proposed to look at this aspect of the matter in some depth later

on it is none the less important that it be stated as a fundamental principle in any application for an interlocutory injunction.

Structure of the courts

Whilst most applications for injunctions are made in the High Court, jurisdiction for an application at first instance is also vested in both the Circuit Court and the District Court. The criteria for choosing the court in which application is made is laid down by the Rules of Court. The District Court has jurisdiction for claims up to £5,000. The Circuit Court has jurisdiction for claims up to £30,000 and over property, the rateable valuation of which does not exceed £200—Courts Act 1991. The High Court has unlimited jurisdiction in respect of both monetary and property claims. Each court is governed by its own rules but in the event of the lower courts' rules being silent, those referrable to the High Court will apply to them. The High Court sits primarily in Dublin although it does sit, on circuit, in a number of the provincial cities throughout the year. In practice the vast majority of interlocutory applications are made to the High Court in Dublin. Broadly speaking it is divided into three principal divisions for the purpose of injunction applications:

(a) *Chancery Courts* these will deal with all matters pertaining to company law, intellectual property, insolvency, sale of property, trust claims and such like.

(b) *Common Law Courts* these deal with claims for breach of contract, personal injuries and tort.

(c) *Family Courts* these deal with all matrimonial disputes.

Most injunction applications in the High Court are taken in the Chancery Courts and the designation of these is carried out by court officials rather than being any conscious choice made by the applicant's lawyers.

The Circuit Court sits throughout the country and the applicant may choose the Circuit Court either in which the defendant resides or where the cause of action arose. It is immaterial where the defendant's assets may be located or where the plaintiff resides. The rules applicable to each Circuit are identical although the interpretation of them may not always be so because different judges will place emphasis on different criteria.

A judgment of the Circuit Court may be appealed to the High Court but the court of final appellate jurisdiction is the Supreme Court. This sits only in Dublin and will comprise either three or five judges depending on the nature of the issue to be tried. It is not a Court of First Instance but has been the author of most if not all of the essential criteria applying to the granting or refusal of injunctions.

The legal team involved in any injunction application should consist of a solicitor specialising in litigation matters; Junior Counsel; and, if the case so warrants it, Senior Counsel as well. Ideally the barristers will be chosen with their specialisation in mind, but since injunctions cover a wide spectrum it is fair to assume that any practising barrister of reasonable standing will have experience in the area. There are no regional qualification requirements within the 26 counties of Ireland as the law (if not the interpretation of it) is identical throughout.

Criteria for obtaining interlocutory injunctions

Main features

All applications for interlocutory injunctions are invariably dealt with by way of affidavit evidence being a sworn statement of the applicant or witness as the case may be. It is extremely unusual for oral evidence to be adduced but there is provision for the cross-examination of deponents as to the contents of their affidavits. In interlocutory applications it is permissible to introduce hearsay evidence in the affidavit provided the source of the information in question is identified. There is sometimes, however, a possibility that a deponent will become carried away and make presumptions as to what might happen if the injunction sought were not granted. In these circumstances it is often a useful tactic to serve a Notice to cross-examine and such examination may take place at the hearing of the interlocutory application or at some date fixed subsequently.

The courts are always at pains to point out that the hearing of an application for an interlocutory injunction is not a trial on the merits and no decision can be made as to the outcome of the substantive claim. It is, however, incumbent upon an applicant to show that a serious question has been raised to be decided at the trial. This criteria is explored in more detail below.

The relevant test

The Supreme Court has considered on a number of occasions the appropriate criteria that must be taken into account when considering any application for an interlocutory injunction. Primarily its deliberations are set out in the case of *Campus Oil Ltd v Minister for Industry and Energy* (1984) ILRM 45. In that case O'Higgins CJ adopted with approval the judgments given in the cases of *The Education Company of Ireland Ltd v W J Fitzpatrick* (1961) IR 232 and *American Cyanamid v Ethicon* [1975] AC 396. The main factors concerned are as follows.

(1) The test to be applied by the court in exercising its discretion as to granting or refusing an interlocutory injunction is whether a 'fair *bona fide* or serious question' has been raised to be decided at the trial by the party seeking relief. The courts however ought not to weigh up the relative strengths of the parties' cases on evidence available at the interlocutory stage, that evidence being then necessarily incomplete (Griffin J in *Campus Oil*). If a fair *bona fide* question has been raised at the interlocutory stage it is not for the court at that time to determine the question since that remains to be decided at the trial.

(2) Interlocutory relief should only be granted where what is complained of is continuing and is causing harm or injury which may be irreparable in the sense that it may not fairly or properly be compensated for in damages. The courts will obviously also consider, in suitable cases, the question of the defendant's ability to pay any damages that might ultimately be awarded at the trial of the action and in cases where the defendant in the injunction is, perhaps, a recently formed company with a two pound share capital or an individual of dubious means, then the relevance of this test becomes obvious. In the case, for instance, where a crude imitation of a product is being marketed with potentially disastrous results to the applicant's reputation, goodwill and business then it would be extremely difficult to assess the damage that might be occasioned to the established product. O'Higgins CJ stated in the *Campus Oil* case that interlocutory relief is given because a period must necessarily elapse before the action can come for trial and for the purpose of keeping matters in *status quo* until the hearing.

(3) What inconvenience, loss and damage might be caused to either party and in whose favour is the balance of convenience. This test is in many respects related to the previous one. The courts must consider the nature of the loss or damage which would be suffered by the defendant on the one hand if the injunction were granted or by the plaintiff on the other hand if it were not. The burden of proof in this instance rests clearly with the plaintiff who is the party seeking relief from the courts. Additionally the requirement that the plaintiff must give an undertaking

as to damages should the injunction have been improperly granted may be a source of comfort to the courts, provided always that the plaintiff is considered to be of sufficient stature to meet such an undertaking should this be required.

(4) Special circumstances. There must be special circumstances existing in a case where a Mandatory injunction is granted by way of interlocutory relief. In the case of *Campus Oil* the presumption that an Act of Parliament was, on its face, valid and to be regarded as part of the law of the land, unless and until its invalidity was established, was considered to be a suitable special circumstance.

The plaintiff's undertaking as to damages

The court will invariably require or expect the plaintiff to give an undertaking to the court that in the event of the injunction being granted to a plaintiff who fails in the ultimate trial then he will compensate all damage suffered by the defendant as a result of the interlocutory injunction having been granted. Lord Diplock stated in *American Cyanamid* that 'one of the reasons for the introduction of the practice of requiring an undertaking as to damages upon the grant of an interlocutory injunction was that it aided the court in doing that which was its great object *viz* abstaining from expressing any opinion upon the merits of the case until the hearing'. (Lord Diplock page 408). He went on to state 'if damages in the measure recoverable under such an undertaking would be an adequate remedy and the plaintiff would be in a financial position to pay them, there would be no reason upon this ground to refuse an interlocutory injunction'. Clearly the court is faced with a problem where the plaintiff in such an application is a relatively new or insubstantial company. Leaving aside the difficulties which any newly formed company might have in sustaining a claim for irreparable damage in any case, it may be required to adduce evidence of paid up share capital and other assets before the court would be inclined to accept its undertaking.

The position in regard to foreign plaintiffs has been simplified somewhat since the introduction in Ireland of the Jurisdiction of Courts and Enforcement of Judgments (European Communities) Act 1988. Prior to the introduction of this legislation, if a foreign company were seeking interlocutory relief in this jurisdiction they would almost certainly be required to provide security for costs, the amount ranging from anything to one third of the anticipated party and party costs to full indemnity costs. The rationale behind such a requirement was because of inherent difficulties in enforcing any award of costs or damages in the jurisdiction of that applicant. However, the 1988 Act greatly simplified the relevant procedures with the result that the courts are now much less likely to make an award for security for costs than they were in the past. However, if such an award is made the amount is either agreed between the parties' legal advisors or ultimately measured by the Master of the High Court following submissions by both parties. Ultimately the amount decided may be provided by way of cash or bank guarantee.

Alternatives to an application for an interlocutory injunction

In certain cases the court may not be inclined to grant an interlocutory injunction even where the plaintiff has satisfied all of the relevant criteria in so far as the legal principles are concerned but there are none the less compelling reasons for not acceding to its application. Such a situation might arise in an action for passing off where a similar and perhaps inferior product is being produced by a defendant company that will damage the plaintiff's reputation. However, the granting of an injunction may result in the (at least temporary) loss of many jobs with a consequent hardship to many families. In such situations the courts will do whatever possible to facilitate an early trial and will often give directions as to shortened or reduced pleadings and accelerated discovery. This will have the effect of enabling either party to go back to court in the event of default of the other in ensuring the matter comes to early trial. However, a practical difficulty is the availability of dates in the court's often hectic schedule.

Another alternative to an interlocutory injunction is perhaps an early application for judgment in default of defence. Having served the writ and Statement of Claim the plaintiff may then apply at an early stage for judgment should the defendant fail to file a defence. In practice, however, the courts will be particularly lenient in allowing extensions of time for a defence to be filed should an application of this nature be made. Where, however, damages are to be assessed the court will have to set a date for this to be done at some later stage but if judgment is granted restraining the act complained of on the part of the defendant then it will be possible to enforce this immediately thus preventing any further breach of contract or unlawful activity as the case may be on the part of the defendant. There are, however, always risks of delays in such a procedure and it would not generally be considered a viable alternative to an injunction application that might be of an urgent nature.

Practice and procedure

Notice

Ex parte

This procedure enables the plaintiff to apply to the court for an interim injunction without notice to the parties affected. Clearly such an application will only be entertained in cases of extreme urgency and where an immediate remedy is required. One High Court judge remarked in the course of an address to practitioners recently that the reluctance of the courts might be best summed up by an example of a case that recently came before him where it was contended that unless interim relief were granted then '2000 one day old chicks would not become two day old chicks' (Mr Justice Costello). Whereas this is, perhaps, an extreme test it does symbolise the attitude of the courts to granting relief where one party may not be represented and therefore incapable of presenting its views.

Secrecy may also be another reason for applications being made *ex parte* where knowledge of the application could perhaps prejudice the plaintiff's ability to obtain the remedy sought in any event.

There are of course occasions when a plaintiff will seek to obtain an interim injunction at a time when the courts are not actually sitting. This may necessitate an application to a Judge in Chambers or, in extreme cases, an application to a judge in his or her home. Generally speaking the first approach is made to the most recently appointed judge but often a practical difficulty can be locating a suitable registrar who must be in attendance on all such occasions, primarily to draw the order made.

A general requirement is that a plaintiff seeking an interim injunction should have either issued his plenary proceedings or provide an undertaking to do so. The application is made on affidavit and will exhibit the draft writ. In exceptional circumstances evidence may be given by way of oral testimony if there has not been time to prepare the papers. A recent example of this was in the case of certain travelling families occupying the proposed venue for a concert the following morning (*RDS v Maughan*, Mrs Justice Denham) when the trespass complained of took place extremely late in the day and any delay in granting the interim order would have had catastrophic results for the organisers of the event. Other examples of where interim injunctions may be justified is to prevent the publication of an article that is potentially defamatory or damaging to the plaintiff where he or she only becomes aware of its content just prior to the publication of the edition in which it is to be contained. Frequently an application for an interim injunction will also include a request for liberty to effect short service of notice of the application for the interlocutory injunction and on some occasions this aspect of the application will be granted without the actual relief sought being given, as a measure of compromise.

Clearly there is an obligation on any party applying to the court in the absence of its opponent to be both frank and informative. An injunction, being an equitable remedy granted at the discretion of the court, is a classic example of the application of the maxim 'he who comes to equity must come with clean hands'. If there has been selective disclosure to the court at first instance by the plaintiff this will undoubtedly prejudice him in the next stage of the proceedings.

Inter partes
This will frequently be the first application to the court but if an interim order has been made it will form the next stage in the injunction process. A prerequisite to the application is the issue of proceedings and the application itself is made by way of Motion supported on affidavit. Service of all High Court documentation must be effected personally on an individual but may be undertaken by registered post in the case of a limited company (s 379 of the Companies Act 1963). If a defendant already has solicitors on record then a minimum of two clear days' notice must be given of any interlocutory application. In the event that no solicitors are yet on record and service must be effected directly upon the defendant then a minimum of four clear days is required. The time limitations in the Circuit Court are identical save that documentation may be served by registered post in the case of both individuals and limited companies (Courts Act 1964, s 7). The court may give directions in an interim order for additional modes of service eg telephone, fax or telex.

In the event that no solicitors have come on record by the return date then the matter will be listed as 'a Motion for the sitting of Court'. The case will be called over at the beginning of the list and so it is important for the plaintiff's solicitor or counsel to be present at that time to ensure that the matter is allocated a time for hearing during the day. If an appearance is entered on behalf of the defendant then the matter will be listed in the normal way.

In addition to the summons, motion and affidavit, the defendant or his solicitors should also be served with copies of all exhibits.

It is most unusual for an application for an interlocutory injunction *inter partes* to be heard otherwise than in court and except in the case of family law applications which are heard *in camera*, they will also be heard in open court. This sometimes results in the unfortunate fact that the defendant in an application for a Freezing order or Mareva injunction will sometimes learn about it for the first time from the newspapers.

Documents required

In any application for an injunction whether it be interim or interlocutory it is essential to produce to the court the documentation upon which one is relying. In the case of any agreement the breach of which is being alleged this should obviously be exhibited with the plaintiff's affidavit. If the plaintiff's claim is in tort then there may be no documentary evidence in existence but clear and precise details of the damage alleged should be set out in the grounding affidavit.

In the exceptional cases where there is insufficient time to prepare affidavits then oral evidence may have to be given by the applicant, but the originals of any documents upon which he may be relying should also be produced.

Generally speaking, the documents prepared in support of the application are drafted by solicitor or counsel. The plaintiff should be represented by both but again the time constraints may necessitate the first draft being prepared by solicitors and subsequently settled by counsel. Much depends on the timing of the meeting of the plaintiff and his lawyers.

Procedures and rules

Generally speaking the following is the chronological order of events in the application for an interlocutory injunction.

(1) Issue originating summons, by stamping and filing it in the High Court Central Office.

(2) Prepare motion and affidavit, the originals of which are also stamped and filed in the Central Office. The motion will identify the date on which the application is to come before the court.

(3) Serve copies of the summons, motion, affidavits and exhibits on the defendant or his solicitors. Most interlocutory applications will at first instance be returnable for a Monday morning, the customary date on which the court will hear such motions.

(4) Certified copies of the summons, motion, affidavits and originals of the exhibits are then handed to the judge on the day of the application. In the case of applications made to the Chancery Court a separate booklet of all relevant documents must also be provided.

In the event of the application being too lengthy for determination on a Monday the court will endeavour to set aside time in the ensuing days to have the matter dealt with. In a complex case that lasts a number of days, the judge may sometimes indicate his decision at the conclusion of the hearing and provide his reasoning at some later date.

Costs

The most normal order in respect of the costs of an interlocutory application are that they be reserved to the trial of the action and a decision can be made by the trial judge when deciding the matter of costs generally. There are, however, occasions on which the court may award costs to either side at the interlocutory injunction stage. Obviously this decision can be prompted if both parties should agree at that time to treat the hearing of the motion as a trial of the action since this will sometimes be the inevitable consequence of an injunction being granted. However the different types of orders to be made are as follows.

(1) Plaintiff's costs of the application.
(2) Defendant's costs of the application.

Both of these orders could entail the immediate measurement and payment of the costs on what is known as the party and party scale. In exceptional circumstances the court may decide to award the costs of one party on a full indemnity basis otherwise known as solicitor and client costs. This, however, would be extremely rare and only justified in circumstances where the plaintiff's application for interlocutory relief was entirely unfounded, frivolous and vexatious. It is virtually unheard of that such an order might be made against an unsuccessful defendant at the interlocutory stage. Once an order for costs is made then it is open to the successful party to immediately enforce their recovery although in practice this often does not happen as the parties prefer to await the outcome of the trial. If the parties' solicitors are unable to agree the amount then provision exists in the High Court Rules to have them measured and assessed by a court official known as a Taxing Master. In practice a full and detailed bill of costs will be prepared by a legal costs accountant who specialises in this particular field and they will undoubtedly be opposed by a costs accountant engaged by the unsuccessful party. Once the hearing has taken place before the Taxing Master he will ultimately issue a certificate indicating the amount at which the costs have been measured. This will then attract stamp duty at 10 per cent but the certificate itself is enforceable in much the same way as any judgment would be. Two matters are important to note in respect of this process:

(1) The costs, once assessed and certified, carry interest at 8 per cent from the date of their initial award, which may be some time before the taxation process has been finalised. (*Cook v Walsh.*)

(2) The charges of the legal costs accountants who prepared the bill for taxation will also be approximately 10 per cent of the amount certified and are payable by the solicitor who engages them and not necessarily by the client unless this has been previously agreed.

Solicitor/client or full indemnity costs are intended to ensure a 100 per cent recovery of costs from the other side. Party and party costs will only ensure the recovery of approximately 65–75 per cent of costs.

Post-injunction factors

Service of the injunction

Any injunction takes effect from the time at which it is pronounced in court subject to the parties affected being on notice. Obviously a defendant who has, unsuccessfully, disputed a plaintiff's entitlement in court will immediately be on notice. The order may, however, also provide that it is to be enforceable against any party having notice of it. This provision is common in cases where a large number of defendants are sought to be enjoined such as in the case of a mass trespass or picket by a substantial number of employees where it is simply not possible to obtain the names of all the parties involved. The normal practice is to try and identify the names of the principal protagonists and cite them as, effectively, representative defendants. If an injunction can be obtained against them and 'all other parties having notice of this order' then a copy of the order or notice thereof will simply be posted in prominent positions so as to be easily read by the appropriate persons. (*McInerney Contracting Ltd and Radio Tara v Guest and others* (1988) unreported.) To be effective, however, against named defendants the order must be served personally on them if they should be individuals. Delivery of the order to the registered office of a limited company defendant is sufficient but often it will also provide for service on individual directors who may be responsible for the particular activity complained of, acting in their capacity as officers of the company.

Service is proved by way of affidavit. It is important to bear in mind that the perfection and availability of any interim order may give rise to some delays and practitioners are then faced with the problem of actually ensuring that a copy of the order is delivered to all of the parties named. In situations where they may be residing at various locations it is important to give sufficient time for the summons server to complete his task before the return date for the interlocutory hearing is scheduled.

Sanctions

Once the order providing the interlocutory injunction is served on the relevant parties the plaintiff should be careful to police compliance therewith. In the event of a continuing breach of the act(s) complained of, or failure on the part of the defendant to carry out the court's direction then the plaintiff's option is to apply back to the court by way of committal proceedings. An essential prerequisite to any application is, of course, personal service of the order itself which must contain the appropriate penal clause cautioning the defendant/recipient that failure to comply may result in his committal to prison because of his breach of an order of the court.

Further application is made by way of motion again supported on affidavit with all relevant details being given of the defendant's failure to comply with terms of the order. This does not extend, incidentally, to non-payment of any costs awarded which might subsequently have been measured and taxed. Service of the latest proceedings must again be personal unless solicitors are on record and will usually provide for the minimum notice period permissible under the Rules. The defendant(s) are obviously given an opportunity to dispute the contentions made. It is not unusual at this stage for oral evidence to be given and very frequently as an alternative to a committal order the court will seek and be given an undertaking by the defendant to forthwith comply with the interlocutory order. This is a way of giving the defendant an opportunity to purge his contempt and the court will view seriously any continued failure on the part of the defendant following the giving of such an undertaking. If a committal order is made then the defendant, if in court, will immediately be remanded in custody, for an unspecified time, until his contempt of the court order is purged. This requirement caused particular difficulties in one case in the past (*Foley v McCarthy* (1985) unreported) where the plaintiff's evidence of contempt was completely contrived yet none the less believed by the court and a number of the defendants were committed to prison despite protesting their innocence. It proved necessary for the defendants' solicitors to effectively dismantle the evidence given by the plaintiff before the application could again be made to the presiding judge to release the innocent parties. The only compensation forthcoming to the defendants was that the judge ordered that papers be submitted to the Director of Public Prosecutions to take action against the plaintiff for perjury.

Defendant's ability to vary or discharge the injunction

There are situations in which a defendant against whom an interlocutory injunction has been granted may apply to vary its terms prior to the trial of the action. Such an application may be justified where the prevailing circumstances may have changed. An obvious example of this is where an injunction is awarded to a local authority restraining a party from developing or building due to the absence of any planning permission. These applications are brought under s 27 of the Local Planning and Development Act 1976 but do not involve any subsequent trial except in circumstances where the application is brought not by a local authority but by a private individual who alleges that they have been prejudiced or disadvantaged by the unlawful development. In such a case, if planning permission does issue subsequent to the injunction being granted, then the order will of course be discharged. Another example might be where the plaintiff's *bona fides* may be subsequently called into question or it emerges that there has been a selective disclosure of facts to the court at the injunction application. As with nearly all our other applications that we have considered this one is likewise initiated by way of Motion and supported on affidavit. The requisite notice period should be a minimum of 10 days but realistically, if the plaintiff is to be given an opportunity to respond to the allegations made, a slightly longer notice period should be allowed.

Financial compensation to defendant when injunction discharged

If a defendant successfully makes an interlocutory application to discharge the injunction prior to the trial of the action it is appropriate at that stage for him to seek compensation for any damage or loss he may have sustained as a result of the injunction being given in the first instance. The court will then look to the plaintiff's undertaking as to damages which it will have required to be given at the initial interlocutory hearing. Frequently, the damage sustained will not be readily identifiable and the quantum of any claim will not therefore be immediately evident. In those circumstances it is normal for the court to direct an enquiry as to the damages and list the matter for further hearing at some later date. If the trial itself is to proceed, notwithstanding the discharge of the injunction, then logically the court will indicate that an assessment of the defendant's loss should be provided at that time. However, if it is not anticipated that the trial will take place for some time and the defendant's loss is likely to be considerable then a court can suggest a further interlocutory hearing to make that assessment. The timing is very much a matter of convenience to both the parties and the court.

Freezing orders

In 1975 the English Court of Appeal decided in the case of *Mareva Compania Naviera SA v International Bolt Carriers SA* (1975) 2 Lloyd's Report, 509 that it had jurisdiction to freeze certain assets of a defendant in advance of the trial of the action. Thus developed the interlocutory injunction known as 'the Mareva'. The practice quickly developed in the Irish Courts of granting such orders, its power to do so emanating from the Judicature (Ireland) Act 1877 and specifically s 28 thereof which provides fairly wide powers to the court to grant interlocutory orders where it shall appear to be just or convenient to do so.

Whereas the party applying for such an order must satisfy the usual criteria set out at pp 158-160 above there are additional principles applicable in the case of a Mareva injunction and which are as follows.

(1) Good arguable case—this has been established as the relevant test which the plaintiff's case must surmount. In the case of *Z Ltd v A* (1982) QB, 558, Kerr LJ stated that it was not necessary for a plaintiff to show that its case is strong enough for summary judgment but that it appears likely the plaintiff will recover judgment against the defendant at the trial. This test was approved by McWilliam J in the case of *Fleming v Ranks (Ireland) Ltd* (1983) ILRM, 541.

(2) Cause of action within the jurisdiction—to actually mount the claim at first instance the plaintiff must show that it has a substantive cause of action within the jurisdiction of the Irish courts. This matter was argued at some length in the case of *Caudron v Air Zaire* (1986) ILRM, 10. In that case, whereas the plaintiffs could identify an asset of the defendants located within the jurisdiction, it could not establish that it had a right to initiate a claim in Ireland and in those circumstances the Supreme Court rejected its right to freeze that asset. To some extent the effects of this decision have been circumvented by the Jurisdiction of Courts and Enforcement of Judgments (European Communities) Act

1988 and in particular s 11 thereof which gives effect to the Brussels Convention of 1968. This matter is dealt with further below.

(3) There must be assets within the jurisdiction—for an action to be grounded in this jurisdiction there must be assets located here which are capable of being frozen. This does not, however, preclude an order being enforced which may have been given in the courts of another EC Member State nor does it preclude the Irish courts from granting orders in regard to assets located in another jurisdiction. The authority for this is the recent decision of *Babanaft International Company SA v Bassatne* (1988) 138 New LJ 203, CA, where the English Court of Appeal held that art 24 of the 1968 Brussels Convention entitled the court in an EC State to make a protective order 'in aid' of a substantive action pending in another EC State in respect of assets located in the UK. Since the Jurisdiction of Courts and Enforcement of Judgments (European Communities) Act gave effect in Ireland (as and from 1 June 1988) to the 1968 Brussels Convention then it is envisaged that a similar ruling would be given by an Irish court although the specific issue has not yet come before it.

(4) Risk that assets will be dissipated or reduced or that defendant will default in satisfying judgment obtained—this is often the most difficult criterion to satisfy as in the absence of any specific evidence it is necessary to impute certain intentions to the defendant. The more obvious grounds for substantiating this requirement is to establish that the defendant has entered into contractual arrangements for the sale of property or assets and is likely to dissipate/distance funds from the applicant, but since often the target of the Mareva injunction is a bank account no such evidence is readily available. Circumstantial evidence will often be the mainstay of the plaintiff's case and the court will often be invited to draw similar conclusions to those of the plaintiff.

(5) Third parties—third parties are often those most affected by the granting of such an order, in particular, banks. Where banks are on notice of or in receipt of such an order their primary responsibility is then to the court but this is subject to any prior undertakings or obligations which may exist and also to any existing rights of set-off or security that banks may normally enjoy with their customers. The effect of the order will often extend to cover joint accounts and the banks ignore the terms of such an order at their peril.

(6) General points—as with any interlocutory injunction the plaintiff is obliged to give an undertaking as to damages but in the case of Mareva orders this extends not just to the defendant but also to any third parties affected by it. Furthermore the cost of compliance with the order may also be something that the plaintiff will be obliged to bear since the

lack of any concrete information may necessitate additional research work on the part of banks or other institutions and they are not expected to undertake this at their own expense.

In many cases the amount of the plaintiff's claim is readily identifiable and the order will be framed in such a way as to restrain the defendant from reducing his net assets below that figure. Where, however, that figure, if specified, actually exceeds the defendant's assets then he may have difficulty providing for his day-to-day living expenses and it is customary for an application to be made to the court in those circumstances following the making of a Mareva injunction. The defendant will be obliged to set out, on affidavit, full details of the living expenses he requires and it is also appropriate at this time for the defendant to obtain payment (at least partial) of his existing and anticipated legal costs in dealing with the substantive action as well as the interlocutory motions.

Upon application being made for a Freezing order it is not unusual for the plaintiff to seek discovery from the defendant either in relation to the funds which are being claimed, or alternatively, as to the defendant's assets. The court may be persuaded that in order to effectively police compliance with the injunction the defendant should be asked to identify all of his assets and the court may view such a requirement as necessarily being in aid of the performance of the order (*Craigie v Mark Synnott (Life and Pensions) Brokers Ltd* unreported (1991) 28 June.

It is important to note that the granting of a Mareva injunction, even while specific assets are identified, does not give any priority to the plaintiff over other creditors of the defendant and the assets frozen are subject to all or any prior encumbrances.

If a defendant should fail to accurately disclose his assets, and the plaintiff becomes aware of this, application can be made to the court to examine the defendant; the court will take a particularly stern view of any attempt by the defendant to hide the full extent of his assets.

Search and seize orders

In appropriate circumstances, and in cases where it is imperative for the plaintiff to ensure that evidence is not removed or destroyed so as to deliberately deprive a plaintiff of the evidence required to prove his case, an application can be made to the court to allow the plaintiff to search the defendant's premises and to seize documents or other items which are referrable to the subject matter of the action in question.

These are commonly known as Anton Piller orders named after the case of *Anton Piller KG v Manufacturing Processors Ltd* (1976) Ch 55. Again the legislative jurisdiction of the Irish courts stems from the provisions of s 28 of the Judicature (Ireland) Act 1877 applying the 'just and convenient' principle.

Because of the nature of such applications they are inevitably made *ex parte* without notice to the defendant for the very reasons which justify the application itself. These types of applications have found favour in claims for breach of copyright, particularly in the film or music industry where the use of pirate tapes is a regular occurrence.

General principles

It is important to note that the granting of an Anton Piller order itself gives no authority to the plaintiff or his solicitor to enter premises. The plaintiff must obtain the defendant's permission to enter and search for documents or other evidence and the defendant is made subject to a mandatory order of the court requiring him to give permission to a limited number of persons including the plaintiff's solicitor to enter the relevant premises within certain hours, to search for evidence, property or other material falling within the ambit of the categories defined in the order and to remove the material from there so that it can be safeguarded. Denning MR stated in the case from which the order obtains its name that '... it [the order] serves to tell the defendants that, on the evidence put before it, the court is of the opinion that they ought to permit inspection—nay it orders them to permit—and that they refuse at their peril'.

Criteria

The criteria applying to a search and seizure order are as follows.

(1) The plaintiff must establish that he has an extremely strong *prima facie* case. It will be seen that this varies from the standard interlocutory injunction (fair question to be tried) and the Mareva injunction (good arguable case) and imposes a stronger burden of proof because of the very serious nature of the relief being sought.

(2) The damage, potential or actual, must be 'very serious' for the applicant.

(3) There must be 'clear evidence' that the defendants have in their possession incriminating documents or things and that there is a 'real

possibility' that the defendants may destroy such material before any application *inter partes* can be made. (Ormrod LJ in *Anton Piller KG* above.)

Plaintiff's obligations

As with the other forms of interlocutory injunction that we have already considered the plaintiff's undertaking as to damages applies equally in the case of Anton Piller orders. However, in this instance, the undertaking must extend to the preservation by the plaintiff of the property that may have been seized or handed over, pending the trial of the action. In relation to such undertaking as to damages it is particularly incumbent upon a plaintiff in these proceedings to be both full and frank in its disclosures to the court where, as in the case of *Manor Electronics v Dicks* [1988] RPC 618 the court discharged the order upon additional facts regarding the plaintiff's solvency subsequently coming to light. The obligation regarding full disclosure is imposed not only on the plaintiff but also his solicitor and if not complied with may not only seriously damage the plaintiff's ultimate case but also the reputation of the parties involved who may be open to adverse comment from the court.

General points

The search itself and any ultimate seizure is generally carried out by representatives of the plaintiff but invariably his solicitor will be present as an officer of the court to ensure the proper and correct compliance with the terms of the order.

Generally speaking it is documentation which is being sought and which will ultimately be seized since it is concern about the destruction of such papers that prompts the application to be made in the first place. The documentation is that which contains some evidence that tends to substantiate the plaintiff's claim and the destruction of which could ultimately negate it. Ancillary orders are frequently made in conjunction with the Anton Piller order restraining the defendant from destroying or damaging evidence or documents described in the order or directing the defendant to disclose the whereabouts of other documents which may be sought. The defendant may be obliged to disclose such information by way of affidavit.

In today's times of computerised databases the information may well be stored on memory or disk and the court may direct that hard copy should be printed out from the computer to preserve it as a tangible piece of evidence. An order to this effect would have been of considerable assistance to a receiver involved in a recent assignment (*Ballybay Meats Ltd (In Receivership)*) since upon his arrival he discovered that the entire accounting records of the company had been wiped shortly before his attendance at the premises and no valid explanation was forthcoming from the company's officers as to how or why this could have been done.

In theory, the terms of the order require almost immediate compliance by the defendants and although they have the usual rights granted to any party to apply for variation or discharge of the order, in practice, however, the time constraints imposed simply do not permit them to do so. The court's attitude appears to be that if they have nothing to hide then they need not fear the effect of the order.

Given the mandatory nature of the direction from the court, the defendants must permit access to the plaintiff and his solicitor. A refusal to do so is considered to be contempt of a court order, the sanctions for which are the committal proceedings described at p 167 above.

Other injunctions

In the introduction to this chapter reference was made to a *Quia Timet* injunction and to the circumstances in which this will be granted. The procedures applicable to the application for such an injunction are identical to those for the ordinary type of interlocutory applications. However, in such a situation the damage has not yet occurred and the plaintiff is expressing a fear of what will ensue if the defendant is not restrained, to justify an order being made. A degree of inevitability will have to be established and because of the difficulties in doing so, and because there is always the element of conjecture, such applications are unusual.

A further type of injunction that is occasionally granted by the courts is known as *Ne Exeat Regno* which precludes the defendant from leaving the jurisdiction of the court. An order to this effect is usually given in conjunction with other orders such as Mareva. The plaintiff must establish that he has a claim to make against the defendant and that he is fearful that the defendant will leave the jurisdiction and not return to face the proceedings where his presence is essential to identify available assets etc. Relief of this nature was recently granted to the official liquidator of the company *Mark Synnott (Life and Pensions) Brokers Ltd (In Liquidation)* where the defendant was a former director of the company and whose assets had been frozen as a result of the liquidator's contention that substantial amounts of investors' money was unaccounted for. The defendant's intention of leaving the jurisdiction to go on holiday with his family, in circumstances where it was rumoured he had a house in Spain, was deemed by the court to be sufficient justification for granting a *Ne Exeat Regno* order and directing him to give up his passport (Carroll J (1991), unreported 2 July 1991).

Terry Leggett

Italy

Introduction

Preliminary remarks

Italy is currently undergoing a crisis over the efficiency of its legal system characterised primarily by a considerable lengthening of the time required to settle legal actions. The so-called 'law problem' is encountered every day in all areas of life, and unfortunately every effort to speed up the processes has so far proved in vain. An increasing demand for justice is without doubt a common characteristic of all industrialised countries, since it goes hand in hand with an acceleration of the economic and social processes, as well as with the extension of the realm of legally defendable claims in other areas (health, the environment, etc). As this demand has increased, however, there has not been a corresponding upgrading of the legal system as a whole.

This is the problem the Italian legal system is having to come to terms with, and it is against this background that Italian lawyers are now considering the importance and the frequent use made of all those procedures whose essential distinguishing feature is the speed with which the appropriate jurisdictional measures are adopted.

It is against this background that the precautionary provisions have reached a position of great importance since they provide the individual with a speedy and effective safeguard in an area where the ordinary expedients are by and large ineffective. By way of example, the Civil Court of Rome had some 140,000 outstanding judgments at the Court of First Instance level in 1991, and, according to the statistics, these have an average duration of around seven and a half years. It is therefore easy to understand the growing use of precautionary measures by lawyers, and this is matched by a keen sensitivity, on the part of the judges, to the problem of correctly interpreting the procedural expedients available, in order to ensure, where possible, a speedy safeguard without running into formal preclusions.

As things stand precautionary procedures are the only ones which would seem to be in harmony with the provisions of art 6, para 1, of the European Convention for the Safeguarding of Human Rights.

Every person has the right to a fair, public hearing *within a reasonable period,* before an independent, impartial court established under the law, with a view to determining both his rights and his duties of a civil nature, and the grounds for any criminal charge brought against him.

Italy is one of the countries which has most frequently fallen foul of the Court of Strasbourg, with charges being brought against its government because of the unjustifiable slowness of legal actions, both civil and criminal.

The Italian legal system has three levels of justice, two of which are based on examining the merits of cases, and one on the legitimacy thereof before the Court of Appeal. All citizens can appeal against all judgments before the Court of Appeal, and obtain legal protection from the actions of the public authorities.

In the Italian system jurisdictional power is divided up into three sub-systems which are independent of one another. Thus alongside civil law and criminal law, there is the so-called administrative law which has a wide range of situations in which legal protection may be sought. This particular branch of substantive law is designed for protecting the citizen in his dealings with the Public Authorities, and it therefore differs from civil law which is designed to regulate relations between citizens in the free exercise of their contractual independence.

It must be borne in mind, however, that recently introduced reforms, and reform initiatives now under way may, we hope, bring about a recovery of efficiency which would be able to shorten the time taken by civil proceedings. In this regard as far as the recently introduced reforms are concerned, we would underline the importance of the following:

(a) Law No 32 of 3 February 1989 increased the number of judges by 329 in 1989, by 105 in 1990 and by 28 in 1991;

(b) Law No 104 of 22 March 1989 increased the number of legal assistants by 1,500 'with a view to ensuring effective assistance and collaboration' with the judges;

(c) Law No 261 of 25 July 1989 increased the number of judges by 550 but this will not come into effect for about three or four years; and

(d) Law No 30 of 1 February 1989 established the district magistrates' courts, laying the foundations for a more practical use of staff throughout the country.

All this means a mammoth task, involving the allocation of staff to ease the workload of the busiest offices and bodies set up to dispense justice.

Types of precautionary provisions

Precautionary provisions are laid down in, and regulated by, book four of the Code of Civil Procedures (CPC). That book is entitled *Special Procedures,* and this definition refers to a number of procedures which have in common the fact that they represent a departure from the basic pattern of the ordinary procedure of cognisance or inquiry.

Although precautionary measures still involve the mediation of a judge, they have this essential difference that they take the form of a regulation without a judgment (see Satta, *Diritto Processuale Civile,* p 740 (Padua, Cedam), 1981), that is to say protection is granted without a full assessment of the facts.

Title I, book four, of the Code of Civil Procedures contains provisions governing this type of procedure: the injunction, the procedure for the granting of an eviction order, the various precautionary procedures such as sequestration, the ban on new work and feared damages, provisions governing preventive investigations, emergency provisions and finally possessory procedures.

It should be pointed out that although these all come under the same general area of procedural activity, the individual characteristics of these various expedients are quite different.

There is a general distinction between precautionary provisions, which we will call 'typical' and the only 'atypical' provision, namely that governed by art 700 of the Code of Civil Procedures.

The atypical feature distinguishing this procedure is that it has been designed fundamentally as a 'closing mechanism' (see Mandrioli, *Corso di diritto processuale civile,* p 297 (Turin, Giappichelli), 1989). It is in fact a mechanism designed to prevent all those situations in which it is impossible to have recourse to any other named precautionary provisions, even though the circumstances of the case appear subjectively to merit immediate protection and therefore require the intervention of the judge who has the power, in such cases, to give instructions for the safeguard(s) sought as a matter of urgency.

Among those procedures which can definitely be regarded as 'typical' we can make a further sub-division. The procedure for obtaining the injunction and the granting of an eviction order are characterised by the fact that they are processes for summary cognisance or inquiry subject to a possible subsequent full inquiry. Precautionary provisions are essentially distinct in that they must be linked to an ordinary action, ie a final judgment. In other words the precautionary procedure cannot have a life of its own, but is always followed, and confirmed, by an ordinary judgment.

Only in the case of the expedient of the injunction and the granting of an eviction order is the subsequent judgment no more than a possibility; it is the defendant who has the power to bring this about if he considers the claim unjustified. Otherwise these provisional orders become final, and this distinguishes them from the other precautionary procedures which are only designed to provide provisional protection for claimed rights, but which, without the subsequent full inquiry to ascertain the legitimacy of the claim, lose their effect.

General characteristics of the precautionary action

Our procedures have been significantly amended following the introduction of Law No 353 on 26 November 1990 (the title of which is *'Urgent Provisions for Civil Proceedings'*) which will come into full effect on 1 January 1993.

The most important new feature here is the introduction of a general procedure applicable to the main precautionary provisions, namely sequestration, the ban on new works and feared damage, and emergency provisions. It also applies to the immediate provisions of possessory procedures and potentially also to all the other precautionary provisions contemplated by the Civil Code and by special laws.

The procedure under examination does not therefore affect the prerequisites for the individual precautionary measures, but has been introduced precisely as a general procedure with the potential for regulating all the various precautionary measures.

With regard to the characteristics of the precautionary safeguard we should underline the instrumental function of the protection provided with respect to the other two types of jurisdictional activity, cognisance (inquiry) and execution (enforcement).

This instrumental status, understood as the placing of the precautionary procedure before the issuing of the final ruling, is unanimously recognised in legal practice as the principal characteristic of the precautionary safeguard.

In practice, since this type of activity is aimed at preventing anything which would jeopardise the function of the jurisdictional safeguard, it is introduced initially by determining the truth of the existence of valid grounds making it necessary and appropriate to grant precautionary intervention. These grounds are as follows:

(1) *Periculum in mora*—justified grounds for fearing that during the time necessary for fully substantiating one's right, that right might be left unsatisfied or irreparably damaged—this represents the essential prerequisite for the granting of any form of precautionary procedure. Conventional legal theory has already made it quite clear that we are not referring here to the general risk of legal damages, nor to a state of risk which is nothing more than a subjective opinion, but we are referring specifically to the risk of the damage which could well be incurred as a result of the inevitable slowness of ordinary forms of defence (see in this context Chiovenda, *Saggi di diritto processuale*, Vol I, p 227).

(2) *Fumus boni iuris*—this expression is used to refer to the probable existence of a right; this means that the judge's inquiries (of a summary nature) must be limited to a judgment of likelihood, which is something more than a mere statement and less than full verification. In short the judge examines the evidence submitted to him in order to determine the existence of a legal situation which on the face of it merits some form of protection, and issues a ruling to this effect. This conclusion may and indeed must be verified more systematically at a later stage when it will be confirmed and modified by the final judgment which concludes the case.

Structure of the courts

Civil jurisdiction

In order to gain a better understanding of the nature of precautionary measures in the Italian legal system, it is appropriate to give a brief summary of the criteria governing jurisdiction.

The judges who administer civil justice in our country are, in ascending order of importance, the Justice of the Peace, the magistrate (judge in a lower court), the Court, the Court of Appeal and the Supreme Court of Appeal.

The criteria governing the allocation of jurisdiction among the different legal venues are essentially territorial ones, the respective sums of money involved in a case, and finally the matter to be tried.

These criteria are laid down with respect to the Court of First Instance;

the competence of the Court of Second Instance follows on from the lower court, where applicable.

At the national level jurisdiction is divided up into various Court of Appeal districts, one for each regional capital throughout the country. Within each district jurisdiction is divided up among the lower judges on the basis of the criteria laid down by law and by the Ministry of Justice.

At the top of the Italian judicial system is the Appeal Court to which recourse may be had in connection with the judgments of all the ordinary judges and specialist judges.

At this stage, however, there is no further investigation of the case; only an inquiry into matters of law highlighted by the petitioner. (Article 360 I of the Code of Civil Procedures: 'Judgments pronounced at the appeal level or at a single level may be challenged through the Court of Appeal: (i) for reasons to do with jurisdiction; (ii) because of violation of the regulations governing competence when competence has not been defined; (iii) because of violation, or incorrect application, of the provisions of law; (iv) because the judgment or procedure is null and void; (v) because of some omission, insufficiency or contradictory grounds in support of a decisive aspect of the dispute, either identified by the parties or automatically verifiable as a matter of fact.').

Administrative jurisdiction

Under our legal system it is possible to take action against the activities of public authorities which are felt to be directly detrimental to the prospects of an individual citizen and which involve an illogical or unfair assessment of the public interest which the public authority is required to satisfy.

The only remedy permissible where public authorities are concerned is removal of the prejudicial act.

It is not therefore possible for the judge to take the part of the public authority in issuing his judgment; he may only rule on removal of the prejudicial acts: there are in fact exceptions in the regulations to this extremely general principle, but there would be no value in mentioning them here. However, there is reason to mention the efforts made by the judges to obtain powers to take the part of or act on behalf of the public authorities, under certain special circumstances, providing for the arrangements which the latter would have to adopt in accordance with the law, but without the power to carry out any discretionary assessments.

Administrative justice operates at two levels only: there is a Court of First Instance for each region, the decisions of which may be appealed against before the State Council in Rome.

Advocacy

The safeguarding of the rights of citizens is entrusted exclusively to a qualified defence counsel who may be either a *Procuratore Legale* or an *Avvocato*. In Italy there is no similar distinction between the two types of lawyers as in the case of solicitors and barristers in England and Wales. It is therefore difficult to find an accurate translation of these terms. If any historical comparison can be made, and it is perhaps a little arbitrary to do so, a *procuratore legale* compares to a solicitor and an *avvocato* to a barrister. The differences however are now almost entirely formal and of very little substance.

Qualifying as a *procuratore legale* is only the first step to becoming an *avvocato* who has all the powers of the *procuratore legale* as well as an additional power to give voice on procedures in the higher courts.

The status of an *avvocato* is acquired upon completion of at least two years' practice in a law firm following graduation, and after having passed a selective State examination. The *procuratore legale* in the interests of the client, is responsible for performing the procedural formalities: he may appear before all judges, with the exception of the Supreme Court of Appeal, with the territorial restriction of having to operate exclusively within the district of the Court of Appeal in which he has his place of residence. He may however avail himself of the services of another *'domiciled'* or local, *procuratore legale* to attend to a matter outside his own district, but he may not validly perform procedural formalities/activities without the collaboration of the domiciled *procuratore legale*. After six years of being a *procuratore legale* or following the passing of a further State examination, which must be at least three years after the first examination, he will become an *avvocato*.

An *avvocato* is able to defend a client at a higher level and also has the powers of the *procuratore legale* when it is necessary to perform individual procedural formalities.

From the strictly practical point of view an *avvocato* is also able to defend clients outside his own Court of Appeal district and to charge higher fees for individual cases. (It would seem appropriate to point out that the fees payable to professional lawyers are not tied to the time devoted to a particular case, but are proportional to the value of the assignment and must take account of the sum gained in the interests of the client. According to the letter of the law, agreements have no validity when they contemplate any other basis for payment of fees, particularly fees based on the time spent on a case or fees in the form of a percentage of the financial advantage gained by the client in relation to a particular professional activity.)

After a further period of eight years (or only two years if he takes the appropriate State examination), a solicitor may also acquire the status of defence counsel before the Court of Appeal, which means that the solicitor in question is now able to defend his client's interests before the higher courts, ie the Supreme Court of Appeal, the State Council (a second level body of administrative justice) and the Higher Court of Water Authorities.

Later in this chapter, we shall look at the various types of precautionary measures available under Italian law in more detail.

Sequestration

In analysing the individual types of precautionary provisions, in order not to give too fragmentary a picture, we have felt it necessary to refer only to the most important remedies, ignoring those provisions which we have considered to be of marginal significance.

The main precautionary measure is the sequestration (seizure or attachment) of assets which is regulated by law in its two essential forms: the judicial attachment (seizure by order of the court) and the protective sequestration. This is a distinction based on aspects which are partly functional and partly structural.

In fact the two types of sequestration are quite different from one another:

(1) The judicial attachment is more of a procedural expedient in the true sense of the word, designed to ensure that as long as the case lasts no situation can arise which would have an adverse effect on the disputed right.

(2) The protective sequestration, on the other hand, has a substantive nature and is designed to keep the creditor's capital guarantee unaltered for the duration of the case so that it may subsequently be satisfactorily resolved from the debtor's assets.

The judicial attachment

The judicial attachment is basically designed for two cases:

The judicial attachment per art 670, CPC

This sequestration may be authorised by the judge on movable or immovable assets, business enterprises or other jointly owned assets when there is a dispute over their ownership or possession and it is necessary to arrange for them to be temporarily impounded or managed. The prerequisites for the granting of this type of sequestration are first and foremost the existence of a dispute over ownership or possession of the assets, and thus the need to provide for their safe keeping or temporary management. Assessment of this need rests, of course, with the judge, and the latter's decision may not be taken to the Court of Appeal unless there have been any defects in the logic used.

The judicial attachment per art 670, II, CPC

The objects of this form of sequestration are books, registers, documents and any other item from which it is hoped to obtain some evidence, when there is a dispute over the right of exhibition or communication and it is necessary to make provision for their temporary confiscation. The right of exhibition is the right to produce before the court a document in the defendant's possession and the right of communication is the right to produce a document in the plaintiff's possession.

This particular type of sequestration is instrumentally linked, not with an enforceable procedure, but with future cognisance (inquiry); indeed the aim is to provide for the safe keeping of certain objects which it is intended to use in a future action as evidence or information for the parties or for the judge. The applicant must show that the documents to be sequestrated are admissible and relevant.

The protective sequestration per art 671, CPC

This remedy is provided in the event that the creditor, in the time required for taking legal action in connection with his right(s), might lose the guarantee of his credit, in that the debtor could fraudulently dispose of formal ownership of the asset in question, thereby depriving the plaintiff of what is rightly his.

The asset is taken into account in its entirety or in terms of its potential for conversion into money; it is for this reason that the judge, in granting a protective sequestration, in contrast with the judicial attachment, does not refer to the individual assets of the debtor on whom the attachment is imposed, but merely states the value up to which the creditor enforcing the sequestration is permitted to impose an attachment on those items among the debtor's assets which he considers most appropriate for guaranteeing his credit.

The risk of losing the guarantee of the plaintiff's credit must be assessed objectively, not subjectively in the mind of the creditor, and must have to do with a situation where there is some real risk and in which there is a possibility that the debtor's assets may be disposed of or reduced to an extent that guarantee of the creditor's rights can no longer be provided (Cass 70/1448). It is possible to freeze the defendant's bank accounts by means of a protective sequestration if the circumstances of the case justify such an order.

For the purpose of controlling the various forms of sequestration the law lays down a single procedure which it closely integrates with certain regulations relating to the various types of sequestration.

The procedure for obtaining a sequestration starts with a petition which is submitted to the competent judge in the appropriate manner for such remedies. If a corresponding ordinary action is already pending, the petition will be submitted to the same judge; if an action is not yet pending, the claim will be submitted to the judge who would be competent to try such an action. At the summary investigation stage the judge will take the action he deems most appropriate for obtaining the necessary information on the basis of which he can accept or reject the claim. The law allows the judge, in certain clearly defined cases, to give his ruling *inaudita altera parte*, that is to say without even hearing the position of the debtor. These defined cases are as follows:

(1) In the case of a sequestration before a legal action; if there is a preventive sequestration or a judicial attachment concerning movable items. If there is a judicial attachment on immovable assets, then there must be some exceptional urgency or a risk involved in delay.

(2) In the case of a sequestration during the course of a legal action, only if there is some exceptional urgency.

In all other cases the judge will give his decision having first heard the parties.

At the same time as issuing his decision authorising the sequestration, the judge may require that the plaintiff provide a security deposit, having first assessed the circumstances of the case, aimed at covering any subsequent compensation for damages (this is the expression of a general principle, and as such applicable to all precautionary measures); he may also order that if the items on which the sequestration is being imposed are subject to deterioration, they may be sold and the proceeds placed under sequestration. However, the debtor has the right to ask the judge to lift the preventive sequestration, providing a security deposit in an amount equivalent to the credit, taking account of the value of the items subject to sequestration.

The effects of sequestration are similar to those of a distraint. The item sequestrated may no longer be used by the debtor (except in proven cases of necessity), nor may it be disposed of against the wishes of the creditor for whom the item or asset in question (independent of any arrangements made by the debtor) remains the guarantee of his right(s).

The instructions to investigate the matter which follow the introduction of the precautionary measure, have the purpose of determining (the confirmation stage) the existence of the conditions which will justify the final judgment, and the eventual confirmation or rejection of the request.

If the final judgment issued is in favour of the plaintiff, the sequestration or attachment will be converted into a distraint, and it will then be possible to arrange for the sale of the sequestrated items in order to satisfy the enforcement of the claim.

Ban on new works and feared damage

The precautionary nature of the ban on new work and feared damage arises out of the purpose for which those actions are designed: the prevention of damage which might result from new work or from other items (the property of others), while waiting to ascertain the right of the plaintiff to prevent the work or have the item or object removed.

The ban on new work is the prerogative of the owner, the title-holder of a property right, or of the possessor who has grounds for fearing that new work started not more than one year ago, and not yet completed, might cause damage or loss to the object which constitutes his right.

The ban on feared damage is the prerogative of the same categories of people who have reason to fear that any building, tree or other object poses the threat of serious damage close to the object which constitutes their right of ownership or possession.

The main difference between these two remedies, which are indeed very similar, and therefore very often considered together, is in the different way in which human activity has brought about the risk, and in the consequent difference in nature of the expedient adopted to resolve the situation. The first of these two types of action has to do with a mandatory order to carry out an act, and the remedy it provides is to prevent some activity which has been undertaken or to make it subject to the adoption of certain safeguards or precautions; the second, on the other hand, has to do with a prohibitory order not to carry out an act, and the remedy it provides is to order the person in full possession or control of the item which is posing the threat, to take the necessary action to eliminate that risk.

It can be seen, therefore, that the interest protected has the effect of preventing or arresting the potential risk while it is taking place or being produced. The actions involved here, therefore, are contingent on the issuing of a provisional, instrumental ruling which loses its effect when the final judgment is issued on the merits of the case.

The request may be submitted either before the court action—in which event the magistrate (or lower court judge) will be competent—or during the court action. In contrast with sequestration, however, the request for the ban must already contain the claim for judgment on the merits of the case, and not only the request for the temporary protection of the rights under consideration. Once the request has been submitted, this marks the beginning of the precautionary stage, during which the judge has powers, at his discretion, to issue an immediate ruling (without hearing the other party), having obtained summary information, if needed, or to summon the parties concerned to appear before him together to put forward their cases. Under the heading 'summary information' would be included such elements as the evidence of witnesses and non-formal, undocumented technical reports. However these powers of the judge do not apply if there is a need for a special investigation, such as the inspection of premises and the questioning of witnesses, in which case it will be necessary to summon the parties involved. Once the necessary arrangements have been made, the judge will fix a hearing at which the parties are to appear before him. This hearing will conclude the special remedy that has been granted, since it will either confirm, modify or revoke the special provision made, and will also act as the initial hearing before the trial of the action which has to follow the precautionary stage.

Article 69 of the Code of Civil Procedures stipulates that if the party which has been restrained from carrying out the damaging activity goes against those instructions, the judge, at the request of the interested party, may order that the objects in question be returned to their original state, at the expense of the offending party. In general terms, culpable non-compliance with the instructions of the judge may be construed as constituting the offence defined in art 388, II, of the Criminal Code, the legislative provisions of which impose a prison sentence of up to three years or a fine of up to two million Lire on anyone who evades the orders issued by a civil judge in connection with precautionary measures in defence of property, possession or a credit.

Procedures of preventive investigation

The term 'preventive investigation' is used to refer to those activities aimed at ascertaining the truth of a fact or situation, through the intervention of the judge and independent of an action, where that fact or situation may not be open to verification at a later stage. It is justified by the fact that, for whatever reason, there is a risk that the evidence will be lost (*periculum in mora*).

It must be borne in mind, however, that the admission, for investigation, of such items of evidence in the context of an ordinary action presupposes, in the first instance, a ruling from the judge who has found this expedient necessary; in addition to which the case itself must have reached a certain level of clarity or 'maturity' so that a precautionary measure of this type is justified. If there is no such assessment of the case by the judge, this can create a number of difficulties. Therefore, the law provides the possibility of taking immediate action, but stipulates that 'the preventive acquisition of evidence in no way affects questions relating to its admissibility and relevance as evidence, nor does it prevent that evidence being brought up again in a subsequent action' (art 698, II, of the Code of Civil Procedures). In the last paragraph of the same article there is a further reaffirmation of the principle of the provisional nature of the findings in question and of the summary nature of the inquiries carried out in terms of admissibility and relevance. Indeed one cannot even refer to reports on the evidence obtained before the evidence has been declared admissible in the corresponding legal action. The purpose of this is to avoid a situation in which a judge might be influenced by evidence which had not yet been held to be admissible, but which had been brought to his knowledge.

The types of evidence for which the law contemplates the possibility of obtaining preventive information are the obtaining of witness accounts (testimonies), technical verification and judicial inspection.

Witness accounts

With regard to the first of these, the law (art 692) stipulates that 'anyone with valid grounds for fearing that there is the possibility of losing one or more witnesses whose statements may be necessary in an action yet to be brought, may request that evidence be obtained from those witnesses for future use'. Prevailing legal practice interprets 'valid grounds' as advanced age, the seriousness of an illness, a state of war or some other public calamity, but it does not extend this concept to persons moving abroad.

Technical verification and judicial inspection

As regards the other two types of evidence art 696 of the Code of Civil Procedures provides that 'anyone who has an urgent need, before taking legal action, to verify the state of premises/property or the quality or condition of various objects, may request that instructions be issued for a technical examination or judicial inspection'. The purpose of the examination or inspection is the state of the premises/property or the quality or condition of the objects; however the technical consultant must limit himself to a description without expressing an opinion on the corresponding causes. Requests for this precautionary measure are to be addressed to the judge who will be competent to try the case. Where there is some exceptional urgency, however, requests may be made to the judge in the place or town where the evidence is to be obtained.

It is normal for such evidence to be obtained with both parties present to put forward their positions, but in cases of exceptional urgency the judge may order the immediate acquisition of evidence *inaudita altera parte*. In this case the clerk will inform the other party no later than the following day.

Urgent provisions

Italian law, as we have already seen (see Introduction, p 177), does not provide precautionary measures with an independent discipline of their own comparable with that of an inquiry, or compulsory enforcement, but limits itself to regulating certain precautionary procedures, defined as 'typical', in the context of specific situations. The precautionary procedures examined so far represent the outcome of this discipline.

Other precautionary measures of less significance are found at random in the Code of Civil Procedures or in various special laws. However large a number of precautionary measures there may be, they are nevertheless 'typical' measures and fail to meet the demand for safeguards in all those cases in real life where the human mind exhibits greater powers of imagination than has the mind of the legislator. Therefore, the Italian legal system has provided, in art 700 of the Code of Civil Procedures, that 'apart from the cases governed by the preceding sections of this chapter, a person who has valid grounds for fearing that, during the time it would take to bring an action in the ordinary way, his case is threatened by an imminent, irreparable loss/risk, may ask the judge to issue the emergency provisions which, in light of the circumstances, seem most suited to providing provisional protection of those elements which will be necessary for the judgment of his case'.

This is a rule, defined as a 'closing rule' by much of legal theory, which is subsidiary by nature and has the function of providing a remedy in all those situations of *periculum in mora* which are not expressly covered by a typical precautionary measure. By way of example we would mention the way in which this atypical precautionary measure was granted to protect a famous trade mark (in this instance: Rolls Royce) with a view to removing the external signs and objects, as well as the advertising materials of an establishment used as a brewery and bearing the trade marks of the plaintiff company (Pret Turin 13 December 1984). Another example was the request for protection from a well-known Italian singer who complained of the discrediting of his name and image as the result of an advertising campaign carried out by the defendant company without the consent of the interested party, the advertisement consisting of someone putting audio cassettes, containing well-known songs of the plaintiff, into a bucket containing a new detergent (Pret Rome 15 November 1986). A reading of art 700 of the Code of Civil Procedures shows that this article actually confers on the judge 'the general power to issue emergency instructions, in keeping with the circumstances of a case, whenever the other specifically named precautionary measures provided by law seem insufficient' (on this question see Apicella, *Unnamed Precautionary Measures* (Citta di Castello 1948); Sapienza, *Emergency Provisions per article 700 of the CPC* (Padua 1982), and in particular Tommaseo, *Emergency Provisions* (Padua 1983)).

It emerges from the text of art 700 of the Code of Civil Procedures, and from the overwhelming body of judicial practice in this area, that recourse to emergency provisions is subordinate to the following requirements for admissibility.

Observance of the residual function of the rule
The only condition that is laid down according to the letter of the law ('apart from those cases governed by the preceding sections') is the negative one of the impossibility of resorting to any other precautionary remedy. It is therefore necessary that the case concerns a fact which cannot be protected by a sequestration or by the other typical provision. (A request for an urgent precautionary ruling in advance was granted to a company which complained that its ex-employees, using confidential technical knowledge, had produced similar products of their own and placed them on the market at a lower price (Pret Rome 10 March 1987).)

The requirement that the legal situation in question concerns personal rights
It is not therefore possible to issue emergency provisions to protect legitimate interests (protecting the citizen before the public authorities) or interests of fact (interests in connection with the observance of all the regulations laid down for the functioning of public powers) which cannot be jeopardised in the absence of an action/judgment.

The requirement that the right claimed is subsequently asserted in an ordinary action for investigation of the facts
The situation constituting the object of the right being claimed must justify a favourable decision on the merits of the case, if it is founded on fact and on a legal right.

In addition to the conditions for admissibility as described, it is also necessary that there be so-called *fumus boni iuris* if an urgent measure is to be granted.

The requirement that delay involves a risk to the plaintiff's rights
Clearly the urgency of a case or *periculum in mora* constitutes another essential requirement for the granting of the provision; therefore the remedy will be rejected in those cases in which valid protection could also be obtained by commencing an ordinary action for investigation of the facts.

The requirement of irreparable damage
Another essential element is represented by the danger that the damage to be suffered by the plaintiff cannot be rectified in any way once it has occurred. This provision would apply in all those cases in which the asset or item protected is irreplaceable, or where the plaintiff is seeking protection of his health, of his good name, reputation (be it private or public) or the good name of a company and of the rights of the individual in general.

In the past legal practice had always stubbornly rejected this protection in cases where what was being sought was a simple restoration of assets or property since damages (in the form of financial compensation) appeared to be an adequate remedy.

However, a more considered interpretation of this rule over recent years has led, in some cases, to the favourable treatment of requests in which even the right to a credit, if not immediately satisfied, could result in irreparable consequences, for instance the bankruptcy of a creditor as the result of a cashflow crisis (Pret Rome, 1987), on the assumption that once it had collapsed the company would not be able to return to the market.

Nevertheless, the interpretations offered by judges with regard to this concept of the 'irreparable' nature of damage are to a great extent dependent on the personal viewpoints of individual judges, and the most varied of solutions have been proposed to resolve such problems (see Andrioli, Comm IV, p 251). As an example, in connection with the reinstatement of a position of employment which was lost through unfair dismissal, due consideration was given to the imminent and irreparable damage suffered by the employee, strictly correlated to the right of compensation to guarantee himself and his family a free, dignified existence (Trib Milan, 1 July 1980); imminent and irreparable damage was also recognised in terms of the threat to the health of the inhabitants of a building due to malfunctioning of a heating installation, taking into account the special needs of the winter season (Pret Molfetta, 23 December 1988).

From the procedural point of view it can be seen that if an action on the merits of the case has not yet been instituted, art 669.3 of the Code of Civil Procedures requires that the request (for a precautionary measure) be submitted to the judge who would be competent to try the said action. If the case is already pending, on the other hand, the request must be submitted to the judge by whom it is being dealt with. In granting a provision in response to the request, which marks the precautionary measure stage, the judge will fix a period of not more than 30 days within which the plaintiff must bring a legal action before the competent judge. The peremptory nature of this period means that if the plaintiff fails to comply with this requirement, the emergency provision will automatically lose its validity and effect. The judge has a discretion to order a period of less than 30 days depending on the urgency of the case.

There is another remedy of a general nature provided for in art 120 of the Code of Civil Procedures which states that in cases where publicity of the decision on the merits of the case could contribute towards compensating for the damages suffered, the judge, at the request of the party concerned, may order the publication of the judgment 'at the expense of the losing party, by inserting an extract thereof in one or more newspapers that he will choose'.

The injunction procedure

The injunction procedure belongs to that category of investigative proceedings which most legal theorists see as 'proceedings whose primary function is that of enforcement' in that, as far as their function is concerned, they are characterised by the requirement to obtain an enforceable declaratory judgment as quickly as possible, and with it the commencement of the compulsory enforcement. From the procedural point of view the most striking characteristic, however, is the summary nature of the investigation, and it is with regard to this aspect that the code equates this procedure with the confirmation of an eviction order and the precautionary measures proper.

In essence the procedure consists of an order from the judge, issued at the request of the creditor and pronounced *inaudita altera parte*, to pay a sum (or a specified quantity of replaceable items or a specified object) within a specified period of time.

Article 633 of the Code of Civil Procedures, under the heading 'conditions for admissibility', states the specific prerequisites for this procedure. These prerequisites relate, in the first instance, with the claim for which protection in this form is being sought, secondly, with the evidence on which the claimed right is based, and finally with a number of procedural formalities:

Concerning the right on which the claim is based this must take the form of a right of credit in the broad sense of those words, that is to say involving a cash sum (or at least a pre-determined sum), or a specific quantity of replaceable objects, or the right to take delivery of a given movable asset. Moreover the credit must be *collectable*.

Concerning the evidence except in special cases, art 633, point 1 requires that written evidence be provided to substantiate the claimed right. This requirement is directly linked to the fact that the function and technique of the injunction procedure require, first and foremost, a strong probability of the existence of the credit, and secondly a speedy verification of its existence.

Concerning the procedural formalities if the right takes the form of a situation in which there was an obligation on both parties to provide a service, the injunction may only be granted if the plaintiff can provide evidence that he fulfilled his part of the agreement or that the conditions were met. Paragraph III of art 633 states, finally, that an injunction cannot be pronounced if it has to be served outside Italian territory.

The preliminary request for the injunction procedure is made to the judge who is competent to deal with the corresponding ordinary legal action. The request, accompanied by the supporting evidence, will be examined at once by the judge who, *inaudita altera parte*, will either accept or reject that request. However, rejection will not in any way prejudice the subsequent resubmission of the claim in the form of an ordinary action. If, on the other hand, he is of the view that the necessary requirements have been met, the judge, stating the grounds for his ruling, will issue an injunction on the debtor to fulfil his obligation within 20 days of receiving orders to do so. 'Where there is just reason, the period for fulfilment of the obligation may be reduced to five days or extended to thirty days' (art 641, II of the Code of Civil Procedures). The judge's order will also contain a clear note to the effect that during the specified period action may be taken to oppose the judgment, in the absence of which the judgment will be enforced.

Upon expiry of the specified period the judge's decision will become final and enforceable if the other party has not appealed against it.

There are, however, exceptional cases in which the injunction may be declared provisionally enforceable. The first of these is contemplated in art 642 of the Code of Civil Procedures. This states that if the credit takes the form of a cheque, bill of exchange, stock exchange certificate or a notarised deed, or any form of public deed, at the request of the creditor, the judge 'will issue an injunction against the debtor to pay or hand over [what is owed] without further delay, granting authority, in the absence of such action, for provisional enforcement of the judgment and fixing the period during which the other party may lodge an appeal'.

Provisional enforceability may also be granted if there is the risk of serious harm in the event of delay; in this case the judge may require the plaintiff to provide a security deposit. The plaintiff must then formally serve the request and corresponding judgment on the debtor within 40 days of the judge making his pronouncement; if this does not occur the judgment will lose its validity. However, this does not preclude the possibility of resubmitting the request or claim.

The summary investigation stage ends with the judge's granting of the appropriate provision. The judge's decision is always appealable. If the defendant appeals, he will effectively become the plaintiff in the ordinary action and will file 'counter-pleadings'. The judge hearing the appeal may revoke the order or make it enforceable. The ordinary action will always conclude with a final judgment revoking or confirming the order containing the precautionary measure. At this stage the proceedings will constitute an ordinary action, but the periods of time allowed for appearing before the court may be reduced by half. If the debtor's opposition is rejected, the judge's ruling, if not already effectively enforceable, will now become so. If the opposition is accepted only in part, the executive powers of enforcement will be based solely on the judgment, but enforcement on the basis of the judge's ruling will retain its effectiveness within the limits of the reduced amount or sum (art 653 of the Code of Civil Procedures). An injunction ruling which has been declared enforceable represents an enforceable declaration for all purposes; moreover those injunction rulings which are declared enforceable in a provisional sense, and those for which opposition has been rejected, allow a plaintiff to register a judicial mortgage in appropriate registers relating to the assets in question.

Precautionary measures in employment law and administrative law

Employment law

Under employment law situations are encountered with the characteristics necessary for the granting of a precautionary measure. In fact the legislator has provided, in art 423 of the Code of Civil Procedures, that at the request of the employee, and at any stage in the legal proceedings, the judge may order payment of a provisional sum if he deems that entitlement to that sum is beyond dispute, and within the limits of the amount for which there is already evidence. This provision by the judge (a provisional ruling), follows the summary investigation of the facts and is also of a precautionary nature.

The obvious justification for this is the need to ensure that the employee, as the supposedly weaker party to the employment relationship in financial terms, has the necessary funds for his maintenance for the duration of the case, provided of course there exists the prerequisite of *fumus boni iuris*. Consequently, in order for the provision to be granted it is sufficient that the judge's investigations keep pace with such provisional rulings. The ruling in question represents an enforceable declaration and can be revoked by the judgment pronounced at the end of the action, but the ruling can never be subject to an immediate challenge.

Administration law

The dividing up of jurisdiction between an ordinary judge and administrative judge is made essentially on the basis that the civil judge deals with subjective rights, whereas the administrative judge deals with legitimate interests—see in this connection the Introduction, p 177. The definition of a legitimate interest is hotly debated by legal theorists and there are many definitions put forward. Without claiming to offer a valid explanation, but simply in an attempt to provide the reader with a general idea, a legitimate interest can be defined as the subjective position of a citizen who, with regard to a particular provision of the public authorities, has a 'qualified' (one might say 'special') interest in a public authority respecting the correct logical and judicial criteria when adopting the provision in question. The legitimate interest operates on the premise that a subjective right and a legitimate interest can be fully distinguished. In reality the two situations often overlap and are indistinguishable. It will also be noted that the jurisdictional protection provided for the two legally defined situations is very different from all points of view. For the protection of a subjective right, in the context of an administrative act, the ordinary courts are required to limit their activities 'to determining the effects of the act' (see art 49, Law No 865 of 1865), and they are forbidden to cancel or suspend the act itself. In short, then, the ordinary courts may not impose on the public authorities anything other than instructions to pay compensation for damage caused.

A legitimate interest, on the other hand, is protected by means of a verification or control of legitimacy by the administrative judge who may cancel the administrative act that has been challenged if he deems it appropriate to do so. It is precisely in a case of this nature that the administrative judge has powers, for precautionary purposes, to suspend the enforceability of the disputed administrative act where there are 'serious reasons' (art 39, TU, CdS) and the plaintiff would suffer serious and irreparable loss from enforcement of the act.

It should be remembered, however, that art 8 of Law No 1669 of 27 May 1975 introduced yet another form of protection. This applies to a situation where a request has been submitted to the administrative judge for the suspension of the enforcement of an administrative provision aimed at the temporary and urgent occupation or expropriation of assets or property for reasons of general public interest. In such a case, the judge has the power to order that, instead of suspending enforcement of the act, a security deposit should be set up by the party on whose behalf the act was introduced, in a sum equivalent to compensation for the expropriation or occupation.

The poverty of administrative justice in the area of precautionary provisions is keenly felt by legal commentators who are in favour of sweeping reforms. Until the legislator chooses to act in this matter, however, legal practice will have to continue seeking to satisfy the need for adequate safeguards, firstly by relying on parallels with civil precautionary remedies, and secondly by squeezing every drop out of the scope provided by the suspensive judgment so that it is able to cover contingencies which are not at all typical.

Fabio Gullotta

Luxembourg

Introduction

Definition

The law authorises the judge to pronounce authoritative orders at the beginning, in the course or upon completion of proceedings. In most cases, such orders are part of the final judgment and may be:

(a) injunctions to do or not to do specified acts;
(b) limited to a certain period of time or perpetual.

Those injunctions issued at an early stage in the proceedings are generally pronounced with a view to maintain the *status quo* or restore and maintain an existing situation, until court clearing of the case (*measures conservatoires*).

Under certain special proceedings and in certain limited situations, specific judges may deliver mandatory and prohibitory injunctions in an accelerated action (*action en référé*).

This chapter will focus on the early-stage injunctions (interlocutory injunctions) as well as on injunctions passed under an accelerated procedure (*ordonnances en référé*). The term *Injunction* shall hereafter designate these two categories of injunctions only, if not otherwise indicated.

Scope of injunctions

Injunctions are used in many diverse areas and may be summarised as follows:

Conservatory measures
Aimed to maintain the *status quo*. For example:

(a) in case of difficulties in inventory matters (art 944 *Code Procédure Civile*). There are disputes which may arise when drawing up the inventory of the assets and liabilities of a deceased person;

(b) to organise the distribution of assets among spouses and the custody of the children during divorce proceedings and pending the final judgment (art 267 *Code Civil*).

Administration measures
Aimed to avoid the depreciation of assets subject to dispute. For example:

(a) provisional administration of vacant successions (art 812 Civil) whereby nobody claims to be a successor after a period of three months and 40 days since the death.

Investigation measures
Targeted to gather evidence so that the judge may form his opinion. For example:

(a) to hear a witness.

Restoration measures
Aimed to bring back a situation to its former condition. For example:

(a) seizure of a newspaper which infringes on privacy;
(b) attachment of a publication to interrupt a breach of copyright.

General principles

During the course of ordinary proceedings, the judge may, at all times, pronounce interlocutory injunctions, *ex officio* or at the request of one of the parties. Appeal of interlocutory judgments cannot be lodged, except when interlocutory injunctions are made together with enforceable decisions (eg dismissal of one of the plaintiff's points *and* designation of an expert to give an appraisal on some other claim). An enforceable decision is one which decides a legal issue and an expert may be appointed to assess the damages due to be paid. In such a case an appeal can be lodged immediately before the final decision is given.

The *référé* proceedings are subject to tighter rules:

General condition—urgency
Ordonnances en référé are passed under quick, discreet and efficient special proceedings, and are therefore always limited to urgent situations.

Non-urgent cases may be brought to ordinary courts. The judge competent for *référés*—the President of the District Court (*Tribunal d'Arrondissement*)—may of course determine whether the condition of urgency is fulfilled or not.

No serious dispute on the substance

Given the general conditions of the proceedings (quick, discreet action), the judge is not meant to examine the substance of the case but only to supply a solution in an urgent situation. However, the judge is once again competent to determine whether there is any serious dispute on the substance. In certain cases where the substance is indeed disputed by the parties, though the judge cannot decide on the claim, he may pronounce certain injunctions (eg investigation measures) when they are justified by urgency.

Conservatory and restoration measures

The judge may pronounce such injunctions to prevent or interrupt illegal prejudice caused to the plaintiff. Here again, urgency is the substance of the action.

Structure of the courts

Description

Civil courts are organised according to the double court instance principle:

(1) At the first level of instance, the *Juge de Paix* (justice of the peace) has special jurisdiction for cases valued at a maximum of LUF 100,000— and specific matters notwithstanding the value of the dispute (eg alimony out of a divorce case, rentals on premises); the *Tribunal d'Arrondissement* (District Court) is the civil court with overall competence on all matters which have not been specifically transferred to the *Juge de Paix*.

(2) At the second level of instance, the Court of Appeal re-examines judgments from the District Court. The District Court hears appeals against judgments from the *Juge de Paix*.

At the top of the civil courts organisation, the Court of Cassation governs the homogeneous application of legal rules by all courts pronouncing final judgments (note that in certain matters, first instance courts may issue final orders which are not subject to appeal).

The president of the first instance District Court (*Tribunal d'Arrondissement*) is competent for all actions in *référé*, whether of civil or commercial nature. His orders are subject to appeal and *opposition* (appeal against a default judgment). Appeal is examined under the special proceedings applying to urgent cases.

Local jurisdiction

The Grand Duchy has two District Courts: Diekirch in the north of the country, and Luxembourg for the southern region. Local competence of the judge of *référés* may be determined in two ways:

(a) the competent judge is either the one having his bench in the same district as the court ultimately competent on the merits of the dispute, or
(b) the judge sitting in the district where the requested injunction is to be enforced.

Procedural rules are identical in Diekirch and Luxembourg.

Legal team

The proceedings for obtaining an injunction are not very technical and do not require a high level of specialisation. The technicality of the claim itself may, however, lead the plaintiff to search for the assistance of an experienced and knowledgeable lawyer, especially in business related cases. Besides, obtaining an interlocutory injunction is often only one of the first steps towards a later trial on the merits, and it is always valuable to have the same legal counsel throughout the entire procedure. All lawyers have a right of audience in all the courts in Luxembourg.

Criteria for obtaining interlocutory injunctions

The criteria are described in broad terms in the statute, and the interpretation of such terms in case law has led to quite extensive concepts. Criteria may be summarised under two headings.

Urgency

This is the general criterion for obtaining an injunction from the judge of *référés*. Urgency is explicitly referred to in art 806 of the Code of Civil Procedure and implicitly in art 807.

Serious dispute

Whether there is a serious dispute or not between the parties, interlocutory injunctions may be requested from the President of the District Court in case of urgency. The aim is here to avoid any brutal and unfair deterioration of the situation for the plaintiff due to the length of the ordinary courts proceedings.

Imminent damage

The President of the District Court has the broadest powers to pronounce interlocutory injunctions aimed at the prevention of damages. Conservatory measures are often requested in cases where privacy is threatened by the press: an injunction to seize to-be-released publications prior to circulation containing material prejudicing the claimant's private life is delivered by the judge to avoid imminent damage occurring, and a trial on the merits can later establish whether or not the claim was justified. Such procedure involves fundamental questioning on the comparative importance of the freedom of the press and freedom of private life, and the preferred protection to be granted to one or the other. Neither the judge of *référés* nor the courts have made clear their position on the subject.

Unlawful disturbance

When the damage is being realised, or has been done and carries continuous consequences, the President of the District Court may be asked to deliver an injunction restoring the claimant to his position prior to the disturbance.

For example, a breach of competition law, once perpetrated, produces continuous effects and the judge of *référés* may take all measures to interrupt the activity thus created.

In all cases, urgency is of the essence of the action: should there be no degree of urgency, the claimant would have to be content with ordinary proceedings. In his request to the President of the District Court, the claimant must of course indicate why his action is urgent. The judge appraises the criterion of urgency on a case-by-case basis (see *Cour* 14.3.66, Pas 20, p 90) and this is of great significance in the case law: by appraising the urgency condition, the judge states whether he is competent or not to hear the case.

Undisputed claims

Certain claims between parties may create difficulties even though they are not seriously contested. In such cases, whether there is urgency is of no relevance. The absence of contention makes it unnecessary to settle the case through ordinary proceedings, and it is preferable to obtain a clear and quick ruling by means of an injunction from the President of the District Court.

The judge then has broad injunctive powers, and they are not limited to interlocutory injunctions: final mandatory or prohibiting injunctions may be delivered. When the claim relates to a debt, the judge may even allow provisional payment to be effected. The judge of *référés*, not being expected to judge on the merits, should only take provisional measures. In practice, however, when the judge is confronted with an uncontested debt, he grants to the creditor a provisional payment which covers the major part of the debt, sometimes even the full amount. This is in fact a decision on the merits, which exceeds the basic competence of the President of the District Court. But this also means simple cases may find a quick and efficient solution without congesting already overworked courts.

Here again, as for the criterion of urgency, the judge himself appraises whether the undisputed claim factor is satisfied or not. The competence of acting as the judge of *référés* is granted only to a senior professional judge. Case law shows that the judges are quite protective of the interests of individuals.

Practice and procedure

Notice

The action *en référé* is made *inter partes*, even when remedies are needed within hours. No *ex parte* action is available.

Notice is given to the defendant without the assistance of a bailiff (*huissier de justice*) being required. This is of particular importance when hearings are scheduled within hours. Given the urgency, there is no time for the usual registration of the notice.

The judge must check and ensure, in his judgment, that the time period left to the defendant was sufficient for the latter to prepare his defence. In very urgent cases, half a day would be considered a reasonable time period granted to the defendant. There is no provision in the law on the duration of such 'reasonable delay' and the judge has an absolute discretion to appraise the time delay, subject to a statement in his judgment, assessing the notice period afforded to the defendant.

In cases of great urgency, notice may be given to the defendant even on Saturdays, Sundays or public holidays, at the court or even at the domicile of the judge 'with open doors' (so that members of the public can still have access to the hearing, as in all court hearings).

Should the judge consider the defendant as not having had enough time to organise his defence, the hearing of the *référé* would of course be postponed to a later date if that is more suitable in the judge's view.

Documents required

The procedure is oral in nature: hearings are to be held mainly based on oral evidence. However, when filing his application with the judge, it is in the plaintiff's interest to provide full details about his claims, including documentary proof supporting his request and all possible evidence that no serious defence can be submitted by the other party or that the claim is urgent.

The judge is not expected to decide on the merits of the case, but shall only grant provisional measures. The stronger the injunction requested of the judge, the more self-explanatory must be the supporting documents.

In urgent situations, it is the urgency criterion which must be carefully documented together with the damage to be remedied or avoided.

Wherever possible, parties must exchange their respective documents. However, this exchange of information need not be made before the hearing if, in the circumstances, there is insufficient time to do so. Once the documents supporting the claims have been communicated by each party to the other, they may jointly wish to be granted an additional time period in which to re-assess their claims. Under normal circumstances, such a request should be allowed by the judge.

Statements of claims do not need to be presented to the judge in written form. However, the parties may choose to prepare such statements in writing and forward them to the judge. Further, when the case is of a technical and/or complicated nature, the judge may require the parties to state their claims in writing.

Procedures and rules

The text of the law does not specifically require parties to appear represented by a lawyer. In theory, parties may appear in person and plead their own case. In practice, parties are always represented and assisted by lawyers.

The application to the judge of *référés* once notified to the defendant is heard at a weekly session held at the District Court. Applications are then fixed for hearing by order of seniority of the claimants' lawyers. This procedure is not followed when the case is urgent and requires the utmost expediency: the defendant is then notified to be present at the hearing—fixed within hours if necessary.

The case will be heard without prior investigation. Should the judge consider the case not to be sufficiently documented, he will adjourn the hearing date or order an investigation injunction. To take full advantage of the speedy procedure, it is vital for the claimant to document his request with the utmost care. The order (*ordonnance*) delivered by the judge is very similar to a judgment, except that the order is not subject to the force of *res judicata*.

The order must contain a brief description of the grounds of the decision before the wording of the order. The degree of urgency of the case governs the timing of when the order will come into force: it may be immediately after the hearing, later on the same day, or one or several days later. This choice is left to the judge's discretion.

One is reminded that the judge of *référés* may not decide on the merits of the case. However, when a provisional payment of the full debt is granted to the creditor, at the very least the order was determined on the merits and in practice eliminates any further need for a judicial trial.

Costs

The costs usually have to be borne by the losing party. The judge does have a discretion to award part or all of the costs to one party if it is appropriate to do so. Such costs include court fees and other disbursements but each party has to pay his own lawyer's fees.

Post-injunction factors

Service of the injunction

No special rules apply here: the injunction is to be served on the defendant by a process server (*huissier de justice*). If the process server has been unable to meet the defendant in person and the injunction is therefore not served personally, service may then be made on the defendant's domicile or residence. The document is handed over in a sealed envelope to any person present at the address with details of the defendant in an 'information' document. If there is nobody there then the process server leaves a copy of the document at the domicile or residence of the intended recipient.

Should the person(s) present at the domicile or residence (neighbours, watchmen, and in general any person present) refuse or be unable to accept a copy of the injunction, service is then validly made on the Town Hall of the defendant's domicile or residence.

An injunction only becomes effective against the defendant upon service. The process server delivers a receipt to the plaintiff, stating the details of his service (ie name of the actual recipient of the served injunction).

Sanctions

Description

When delivering an injunction, the judge may decide additionally on a penalty fine sanctioning each day of delay by the defendant in complying with the injunction. This sanction, though very efficient, is only optional and left to the discretion of the judge. Despite not being a final judgment, injunctions are provisionally enforceable. Enforcement may be obtained with the assistance of the police where and when required. A breach of the injunction by the defendant cannot lead to imprisonment. The penalty fine is the only available sanction in the event of non-compliance with the injunction.

Procedure

As already mentioned, the most efficient sanction against a solvent but reluctant defendant is certainly the penalty fine. It is in the plaintiff's best interest always to ask the judge to supplement the injunction with such a measure. However, the judge may or may not enter a penalty fine, and for such amount as he deems appropriate.

The fine may sanction each day of delay in complying with the injunction by the defendant, or each breach of the injunction. The fine is paid to the plaintiff, and is deemed to be damages in favour of the latter.

Application to vary or discharge the injunction

The defendant may apply to vary or discharge the injunction by using an action during the special procedure held before the President of the District Court: the action *en référé* is made *inter partes* and the defendant is given notice of the action started against him (see also p 204). The defendant may contest the application upon any ground, but in accordance with the general rules governing evidence in courts.

However, as has already been emphasised, the plaintiff's application is only heard by the President of the District Court if the case is not subject to any serious dispute. It is therefore unlikely that the defendant has any valid points to make in his application to discharge the injunction made in the course of the urgency procedure (the *référé*).

If the defendant has a substantive defence, the case would then be considered seriously disputed and submitted to the District Court for a decision on the merits. The urgency procedure of *référé* would then cease to be applicable. Therefore, in certain circumstances, if there is a serious dispute, an injunction cannot be granted even if the matter is one of great urgency.

Enquiry into damages

Although no precedent can be found in the case law on *référé* decisions, it is possible for a defendant to ask for damages if an injunction is discharged (or varied). Such an inquiry would be based on the charge of abusive proceedings by the plaintiff, and would be heard at a trial as a subsidiary application.

Freezing orders

Article 807 authorises the President of the District Court acting as a *référé* judge to take all conservatory or restoration measures deemed necessary to prevent any imminent damage or to put a stop to an obviously illegal activity. The text does not contain any limitation in respect of the scope of the measures the judge may pronounce, and an injunction for the distraint or sequestration of part or all of the defendant's assets can be made.

The extent of such an injunction is left to the discretion of the judge although the plaintiff may make an application for the general distraint of the defendant's assets. However, it is unlikely that such a radical injunction would be pronounced against a private person. There is also a special provision in the Code of Civil Procedure which deals with the freezing of a person's assets, including his bank accounts, in special circumstances. The plaintiff must demonstrate that there is a risk of the person removing, or disposing of, his assets, and the case must be one of real urgency. In order to apply under this special procedure, a request is filed with the President of the District Court. If the legal requirements and criteria are satisfied, an order can be granted attaching any assets of a debtor with a third party, including a bank account.

No notice is given to the debtor of this procedure. A court bailiff will then serve the attachment order on the third party, and subsequently serve a writ of summons on the debtor. The creditor must pursue ordinary proceedings and obtain a judgment which will validate the attachment. Only after judgment is obtained can the plaintiff levy execution on the attached goods.

General distraint would be more applicable to companies although private persons can also be subjected to limited freezing orders. At least part of the assets of private persons may not be subject to distraint; those representing the 'normal living expenses'.

Once served on concerned parties or entities, the injunction must be executed, and third parties who are depositories of the defendant's assets (such as banks) have a duty to comply with the provisions concerned in the injunction. A customer's instructions received after the injunction was served to the custodian must be overruled by the latter.

Search and seize orders

Finally, there is also a special procedure in the Civil Code, for court officials to seize evidence in intellectual property cases.

The procedure is called *saisie-description*. The plaintiff requests an order with the President of the District Court. No notice is given to the defendant of the application. The order will allow a bailiff to attach (seize) samples of the infringing products. This attachment will allow the plaintiff to compile sufficient evidence to demonstrate that the rights in his genuine product have been infringed.

Alex Schmitt

The Netherlands

Introduction

Preface

This chapter describes provisional remedies under the laws of the Netherlands and, specifically, preliminary injunctions obtained through preliminary relief proceedings before the President of the district court. Given the fact that this book provides a survey of the different systems of injunctive relief in the EC, a uniform outline has been chosen for all of the chapters. Because of the differences among the various legal systems, the outline may fit some systems better than others. In order to preserve the consistency of all chapters, thus enhancing the book's accessibility, the outline has been followed in this chapter as best as possible. In order to obtain proper advice on the possibilities and limitations of injunctive relief in the Netherlands in each particular case, one should always consult an attorney admitted to practice in the Netherlands. This chapter cannot, of course, replace such consultation.

Various types of provisional remedies in the Netherlands

Provisional remedies
Various types of provisional remedies are available to the parties in a civil dispute under the law of the Netherlands. A number of important provisional remedies could be classified as preliminary injunctions; they will be the main subject of this chapter. Other provisional remedies in civil matters include:

Preliminary hearing of witnesses (*voorlopig getuigenverhoor*; arts 214 *et seq* of the Code of Civil Procedure (*Wetboek van Burgerlijke Rechtsvordering*) in effect as at 1 January 1992. Unless otherwise indicated, references to numbered articles refer to the Code of Civil Procedure.

A party may petition the competent court for a hearing of witnesses concerning a matter in which no proceedings have (yet) been issued.

This procedure may be used for one or more purposes:

(a) to preserve the testimony of a witness which might be unavailable at a later stage (when the court would rule in an interlocutory decision in pending regular proceedings on the merits that witness testimony be allowed);

(b) to preserve the quality of a testimony by arranging for the hearing of a witness shortly after the relevant facts occur;

(c) to obtain or confirm the identity of the party against whom the proceedings should be issued (Netherlands law has no equivalent to the discovery proceedings known in Anglo-American jurisdictions); or

(d) to assess the chances of success in a contemplated law suit.

Witnesses are heard by a district court judge after a request to that effect is granted by the district court; the potential defendant, who—if known—should be identified in the request, has the opportunity to object to the preliminary hearing and, if the objections are overruled, to attend the hearing and to question the witness or witnesses (through the judge). At the end of the hearing, the judge will dictate, in his own words, the relevant statements made by the witness; no verbatim transcript is made.

Preliminary expert advice (*Voorlopig deskundigen-bericht*; arts 227 *et seq.*) In a procedure similar to that of the request for a preliminary hearing of a witness a party may request the competent court to order expert advice on complex, often technical matters which are relevant to a dispute in respect of which no proceedings have yet been issued. The court is free to determine the evidential weight of the expert's advice. The procedure for obtaining preliminary expert advice was introduced in 1988 and has—so far—rarely been used.

Notice

The term preliminary injunction could be used for a number of important provisional remedies. Generally, only one such preliminary injunction can be obtained by *ex parte* proceedings: the conservatory attachment of tangible or intangible assets (sometimes also referred to as 'conservatory arrest'). Conservatory attachment will be separately discussed at p 231 below. There is no equivalent in the Netherlands for so-called search and seizure orders.

The other preliminary injunctions are generally available only through *inter partes* proceedings, designed to allow the parties on both sides to be heard. This does not mean, of course, that such preliminary injunctions could not be granted by default judgment, in cases where the defendant, though properly notified of the proceedings, fails to appear.

Preliminary relief proceedings

The majority of all preliminary injunctions issued in the Netherlands in civil cases are obtained by means of preliminary relief proceedings (*kort geding*) before the President of the competent district court. These proceedings are rather informal and have been designed especially to provide immediate and provisional relief in matters too urgent to await a judgment in regular proceedings on the merits (sometimes also referred to as 'principal proceedings').

Preliminary relief proceedings may be used regardless of whether regular proceedings have been or will be issued. Preliminary relief granted by the President does not prejudice the legal positions of the parties in regular proceedings which may, or may not, follow; the relief does not usually become inoperative by failure to issue regular proceedings or by lapse of time. In fact, only a small number of the matters in which preliminary relief is requested result in regular proceedings for permanent relief of the same type.

This chapter will discuss preliminary injunctions within the framework of preliminary relief proceedings, given the practical importance of these proceedings.

Regular proceedings

It should be noted, however, that preliminary injunctions can also be granted in a provisional (interlocutory) judgment rendered in the regular proceedings on the merits (see arts 51 and 100). This mainly happens in cases within the jurisdiction of the Cantonal courts, see p 217 below. Regular proceedings before the district court often take a year or more before the court's first judgment is delivered (even an interlocutory one). As a result, preliminary injunctions in provisional (interlocutory) judgments are rarely requested in regular proceedings before the district court. If granted, such preliminary injunctions are superseded by the final conclusive judgment on the merits, in which final relief may be granted or denied.

There is no principle of Netherlands law that restricts the availability of preliminary injunctions to cases in which damages awarded in regular proceedings would not be an adequate remedy. An injunction may be sought to prevent damage or further damage, even if such damage could be fully compensated financially. The mere threat of damage could (and often does) warrant the issue of a preliminary injunction.

Arbitral preliminary relief

The parties to an agreement to arbitrate may agree to give the arbitration tribunal (or its President) jurisdiction to hear and rule on petitions for preliminary relief instead of having to submit to the general jurisdiction of the President of the district court in preliminary relief proceedings (art 1051). The jurisdiction vested in the arbitrations tribunal in this respect may not exceed the limits of the President's general jurisdiction, see p 218. If the President of the district court is requested to grant preliminary relief, despite an agreement to seek arbitral preliminary reliefs, he has a discretionary power to deny jurisdiction; all relevant circumstances will be taken into account, such as the speed with which arbitral preliminary relief may be available and the plaintiff's reasons for not applying for arbitral relief. A decision in arbitral preliminary relief proceedings is regarded as a regular arbitration award for all procedural purposes.

Types and scope of injunctions

The statute

As discussed above, preliminary injunctions in the Netherlands are usually obtained through preliminary relief proceedings. Article 289 reads as follows [unofficial translation]:

1   In all cases that—given the mutual interests of the parties—urgently require an immediate remedy in anticipation, a claim may be filed at a court session to be held for this purpose by the President of the district court on week-days to be determined by him.

2   In very urgent matters the session may be ordered on the basis of an oral application by the interested party on the day and at the hour, Sundays included, to be determined by the President in accordance with the circumstances of the case. The President may order that the court session take place at his home.

3   In the cases mentioned in 2 the President shall provide the bailiff with an oral mandate to serve the writ of summons, to which the bailiff shall refer in the heading of his writ.

Types of injunctions

Provided the relevant three-tier test of this article is met (ie (i) an immediate remedy is urgently required by a plaintiff (ii) whose claim is likely to succeed in regular proceedings, and (iii) whose interests in obtaining such remedy outweigh the interests of the defendant; (see also p 222) the President may issue the following preliminary injunctions in preliminary relief proceedings:

(i) he may order a party to do something (a mandatory injunction or *gebod*); or

(ii) he may order a party to refrain from doing something (a prohibitory injunction or *verbod*).

In addition, the President may grant some forms of ancillary relief described at p 216. The President may not issue a declaratory judgment, since such a decision would not be provisional in nature. Similarly, the President may not generally alter or annul the legal relationship between the parties, for instance by declaring an existing agreement null and void.

Scope of injunctions

In practice, however, judgments in preliminary relief proceedings can have a very important and often decisive influence on the practical positions of the parties. This results in part from the fact that the President may not only order a party to do a specific physical act, but also to perform a specific transaction (for instance to convey real property pursuant to an existing obligation). Similarly, the President may not only prohibit the defendant from performing a specific act, but also from exercising an existing right (for instance an order prohibiting a former employer from enforcing all or part of a non-competition clause against a former employee). Such a preliminary injunction will—of course—not be phrased so as to constitute an alteration to the legal relationship between the parties (which would be outside the provisional scope of preliminary relief proceedings). Rather, it will be phrased as a limitation on a party's power to exercise a pretended or existing right. Such limitation may arise out of the principles of good faith which the parties owe one another under the specific circumstances of their situation. Although judgments of the President in preliminary relief proceedings can be appealed to a three member Court of Appeal and thereafter to the Dutch Supreme Court, see p 217, preliminary injunctions are invariably enforceable notwithstanding appeal (sometimes referred to as enforceable in anticipation). Often, the nature of the relief granted is such that, once the injunction is enforced, it cannot be undone even if the judgment should be overturned on appeal. Also, it is relatively time consuming and expensive to lodge an appeal both in preliminary relief proceedings and regular proceedings. For all of these reasons the practical result of a 'preliminary' injunction issued by the President in preliminary relief proceedings is often a final determination of the issue in dispute.

Examples

A wide variety of injunctions are regularly issued in preliminary relief proceedings in the Netherlands. The following are examples.

(1) A newspaper may be ordered to publish an announcement rectifying earlier statements which were held unlawful in respect of the plaintiff; the judgment of the President often specifies the exact wording and size of the announcement.

(2) A newspaper may be prohibited from publishing certain specific information in the future; the threat of non-pecuniary damage may be sufficient to warrant injunctive relief.

(3) In libel cases, a newspaper may be ordered in preliminary relief proceedings to pay a certain sum as an advance payment of pecuniary damages; the reason for allowing such a claim in preliminary relief proceedings is that the court takes account of the plaintiff's overriding interest in receiving some form of satisfaction relatively quickly after the libellous publication.

(4) An employee may be ordered to comply with a non-competition agreement with his former employer, but the former employer's request for such an order may also be denied if the request is deemed to be contrary to the principles of good faith given the particular circumstances of the case.

(5) A party may be ordered to return to the negotiating table if he terminated negotiations in bad faith.

(6) An offender may be prohibited from frequenting a certain limited area of a town to allow the plaintiff to move around without the risk of being followed or harassed.

(7) The owner of a trade mark may require the seller of products which infringe the trade mark (i) to identify his supplier; (ii) to deliver to the trade mark owner an auditor's statement evidencing how many products have been sold and to whom; (iii) to withdraw from the market any products not sold thus far; and (iv) to surrender to the trade mark owner all such products and all products in stock for subsequent destruction.

(8) The government may obtain a civil injunction based on tort to avoid (further) damage to the environment.

(9) The President may lift a conservatory attachment with immediate effect; such a judgment—although not final—permanently changes the relative positions of the parties.

(10) A debtor of an undisputed debt may be ordered to pay (collection through preliminary relief proceedings—see p 223); a debtor who acknowledges his liability as such, but disputes the amount of the claim, may be ordered to make an advance payment of damages.

Structure of the courts

Summary of the structure of the courts

Different courts

In most types of civil proceedings the parties may have their case heard by courts at three different levels. The following four types of courts serve in the Dutch system.

(1) Cantonal courts (*Kantongerechten*) have first instance jurisdiction to hear all civil claims up to NLG 5,000, as well as all disputes regarding labour law, agency contracts, rental of real property and lease-purchase agreements. There are 62 Cantonal courts in the Netherlands. The Cantonal courts have single judge panels.

(2) The 19 District Courts (*Rechtbanken*) in the Netherlands serve as appellate courts for decisions of the Cantonal courts and as courts of first instance for all civil matters not within the jurisdiction of the Cantonal courts. The District Courts have both one and three member panels.

(3) Five Courts of Appeal serve as the appellate level for matters within the first instance jurisdiction of the district courts. Appeals are heard by a panel of three judges. One division of the Amsterdam Court of Appeal, called the Enterprise Chamber (*Ondernemingskamer*), has first instance jurisdiction in certain specific corporate law proceedings (regarding, *inter alia*, annual accounts, works councils, and other corporate matters).

(4) The Dutch Supreme Court (*Hoge Raad*) is the highest civil court in the Netherlands. It may review decisions of a lower court, but only with respect to questions of law. The facts are irrevocably established by the lower court. The Supreme Court is obliged to review all lower court decisions presented to it, provided of course that review by the Supreme Court is not excluded by law. The Supreme Court usually sits in panels of five justices.

Appeal in preliminary relief proceedings

Judgments delivered by the President of a District Court in preliminary relief proceedings may be appealed to the competent Court of Appeal by serving a notice of appeal and summons within 14 days. In practice, two types of appellate proceedings have been developed. A speedy appeal is initiated when the appellant includes his grievances (the grounds for the appeal) in the notice of appeal and summons. The respondent should then file a memorandum of answer within two to three weeks, after which a brief oral argument is heard. Thereafter, the Court of Appeal's decision may be available within two months after the initial judgment of the President of the district court. A regular appeal in preliminary relief proceedings may take six to nine months.

Review
Decisions by the Court of Appeal in preliminary relief proceedings may be submitted to the Supreme Court for review on a point of law. The completion of hearings at three different levels in preliminary relief proceedings usually takes between 18 and 24 months.

Regional considerations and jurisdiction

General
As in most legal systems, there is a distinction between subject matter or absolute jurisdiction, and venue, or relative jurisdiction. There is no separate doctrine of personal jurisdiction in the Netherlands. Questions relating to personal jurisdiction are resolved within the framework of absolute or relative jurisdiction.

Absolute jurisdiction
The principal rules of the jurisdiction of the various Dutch courts in regular civil proceedings have been set out at p 217, above. The President of the district court has absolute jurisdiction—provided the three-tier test of art 289 is met, see pp 214 and 222 in all matters in which any Dutch civil court has absolute jurisdiction, as well as in all matters in which the requested preliminary relief has effect in the Netherlands, even if both parties reside outside the Netherlands. However, the absolute jurisdiction of a President in preliminary relief proceedings is limited to the issue of preliminary injunctions, as discussed at p 214.

Relative jurisdiction
The basic rule on relative jurisdiction (or venue) is that an action should be brought before the competent court of the place where the defendant is domiciled. In preliminary relief proceedings a second basic rule applies: the action may also be brought in the district where the injunction requested will have effect.

Other general rules of relative jurisdiction also apply to preliminary relief proceedings. If there are several defendants the action may be brought before the competent court of the place of domicile of any one of them, at the option of the plaintiff. This rule applies even if one or more defendants have their domicile abroad, as long as one defendant is domiciled in the Netherlands. In certain cases the venue provisions are more specific. If the dispute concerns real property, the action should be brought before the court of the location of the real property. In the case of bankruptcy claims, the competent court is the court that declared the bankruptcy. In disputes concerning partnerships or corporate matters, relative jurisdiction lies with the court of the place in which the partnership or company has its official seat. If there is a chosen domicile, the competent court is the court of that domicile. If the defendant is a legal entity with a corporate seat in one place and one or more branch offices in another, the competent court for matters relating to a particular branch office is both the court of the place of the corporate seat and the court of the place of the particular branch office.

Foreign defendants

Dutch courts have jurisdiction in most cases in which a plaintiff domiciled in the Netherlands brings proceedings against a Dutch or foreign national not domiciled or residing in the Netherlands. The competent court is the court where the plaintiff is domiciled. There is, however, no such jurisdiction in the Netherlands over claims against Dutch or foreign nationals domiciled in one of the other Member States of the Brussels Convention (on Jurisdiction and Enforcement of Judgments in Civil and Commercial Matters), to which the Netherlands is a party. An exception to this rule applies in preliminary relief proceedings if the relief sought has effect in the Netherlands (art 24 of the Brussels Convention).

Attachment creates jurisdiction

An attachment of assets located in the Netherlands generally establishes jurisdiction over the cause of action for which the attachment is made, even if one or both parties is not domiciled in the Netherlands, provided that no applicable international treaty or choice of forum clause provides for a different venue. The court competent to hear the claim is the court in whose district the attachment was made. Preliminary relief proceedings regarding attachments may be brought before the President in whose district the attachment was made or the President who granted leave for the attachment.

Forum non conveniens

The doctrine of *forum non conveniens* has limited significance in the Netherlands. It is sometimes applied in family or estate law cases. Apart from these areas there is little need for the doctrine. Thus, as long as venue is proper according to the applicable rules, the defendant cannot argue that another venue would be more convenient or appropriate.

Differences between districts

Differences between the various districts in the Netherlands are limited. As the Netherlands is one jurisdiction, both substantive law and procedural law (the Code of Civil Procedure) are the same in all districts (in fact, the substantive law in certain cases—trade marks, models and designs—is uniform throughout Belgium, the Netherlands and Luxembourg, the Benelux). However, practices which are sometimes laid down in local court rules may differ from district to district. The number of preliminary relief proceedings handled in each district varies widely. In the busiest districts (such as Amsterdam, Rotterdam and The Hague) the President of the district court and up to five Vice-Presidents are fully engaged handling the preliminary relief proceedings (which may average 10 per weekday per district). Cases in certain areas of substantive law (such as immigration law) are assigned, in the larger districts, to specialised (Vice-)Presidents; other cases are assigned randomly. In quieter districts the President may handle most preliminary relief proceedings himself.

Attitudes of the various Presidents may vary widely as well. Some Presidents are rather passive, simply allowing each party to make its statement and to respond to the other's, without asking any questions. Other Presidents actively try to resolve the dispute before them, sometimes practically forcing the parties into a settlement. If preliminary relief proceedings can be brought in more than one district, the choice can rarely be made on the basis of the reputation of a particular President, as it is usually impossible to predict, prior to initiating preliminary relief proceedings, who will preside. After a hearing date has been set in a particular district, the parties may enquire a few days in advance who the acting President will be. Sometimes, attorneys will take this into account when planning the strategy for oral argument.

Supreme Court

The role of the Supreme Court in preliminary relief proceedings is discussed at p 217, above.

Divisions of the courts

Divisions
The Dutch Supreme Court as well as the five Courts of Appeal each have three divisions: the Civil Division, the Criminal Division and the Tax Division. The district courts have a Family Division, a Bankruptcy Division, a (general) Civil Division and a Criminal Division (Courts of Appeal have first instance jurisdiction in taxation cases). Judges and justices rotate through the various divisions of their court. The larger district courts have subdivisions within the Civil and Criminal Divisions.

Tactical considerations
Given the fact that each type of case is exclusively assigned to a particular division, the plaintiff has no choice as to the division that will hear his case. As a result, there are no tactical considerations involved.

Legal team

Admission to the bar
In the Netherlands, an attorney (*advocaat*) is admitted to practice in his district. Only independent lawyers or lawyers employed by an independent lawyer or by a firm of independent lawyers can be admitted to the bar. Lawyers employed by business corporations or by the Government cannot be admitted. There is no distinction such as that between barristers and solicitors.

Local counsel
An attorney admitted in one district should involve local counsel (a *procureur*) for his contacts with the courts in other districts. This involvement is very limited, however, so that a Dutch attorney can argue cases before all Dutch courts (and indeed before the courts of the Netherlands Antilles and Aruba) after having been introduced by local counsel (which in most districts can be done by letter).

Preliminary relief proceedings
Preliminary relief proceedings in very urgent matters may in some districts be initiated (by a request to determine a date and hour for the hearing, see p 226) by an attorney from another district without involving local counsel. However, after a hearing date is determined, local counsel must be involved by the plaintiff.

Experience

Although many Dutch lawyers conduct preliminary relief proceedings occasionally, relatively few have extensive experience in this type of litigation. Many lawyers will do one or two preliminary relief proceedings each year. Few lawyers do many more than that, but those who do, will be very experienced, which will give them an advantage in conducting such proceedings.

Criteria for obtaining preliminary injunctions

Features

Affidavits

No affidavit evidence is necessary in the Netherlands to apply for preliminary injunctions in preliminary relief proceedings. Sworn statements by witnesses are not often used in the Netherlands. A party could request a preliminary hearing of witnesses (see p 211) before initiating preliminary relief proceedings, but this is not done frequently. The role of evidence in preliminary relief proceedings will be discussed at p 227.

Preliminary assessment

As stated above, the provisional character of preliminary relief proceedings prevents the injunction issued from being constitutive. Nevertheless, the decision taken by the President must be based on his preliminary assessment as to who is right and who is wrong.

The relevant test

Three requirements

In order to obtain an injunction in preliminary relief proceedings the following three requirements must be met:

(1) Urgency—the claim for an immediate preliminary injunction must involve a matter of urgency. The various Presidents of the district courts judge the requirement of urgency differently. Case law shows that, in general, claims are not often rejected due to lack of urgency, unless the plaintiff has waited too long before starting the proceedings. With regard to certain cases, urgency is simply assumed on the basis of the

nature of the case, eg when an order is sought prohibiting the defendant from allowing an unlawful situation to continue. The urgency should of course relate to the immediate relief sought.

(2) Preliminary assessment—the President will try to anticipate the potential outcome of the case in regular proceedings by examining the soundness of the principal claim. If at the hearing the case turns out to be very complex, the President can deny the claim for relief on the ground that the case is unsuitable for preliminary relief proceedings. It is a well known defence tactic to put up a 'smoke screen' of complex facts to make it more difficult for the President to grant injunctive relief.

(3) The balance of convenience—the President must balance the mutual interests of the parties taking into account all specific circumstances of the situation at hand and the principles of good faith if they govern the relationship between the parties. The President of the district court must be convinced that the plaintiff's interests in obtaining the provisional relief requested clearly outweigh the interest of the defendant in having the plaintiff's request denied. The suitability of the provisional relief sought plays an important role in the weighing-up of interests. If no immediate relief is required to prevent serious or irreparable (pecuniary or non-pecuniary) damage, the claim in preliminary relief proceedings is usually denied.

Collection matters

In collection matters in preliminary relief proceedings the President may issue a payment order if:

(a) the plaintiff urgently requires a payment order; it is not required, however, that the plaintiff himself be in financial distress;
(b) the existence of the plaintiff's claim against the defendant is beyond reasonable doubt; and
(c) the balance of convenience weighs in the plaintiff's favour; this will not be the case if there is a substantial risk that the plaintiff will be unable to repay the sum he now wants to collect in the event he would be unsuccessful in regular proceedings on the merits.

Cross-undertaking

Security

In the Netherlands a plaintiff does not have to provide security to the court to guarantee that, if a preliminary injunction is granted but the court in subsequent regular proceedings holds that there was no entitlement to the relief granted, the defendant will be compensated for any losses incurred. According to art 152, a defendant may require a foreign plaintiff (both in regular proceedings and in preliminary relief proceedings) to provide security, but only for the liquidated costs of the lawsuit (a nominal amount, see p 226) and not for possible damages which may result from the enforcement of an injunction which would later prove unwarranted (see p 225). This is intended to prevent the defendant from having to bear his own legal costs in the event that he wins the case but cannot enforce the judgment in the plaintiff's home country. Most European nationals are not required to offer security for costs, since their countries are party to the Conventions on Civil Claims of 1905 and 1954. These conventions contain, among other things, a provision concerning mutual recognition of the signatories' court decisions concerning legal costs. Nationals of other countries may be protected by bilateral treaties with the Netherlands that prevent a defendant from obtaining security for legal costs.

Subsequent regular proceedings

Article 292 provides, as a principal rule, that preliminary injunctions shall not prejudice the case in the principal lawsuit. If regular proceedings are instituted after preliminary relief proceedings were held, the decision in such regular proceedings may hold that the preliminary injunction obtained in preliminary relief proceedings was unjustified. The defendant in the preliminary relief proceedings may then want to recover all damage he incurred as a result of the enforcement of this 'unjustified' preliminary injunction. Three rules should be distinguished.

(1) Pursuant to art 6:203 of the Civil Code, the defendant in preliminary relief proceedings has, in such cases, a right to reclaim from the plaintiff in the preliminary relief proceedings all payments he made and the value of all other actions he performed in order to comply with the preliminary injunction.

(2) The successful plaintiff in the preliminary relief proceedings who enforced or threatened to enforce the preliminary injunction, must pay damages to the defendant, in the event that the regular proceedings establish the unlawfulness of the preliminary injunction.

(3) The unsuccessful defendant in preliminary relief proceedings is obliged to comply with the preliminary injunction issued. In case a penalty was connected to the observation of the preliminary injunction, and the defendant failed to observe the injunction, he owes the plaintiff the amount of the penalties incurred, irrespective of whether the regular proceedings deemed the preliminary injunction unjustified. However, such penalties will be considered to be due only if it is beyond reasonable

doubt that the behaviour of the defendant did infringe the restraints or orders of the President, taking into account the grounds on which the injunction was based.

Appeal

If a judgment of the President containing a preliminary injunction is overturned on appeal, the injunction is deemed to have never existed. Penalties forfeited as a result of non-compliance with the injunction are no longer due and must be refunded to the extent paid.

Alternatives to preliminary relief proceedings

No summary judgment

In the Netherlands there is no realistic alternative to preliminary relief proceedings. Summary judgment is unknown in the Dutch legal system. The only way to speed up regular proceedings is to initiate so-called short-term proceedings on the merits. Regular proceedings start with the service of a writ of summons and complaint (*dagvaarding*), followed by the filing of a statement of claim (*conclusie van eis*). The defendant then has the opportunity to file a statement of defence. Thereafter, the plaintiff may file a statement of reply to the defence and the defendant may respond with a rejoinder. Oral argument is requested by the parties only in a minority of all cases in regular proceedings.

Short-term proceedings

In order to shorten the proceedings on the merits, the plaintiff may choose to initiate so-called short-term proceedings (technically called proceedings in urgent matters; art 145), in which only a statement of claim and a statement of defence are exchanged, after which oral argument will usually take place. Short-term proceedings will lead to a final and conclusive judgment on the merits, which may well contain a perpetual injunction. They are practical for matters in which the facts are relatively simple or even undisputed. Most courts in regular proceedings take at least several months to render judgment, which may well be an interlocutory one: in short-term proceedings most courts attempt to render judgment somewhat more quickly. Therefore, in suitable cases, short-term proceedings may quicken the final resolution of the suit, although it is not a realistic alternative to preliminary relief proceedings, which may provide injunctive relief (be it preliminary) much more rapidly, see p 226.

Practice and procedure

Notice

Not ex parte

As stated at p 212, conservatory attachment (arrest) is generally the only preliminary injunction in the Netherlands that can be obtained *ex parte*; it will be separately discussed at p 231, hereinafter. The other preliminary injunctions are available only through *inter partes* proceedings, although injunctions may be granted in default judgment in cases where the defendant fails to appear.

Initiation

Preliminary relief proceedings are initiated by a unilateral request by the plaintiff's attorney to the President of the competent district court to determine a date and hour on which the case shall be heard. The request for a date is usually accompanied by a draft writ of summons. In extremely urgent cases the request can be made by telephone.

Timing

The hearing date will usually be two or three weeks after the request therefor, but in very urgent matters the hearing may take place within days or even hours of the request, even on evenings or weekends. A writ of summons should be served on the defendant as soon as possible after the date is set, unless the defendant has indicated he will appear voluntarily (art 290). He may have an interest in so doing to avoid liability for damages due to a further delay; for instance in cases where the plaintiff seeks a court order lifting an arrest of an aircraft or ship made by the defendant. The statutory notice periods for service of summons in regular proceedings do not of course apply; although when determining the hearing date the President may order that the writ of summons should be served within a specific period of time.

Procedure at the hearing

Hearing

The emphasis in preliminary relief proceedings is on the oral argument, where the parties themselves are often present. At this hearing the plaintiff must be represented by an attorney-at-law. The defendant may appear in person or be represented by an attorney (art 290). The relief requested and the grounds therefor must be set forth in the writ of summons. Even if the defendant appears voluntarily, there is usually a draft writ of summons which is made available to the President and the defendant or its counsel in advance. The writ of summons is the starting point for the hearing. The plaintiff's attorney is usually given the opportunity to explain his claim and the defendant may then state his defence. Each attorney will prepare a written document (*pleading notes*) containing all facts and arguments to be presented at the hearing. These pleading notes are exchanged between the parties and filed with the court at the end of the hearing. The plaintiff may amend or even expand his claim before or even during the hearing. The defendant may file a counterclaim (which may or may not be related to the issue raised by the plaintiff), provided (i) he is represented by an attorney, and (ii) the counterclaim meets the three-tier test for preliminary injunctive relief (see p 222).

Evidence

In general, under Netherlands law, the party which makes a certain statement or allegation has the burden of proving it. Article 177 of the Code of Civil Procedure reads as follows [unofficial translation]:

The party which relies on the legal consequences of facts or rights asserted by that party, carries the burden of proof of these facts or rights, unless the burden of proof should be shifted pursuant to any special legal provision or principles of reasonableness.

Facts need only be proven if they are specifically disputed by the other party. The court is generally free in its assessment of the evidence introduced before it (art 179), although there are a few exceptions to this rule. In preliminary relief proceedings the President is not bound by the statutory provisions on evidence. All documentary evidence should be submitted to the President and the other party prior to the hearing. A plaintiff will try to limit the volume of documentary evidence he submits to the court, because the President may hold the matter too complex for preliminary relief proceedings. Occasionally, a party brings a witness to the hearing for examination by the President. The President will rarely allow a plaintiff to gather and submit further evidence, because this would require a second hearing to discuss it.

Attitude

The President in preliminary relief proceedings may well assume a far more active role during the hearing than would be the case in regular proceedings. He may start the hearing by questioning the parties themselves and/or their attorneys on the facts stated in the writ of summons, before allowing the attorneys to state their case. Some Presidents actively try to force the parties into an amicable settlement.

Judgment

In very urgent cases, the judgment may be rendered during the hearing or immediately thereafter. However, in most preliminary proceedings, it will be one or two weeks before the preliminary injunction is granted or denied.

Costs

First instance

The losing party in preliminary relief proceedings is usually ordered to pay the successful party (i) an amount of NLG 250 to fully compensate the successful party for the court fee he incurred; and (ii) a nominal amount between NLG 700 and NLG 1,500 for attorney's fees, which will not compensate the actual attorney's fees incurred. There is no possibility of recovering the actual costs of litigation from the losing party unless the litigation is based on an agreement between the parties which creates an obligation to reimburse actual costs. It is not at all uncommon for a party in preliminary relief proceedings to incur approximately NLG 10,000 in attorney's fees for the first instance.

Liquidated attorney's fees are calculated as follows: each part of the lawyer's involvement in a case is awarded a certain number of points (filing of written pleadings one point, oral argument two points, hearing of witnesses one point etc). The number of points corresponding with the activities of the lawyer in the particular suit are then multiplied by a certain value per point which depends on the monetary amount involved in the litigation.

Appeal

If a judgment is overturned on appeal the successful appellant is granted compensation for the court fees and the nominal attorney's fees of both instances.

Subsequent regular proceedings

As there is no obligation for the plaintiff in preliminary relief proceedings to institute regular proceedings on the merits (and indeed such proceedings are initiated in only a minority of the cases decided by the President), the award of costs in the preliminary relief proceedings will not be made expressly dependent on the outcome of the suit on the merits. However, in practice there may well be a dependency. If a court in regular proceedings holds that an injunction granted in preliminary relief proceedings was not warranted after all, the successful party in the regular proceedings is entitled to claim a refund of costs paid to the other party pursuant to the judgment in preliminary relief proceedings containing the unwarranted injunction. The reverse is not true: if an injunction is denied in preliminary relief proceedings, but granted in regular proceedings, the successful plaintiff in the regular proceedings has no right to reclaim the costs he may have paid to the defendant who succeeded in the preliminary relief proceedings but lost the suit on the merits.

Post-injunction factors

Service of the injunction

Service
Judgments in preliminary relief proceedings, as with most other Dutch judgments, will take effect only after they have been served on the defendant by a court bailiff. Service need not be made in person; the regular provisions on service of process (arts 4 *et seq*) apply. The regular provisions govern service of all official documents by a court bailiff such as writs of summons. For example, individuals may be served in person or at their home address either by service on family members or by means of leaving the document in a closed envelope; legal entities may be served either at their registered office or at the home address of the managing director. Foreign defendants may be served in accordance with the various treaties on the subject. Service by post is not as such a valid means of service of the injunction. Enforcement may generally be initiated when the defendant fails to comply voluntarily within two days after service is effected, unless the judgment specifies a different term.

Enforceability notwithstanding appeal
Judgments granting preliminary injunctions are invariably declared enforceable notwithstanding appeal. The President may issue such declaration when he sees fit, according to some writers even if the plaintiff did not ask for it.

Sanctions

Penalty
At the request of the plaintiff the President may—and usually will—stipulate in his decision that the defendant shall forfeit a penalty for each day (or other time period) or for each time that he acts in

contravention of the decision. If the decision is an order to pay a certain amount of money, no penalty can be imposed, although the plaintiff may request an order that statutory (also called legal) interest will be paid on the sum due. The rate of this interest is fixed by statute at a level somewhat above market rates, so as to provide an incentive for debtors to discharge their obligations.

Imprisonment

In the case of an injunction (i) to give a specific thing, (ii) to do a specific act which only the defendant can do, or (iii) to abstain from specific action, the President may grant, on a plaintiff's request, leave to enforce the injunction by means of civil imprisonment (arts 585 *et seq*). This sanction is imposed rather infrequently.

Discharge of preliminary injunction

Appeal

A defendant who loses preliminary relief proceedings may appeal from the President's judgment to the Court of Appeal; this procedure is described at p 217, above. The consequences of a decision of the Court of Appeal overturning the President's ruling are set out at p 225.

Opposition

If the defendant failed to appear in the preliminary relief proceedings in which the injunction was granted (ie by default) the defendant may file a claim in opposition which will be heard in new preliminary relief proceedings before the full district court (art 294).

Staying order

If a defendant believes that the enforcement of a judgment (whether or not rendered in preliminary relief proceedings) is unjustified, he may initiate (new) preliminary relief proceedings to try to obtain an order staying the enforcement. Such an order is often based on a change of circumstances from when the initial judgment was issued. A staying order may be requested from any competent President, or from the President who issued the original injunction.

Regular proceedings

Finally, the unsuccessful defendant in preliminary relief proceedings may initiate regular proceedings to obtain a final judgment on the merits in his favour. This may take the form of a declaratory judgment stating that the injunction granted to the defendant (as plaintiff in the preliminary relief proceedings) was unwarranted.

Damages

The issue of damages on the discharge of a preliminary injunction is discussed at p 228.

Conservatory attachment

Introduction

In the Netherlands there are several kinds of attachments. An essential distinction exists between an attachment made to enforce a judgment or an obligation arising under a document drawn up by a civil law notary, and an attachment to freeze assets as a pre-emptive remedy until there is a judgment. Only the latter, referred to as *conservatory* attachment, will be discussed here. Search and seizure orders are not available in civil matters in the Netherlands.

General principles of conservatory attachment

Purposes

Conservatory attachments are usually meant to secure the availability of assets against which a future money judgment against the owner of the assets can be enforced. (The most important exception to this rule is the conservatory attachment made by someone entitled to possession or delivery of specific property now in the hands of a third party (*beslag tot afgifteof levering*). For instance, the owner who finds his property in the hands of another may effect a conservatory attachment to secure the surrender of this property once a judgment ordering such surrender has been issued. Similarly, a purchaser may prevent the seller from selling and delivering the purchased property to a third party by means of a conservatory attachment. This specific type of conservatory attachment will not be dealt with in this chapter.) A conservatory attachment to secure a claim for money prevents a debtor from frustrating the recovery of any amount due to his creditor by, for instance, alienating, removing or hiding his assets. A direct result of the conservatory attachment, and often a purpose in itself, is the pressure it exerts on the debtor. He is not allowed to dispose of or move or transfer any attached property. Although he may be hindered in his business or personal life, and may suffer damages, this does not, in general, constitute a compelling reason for denying or lifting the attachment.

Types
There are different kinds of conservatory attachment such as:

(a)   attachment of assets owned and held by the debtor;
(b)   the garnishment of assets of the debtor held by third parties (*derdenbeslag*, literally: third party attachment; arts 718 *et seq*);
(c)   attachment of assets of the debtor held by the creditor himself (*eigen beslag*: art 724);
(d)   attachment of assets located within the Netherlands owned by a debtor without a domicile in the Netherlands (*saisie foraine* or *vreemdelingenbeslag*: art 765 *et seq*).

Both tangible assets (movable property, real property, aircraft and vessels) and intangible assets (accounts receivable, shares in a company) may be subject to conservatory attachment.

Procedure

Leave to attach
Any party with an apparently justified claim may request the President of the competent district court to grant leave for the attachment, garnishment, or arrest of the assets described in the request. The jurisdiction of the court may be based on either the debtor's domicile, the location of the assets, or, in the case of a garnishment, the domicile of the third party. The President may make his leave conditional upon the petitioner providing security (in an amount to be determined by the President) for any damage that the debtor would incur in case the petitioner's claim would eventually be denied.

The actual attachment
After the President's leave has been obtained, the creditor instructs a court bailiff to make the attachment. The bailiff's official report, one copy of which is left behind at the place of the attachment and one of which is sent to the creditor, serves as proof of the attachment.

Subsequent proceedings
In his leave, the President will determine the period following the attachment within which the creditor must bring proceedings against the debtor on the merits of the claim for which the attachment was made. This period is usually 14 days, but in no event less than eight days. The creditor may request a longer period, for instance, in the

event that competent forum for the main claim is a foreign court, or even an arbitration tribunal. In the case of a garnishment, the bailiff's official report and the President's leave must be served on the debtor within eight days of the garnishment. Also, the summons initiating the proceedings must be served on the third party within eight days of the date of service on the debtor. Non-observance renders the garnishment void. The third party does not, however, become a party to the proceedings. The third party is obliged to declare in writing within four weeks of the garnishment which of the debtor's assets it holds. As stated before, attachment of assets in the Netherlands generally establishes jurisdiction over the claim for which the attachment is made.

Lifting of the attachment

The debtor can, of course, cancel the attachment by paying his debt together with the costs of the attachment. Alternatively, the debtor can start preliminary relief proceedings claiming that the attachment should be lifted. The President will lift the attachment when the debtor furnishes sufficient security (art 705(2)) or when the debtor shows that the underlying claim is *prima facie* without merit or the attachment is unnecessary. This could be the case when the debtor's financial position is such that the creditor's recovery is sufficiently warranted without the attachment. A conservatory attachment (other than the one described at p 231) will automatically become null and void as a result of the bankruptcy of a debtor whose goods have been attached.

Peter Eijsvoogel

Portugal

Introduction

Portuguese Civil Procedural Law has established judicial measures aimed at *preventing or avoiding* the dangers arising out of natural delays—*mora iuditii*—in the issuing of judgments or out of the time taken to process an action.

Thus the precautionary measures contemplated are special legal means for 'safeguarding the useful effect of an action' (art 2 of the Code of Civil Procedures).

The precautionary measure will be considered null and void if the plaintiff fails to initiate the main action within 30 days of notification of the court decision granting the injunction. Further, the injunction will also be declared null and void if the trial judgment in the main action does not confirm the earlier precautionary measure in the provisional proceedings.

The Civil Procedural Law lays down the following specific precautionary measures (which it refers to as security procedures):

- seizure (arts 402–412 of the Code of Civil Procedures);
- inventory (arts 421–427);
- embargo on new works (arts 412–420);
- provisional allowances (arts 388–392);
- provisional restoration of ownership (arts 393–395);
- suspension of company decisions (arts 396–398).

In addition to these measures it was felt necessary to create a provision aimed at acting in an ancillary manner whenever it was necessary to safeguard situations having some direct bearing on the right in question, without any specific precautionary measure being available to the applicant. This non-specific, ancillary measure is residual. It is the last safeguard of the procedure system and it is what is referred to as non-specific precautionary measures (arts 399–400).

Therefore, if one party fears, before or during the main action, serious harm to his rights, he can apply for a non-specific precautionary measure. The courts can order mandatory or prohibitory injunctions in these circumstances, or the delivery up of movable or immovable assets (which are the object of the main action) if none of the specific security procedures apply to the case (art 339).

Structure of the courts

The courts

Procedural law takes only one form and applies to the whole country. Therefore there are no tactical or strategic advantages to be gained from one court in preference to another. For obvious reasons, when the law permits an action to be tried in various courts it will naturally choose the nearest.

Portuguese courts are divided up into three general categories (Law of 23 December 1987, No 38).

(1) The High Court of Justice (*Supremo Tribunal de Justiça*) in Lisbon, which has competence for the whole country. It has sections for civil matters (contracts, civil liability, ownership and other property rights, industrial rights, etc), for criminal matters (crimes), and for social matters (employment relationships, family relationships, etc). It also has competence to decide on questions of law.

(2) The Regional Courts of Justice (*Tribunais da Relação*), located in Lisbon, Oporto, Coimbra and Evora, each with jurisdiction over a judicial region; they too have special sections.

(3) The District Courts (*Tribunais Judiciais de Primeira Instância*); these may have jurisdiction over a county area, over a smaller district, or over some other specified area, in accordance with the relevant territorial competence. There are around 220 such District Courts and 48 area courts. These area courts are regional courts which have jurisdiction over a county area. The District Courts have jurisdiction over a smaller District of the respective county area. There is no hierarchic relationship between them. They have different areas of competence, defined by the legal issues involved, but they are both courts of first instance.

Furthermore, these courts are also District Courts; they may have general or specific competence. According to the importance of the respective district area, these District Courts may also comprise labour courts, criminal courts, family courts, courts for minors, maritime courts and courts for the enforcement of fines.

As regards the international competence of Portuguese courts, as a rule they are competent to act when there exists some connection (subjective or objective) with Portuguese judicial matters—for example when the events giving rise to the action occurred in Portugal; when the offender is a foreigner, but the injured party is Portuguese, since, conversely, the Portuguese participant could be judged by the courts of the country of the offender. It is necessary, of course, that these rules be implemented taking into account the rules applying in the country in which it is intended the judgment is to be enforced.

In this context it will be noted that Portuguese law stipulates exclusive jurisdiction in the case of actions involving immovable property situated in Portugal, bankruptcy on the part of companies with registered offices in Portugal, and for actions relating to employment relationships. Thus no court judgments issued in foreign countries in these matters may be enforced in Portugal. The 1968 Brussels Convention has not yet been adopted by Portugal.

Legal representatives

Lawyers registered with the Portuguese Bar (*Ordem de Advogados Portuguesa*) have exclusive competence to act as the legal representatives of parties to actions. Lawyers have a Master of Law degree and can be registered with the Bar after a two-year probationary period.

It is required that a lawyer be appointed (in accordance with art 32 of the Code of Civil Procedures), (i) in actions, whatever the sum involved, which are subject to ordinary appeal; (ii) in actions involving sums in excess of 500,000 Escudos; (iii) in appeals and in actions brought before the higher courts (the Regional Courts and the High Court).

A *solicitador* is a sort of paralegal who may act in cases with a value up to 500,000 Escudos. They must have academic degrees at least of High School course standard, be registered with the Paralegals Association and be competent in all practical and bureaucratic proceedings with official or private entities.

Criteria: precautionary measures and security procedures of a non-specific nature

Seizure

Seizure, as defined by art 402 of the Code of Civil Procedures, consists of 'the judicial confiscation of assets or goods'. Seizure may be *preventive* or *repressive*.

Seizure presupposes the *justified fear* of loss of guaranteed ownership of a credit; the Civil Procedure Law does not require that this fear be certain, only that it be *probable*. It is aimed at removing the risk that the creditor may suffer before seizure of the goods in his favour, and the court may require that the applicant provide a *security* (art 620 of the Civil Code).

If a justified fear exists, the applicant must submit the facts that render loss of the credit probable, in support of the said justified fear—art 403—the seizure being enacted *ex parte*, and the judge having powers to limit the seizure to assets which are sufficient to cover the obligation in question (art 404).

It is important to note that if the credit for which cover is being sought is commercial in nature (arising out of an act of commerce on the part of the defendant) a request for seizure may only be brought against traders or commercial companies in the following cases:

(a) if the trader or commercial company is not registered;
(b) if the registered trader or commercial company has never traded before; or
(c) if the registered trader or commercial company has traded but has not done so in the three months prior to the court application (art 403(3)).

It is also important to note that jurisprudence and legal theory concur that the applicant may not avail himself of any of the other security procedures or measures (namely, the non-specific precautionary measures) of a judicial nature and invoking the corresponding legal terms, in order to obtain in practice the same result as that contemplated in the seizure.

The only exceptional case in which the law allows for a seizure of goods to be imposed on a trader, in the terms described, is that relating to ships or to their cargoes (art 403).

Without prejudice to the above provisions, the following examples should be noted:

(1) The case of a company which supplies construction materials to a hotel, where the supplies are not paid for and the hotel has not yet started business; there being a justified fear that the hotel may be sold by the owner (a registered trader) for whom the hotel represents his sole property.

(2) The case of a shareholder who discovers, to his loss, with justifiable fear, that dividends have been distributed to other partners illegally by the company's directors, and who is therefore entitled to request the seizure of the company's property/assets in order to safeguard his rights.

In these examples seizure is admissible because, although the defendants are traders, the acts which gave rise to the seizure are not commercial acts in the sense understood by the requirements.

Seizure has the general effect of confiscating goods (or assets); among other things this means that actions involving the disposal of such assets that have been seized are ineffective with respect to the party requesting the seizure once the seizure has been registered; the party requesting seizure of assets takes precedence in the payment of credits compared with creditors who have no prior guarantee (ie prior to registration of the security procedure), arts 622, 819–823 of the Civil Code.

A *repressive seizure* has to do with the counterfeiting or illegal use of industrial or commercial trade marks (art 228, para b of the Code of Industrial Property and art 407 of the Code of Civil Procedures).

It is dependent on two conditions: (i) proof of literary, artistic, industrial or commercial ownership (by means of deposited deeds or a corresponding registration); (ii) proof of an infringement of such ownership.

As in the previous case, this is decreed without hearing the other party.

Inventory

As with seizure, the inventory procedure is designed to remove the danger of a right not being satisfied as the result of delay in the issuing of a judgment, in the form of a claimed justified fear of embezzlement or disposal of the assets, be they movable or immovable, or fear of the loss of documents.

If a person claims a right to, or interest in, certain assets, and is able to point to certain facts or circumstances which give him justified grounds for fearing that the holder or possessor of those assets is misappropriating them, before it is legally recognised once and for all that he has a right to, or interest in, those assets, the said person may request an inventory. By way of example this procedure covers cases of inventories of estates (where an inheritance is involved), cases of divorce, cases of the dissolution of companies or inspection of the relevant accounts, the annulment of wills and bank accounts, etc.

An inventory may be requested by any person who has an interest in the preservation of the property or documents (art 422).

An inventory consists of the description, valuation and depositing of the assets (art 424); the trustee may actually be the possessor of the assets if the judge deems this appropriate. An inventory may be replaced by a security provided by the defendant if the court considers the latter to have a worthy case. An inventory prevents the defendant from disposing of or using the assets listed. The use of inventory procedures is an effective method of freezing a defendant's bank account(s): a defendant cannot dispose of money in the account below the amount shown on the inventory.

Embargo on new works

As in the case of the above precautionary measures an embargo on new works is aimed at safeguarding and/or insuring a right. The legal pattern of this measure is as follows:

(1) A person or company undertakes some work or service (a building, a book, a scientific study, a film, an advertising campaign, etc);

(2) another person or company perceives an injury because it is of the view that the work or service is an infringement of its property (or joint-property) right, right of possession or of any other right of use which will cause a loss to its business;

(3) if the court is convinced of this (on the basis of summary evidence), it will recognise the right of the offended person or company to immediately suspend the work, or the right to place an embargo on the work (art 412).

The purpose of this is prevention, providing the applicant with rights of action in those situations where infringement of the right invoked is imminent or already taking place (it is not necessary that this be recognised, but simply that there be sufficient grounds for a judgment of probability).

The applicant has a period of 30 days, after discovery of the offending activities, in which to request this security procedure. An interesting possibility here is that the offended party, in the presence of two witnesses, may serve legally valid notice on the person or company performing the work for that work to cease, provided that during the five days which follow he requests judicial *ratification* of the embargo, failing which that embargo would have no effect (art 412).

Such embargoes may not be introduced in connection with works of the State on public land, or works of the local authorities on municipal land (art 414); however an offended party does have the right to compensation for such acts.

If the party on which the embargo is served continues with the work, without authority to do so, after receiving notification of the embargo, and providing there are valid grounds for the latter, the party serving the embargo notice may request that the new part of the work be destroyed (arts 420 and 421).

The party to which the embargo is served may ask to be allowed to continue with the work in cases where it can be seen that the loss to be incurred from suspension of the work is greater than that which would be incurred if it were to continue (art 419).

Provisional restoration of ownership

Article 379 of the Code of Civil Procedures states: 'that in the event of violent misappropriation the possessor may request that his property be provisionally restored to him, stating the facts in support of his ownership, and the facts relating to the misappropriation and the violent way in which it has been carried out', provided that this measure is invoked within one year of the offence being committed or of its coming to light if it was committed in secret (art 1282 of the Civil Code).

It is not necessary that the plaintiff be the owner, but simply that he be acting in a manner that is in accordance with the exercise of this right (he might for instance be a tenant, a trustee or a lessee, etc).

Misappropriation takes the form of the deprivation (in full or in part) of the right to retain or use the possessed object; there is no judicial concurrence on the concept of violence in this context. There are judgments in which it has been assumed that this must mean violence against the possessor from whom the property has been misappropriated, and not only against the object of the misappropriation.

If from his examination of the evidence the judge recognises that the plaintiff is entitled to possession, and has had the property taken away from him violently, he shall order that it be returned to him, without summoning or hearing the person guilty of misappropriation (art 394).

Suspension of company decisions

This security procedure consists of a *tertium genus* in that it is aimed at guaranteeing the right of protest by a shareholder for cancellation of a company decision.

The legal pattern of this measure is as follows.

(1) A company or an association (or, for that matter an assembly of joint owners of a property) takes decisions which are against the law or against the articles of association.

(2) Once this fact has been ascertained, any shareholder may call for those illegal decisions to be cancelled within five days of their being taken or of their coming to the attention of the partner concerned. For this purpose he must provide proof that he is a shareholder and show that implementation of the decision would result in significant or substantial damages.

(3) The company will then be summoned to respond, but until a judgment has been issued on the matter the company may not implement the disputed decision (arts 396, 397 and 398).

The judge may decide not to suspend the disputed decision, despite the existence of two requests to that end if he is of the view that the loss which would arise out of suspension is *greater* than the sum, or the rights, which the plaintiff is claiming to want to safeguard.

This security procedure is always a preliminary to action involving cancellation, which means that it will only be admissible in cases contemplated by substantive law (for example, unlawful voting, restriction of the right to vote, failure to comply with essential formalities such as the way in which general meetings are convened, etc).

Non-specific precautionary measures

In addition to the security procedures discussed above, the law also provides a general security procedure referred to as 'non-specific precautionary measures'. These may be invoked wherever there is a justified fear of the serious infringement of a right, for which reparation would be difficult, but where it is not permissible to invoke the special procedures provided by law, eg seizure, inventory, embargo on new works, etc.

A potentially injured party may request the implementation of the measures he considers appropriate for avoiding the injury in question, that is to say authorisation to carry out certain actions, eg action whereby the defendant is ordered to refrain from certain behaviour, or the handing over of movable or immovable assets which are the object of the action to a reliable third party who will act as trustee thereof (art 399).

The list of measures given in art 399 is only meant to be regarded as illustrative, as can be deduced from the expressions it uses: 'may request' and 'such as'; it is therefore possible for a potentially injured party to avail himself of them on the basis of a right or interest he has which is not covered by the other security procedures.

The legal prerequisites for non-specific precautionary measures are:

(a) the non-existence of a special provision to safeguard the right in question;
(b) a serious probability of the existence of a right being the subject of a law suit already filed or to be filed; the law is content with a judgment of serious probability;
(c) a justified fear that somebody else may seriously jeopardise the right in question such that reparation is difficult. There must be threats if there is nothing to avoid or prevent;
(d) the loss caused by implementation of the precautionary measure must not exceed the damages that measure is designed to protect;
(e) adaptation of the requested measure so as to avoid damage/loss, or an order from the judge to determine the most suitable measure for ensuring maintenance of the *status quo*.

It is for the court to decide whether or not to hear the defendant, depending on whether this would adversely affect the purpose of the measure contemplated.

These measures can be applied to the most varied of circumstances, including, by way of example, the case of an ex-employee divulging company secrets, the requirement that employees should not engage in competitive activities for a given period, or a ban on a company from selling a property it owns and taking account of the right of the applicant/plaintiff (shareholder) and the loss which might be incurred from the sale, etc. It is also possible that this type of measure could be used to safeguard the rights arising out of industrial ownership, such as the right of recourse the holder of a patented invention has when the terms of his claim affect the future activities of the defendant, etc.

Practice and procedure

Alternative courses of action

Portuguese law does not have any preferable, realistic alternatives, for the desired ends, apart from precautionary measures.

On the other hand it is always possible to make use of procedural mechanisms which prolong an action, even though the defendant is clearly in the wrong.

The judge may of course bring an early end to proceedings (art 510) when there are circumstances which justify an early judgment (for example loss of a right, the unlawful position of a party, etc), or when the matter under examination is simply a point of law, or again when it is a question of fact and when there is sufficient information for issuing a reliable judgment, which is rarely the case.

Liability of the plaintiff if he loses the case

It should be noted that these measures or procedures do not result in decisions on the merits and facts under examination.

Although recourse to such precautionary measures is guaranteed it is possible for the plaintiff to ultimately lose the case, thereby incurring liability for the losses his action may have caused the successful defendant (art 483).

This liability is determined on the basis of the (culpable) conduct of the plaintiff and the onus of proof rests with the successful defendant.

There are no special rules applying to foreign entities.

Instrumental nature and guarantee aspects

These precautionary measures have an instrumental and a safeguarding function in connection with a given action geared towards the right being secured, and must be implemented as preliminaries and as an incidental factor in that action, ie they may be invoked either before or during the action in question. Nevertheless, refusal to grant a particular measure does not prevent the plaintiff from proceeding with his action.

The instrumental nature is a result of the fact that the measures cease to have any effect (art 382), if the plaintiff:

(i) fails to bring an action within 30 days of notification of the decision;
(ii) if the action is found to be inadmissible;

(iii) if the defendant is absolved by the court, and no further action is brought within a period of 30 days;

(iv) if the right the plaintiff is seeking to safeguard comes to an end; or

(v) when the precautionary measure is replaced by a security or guarantee, without affecting the right of appeal against the decision ordering its replacement.

All these reasons for a precautionary measure ceasing to have any effect are extremely important because 'if the measure ceases to apply for any reason, the interested party may not request implementation of another measure on the same grounds (art 387).

The applicant is considered liable, if the measure ceases to have effect or is judged to be unjustifiable, for the damage caused to the defendant and is therefore under an obligation to compensate the latter for these losses (art 387).

As described above, the precautionary measures may be replaced by a security or guarantee provided by the defendant if the judge deems this appropriate (art 383, point 3, and 401 of the Code of Civil Procedures). In this case the measure will cease to have any effect.

Requirements

Although we have already mentioned the prerequisites for each of the precautionary measures, and their various nuances, it is important to mention that there are two basic general requirements.

(1) The allegation and proof of the likelihood of an offence against the right addressed by the action; the judge need only require a summary understanding of the matter (*summaria cognitio*), or the allegation and summary proof of an offence against that right;

(2) proof of *periculum in mora*, which is the actual or potential existence of a threatened infringement of a legal right.

Proof

With respect to the summary proof required for all the different precautionary measures, the law lays down special provisions in terms of the proof or evidence required.

Thus in his initial written application the plaintiff must state the facts and reasons which he considers provide sufficient proof in support of his request, and must submit a list of witnesses (a maximum of three witnesses for each fact, the total number of witnesses not exceeding eight—arts 381 and 302–304 of the Code of Civil Procedures) and request the submission of other forms of evidence, attaching all the documents, in support of the alleged facts, which strengthen his position and are geared towards making his case successful (all sorts of documents may be submitted, provided that they were obtained legally).

The defendant's means of recourse

Generally the defendant may reject the claim, even if he is not summoned to respond, in the form of (i) an embargo or (ii) an appeal, thereby attempting to avoid implementation of the precautionary measure.

In terms of an embargo the defendant will attempt to refute the facts put forward by the plaintiff. In an appeal the defendant will attack the court's decision and seek to demonstrate that the measure was granted incorrectly (A dos Reis, CPC Note 2, 43), for example, if the court lacked jurisdiction to grant the injunction.

Costs and responsibility for their payment

The costs arising out of the implementation of precautionary measures will be paid, for the time being until the main action is concluded, by the plaintiff if the defendant objects to paying the costs, but they are subsequently taken into account in the main action brought against the defendant. If the defendant does object, the costs will be the responsibility of the party who ultimately loses the main action. If more than one party loses the case, the costs will be divided among them proportionately (arts 453, 446 and 447).

Costs are to be settled on the basis of the value of the case, incidentals and costs incurred in connection with the procuring of evidence, etc, and become payable upon completion of each action or upon completion of the measure or procedure.

The value of the case in connection with precautionary measures is determined on the following basis:

(a) in terms of the provisional restoration of ownership, on the basis of the value of the object misappropriated;
(b) in terms of the suspension of decisions, on the basis of the amount of damages;
(c) in terms of embargoes and non-specific precautionary measures, on the basis of the loss it is hoped to prevent;
(d) in terms of seizure, on the basis of the value of the credit for which

a safeguard is being sought, or the value of the assets confiscated; and

(e) in terms of an inventory, on the basis of the assets listed.

Non-compliance by the defendant

We must begin by distinguishing the nature of the obligation to which the defendant is bound. This may take the form of a *de facere* (the handing over of some object or performance of some action) or of a *non facere* (refraining from certain action or conduct) (art 398).

With regard to the first category, in the event of non-fulfilment of the obligation the plaintiff may then proceed to enforcement of the precautionary measure, requesting the police or the public authorities to execute the court's decision. Non-compliance with the injunction can be a criminal offence and subject to the criminal process.

With regard to the second category, the situation is more complicated. In fact if the defendant sells something he has no right to sell, it is still possible to bring a charge of civil liability because the defendant has engaged in an unlawful activity, but this will be somewhat academic if the defendant has no other assets. Furthermore, with respect to immovable assets, or movable assets which are subject to registration, such as cars, the problem becomes irrelevant because the precautionary measures are subject to registration in favour of the plaintiff, which prevents any form of disposal of the item by the defendant.

In all other cases the plaintiff only has the recourse of seeking the criminal punishment of the defendant, on the basis of the crime of disobedience which can be punished by imprisonment.

Special precautionary measures

In concluding, it is important to make a brief mention of two special types of precautionary measures.

(1) The suspension, at the request of the employee, of dismissal attempted by an employer (art 38 *et seq* of the Code of Employment Procedures). A hearing of the parties must take place within a maximum of 15 days of the request. Only documentary evidence will be admitted. Suspension of dismissal action will only be ordered if no disciplinary action had been taken against the employee by the employer, or if this action was invalid, or again if there are any relevant circumstances

indicating the serious probability of the non-existence of a just cause for dismissal.

(2) The suspension of Customs clearance to imported goods when the holder of a trade mark/brand name suspects that these goods are counterfeit, and submits a claim to the General Directorate of Customs to this effect; in such cases the latter may require a guarantee from the plaintiff to cover his liability to the importer (Dec Law No 160/88 of 13 May 1988 implementing EEC regulation No 3842/86 issued by the Council on 1 December 1986.

Cesar Bessa Monteiro

Spain

Introduction

The concept

Under all systems of judicial regulations the declaration process involves a period of time between the claim filed by the creditor aimed at obtaining legal protection of a right, and the final recognition and practical granting of the said right.

In order to go some way to reducing the risks incurred from the delay in pronouncing the final judgment, a system of protection exists which, under our own legal system is referred to by the term *precautionary measures*.

Precautionary measures under Spanish law are extremely dispersed and are not regulated in a uniform fashion. Because our law does not contain a concept to provide a general definition of precautionary measures in their true sense, it has been left to legal practice in Spain to formulate such a concept in order to give the coherence which it would otherwise lack. Jurisprudence has also contributed to the drawing up and definition of the concept of a precautionary measure, formulating the characteristics which are an essential part of its nature, containing a number of features which distinguish it from other preventive measures which are not truly of a precautionary nature.

Against this background we can define precautionary measures as those remedies which the law places at the disposal of a claimant whereby he can secure a possible, future enforcement of his rights. In a certain respect the precautionary measure provisionally anticipates enforcement from the outset of the procedure, with a view to guaranteeing legal protection for the subject matter of the proceedings, and until the point at which the binding judgment is pronounced.

The basic characteristics relating to the precautionary measure, according to Spanish practice and jurisprudence, are as follows.

(1) Under Spanish law the precautionary measure exists on the basis of an initial action which has already been instituted or which is on the point of being instituted, to which it is an ancillary issue. Its basis rests not so much in the disputed issue of the action, as in the disputed relief sought in that action, hence its clearly ancillary nature.

For this reason precautionary measures are described as *instrumental*, ie being ancillary to an initial or primary action the enforcement of which they intended to guarantee, or they are described as *provisional* in that once the initial action has come to an end, the precautionary measure as such disappears, as it had either been affirmed or finally rejected.

(2) Jurisprudence highlights the need for there to be some similarity between the precautionary measure sought and the enforceable measure which is adopted at the end of the action when the judgment is issued. That is to say, the precautionary measure must be marked by its homogeneity. This means that when allowing the introduction of a certain measure the judge must consider that the measure in question is in some way a means of advancing the enforceable remedies to be adopted ultimately, but without involving an impairment of the assets of the defendant in terms of the final enforceable judgment.

In essence the judge has to achieve a balance between the precautionary measure to be granted and the final enforceable measure, so that they are similar, homogeneous, but not identical.

(3) Another relevant aspect of the precautionary measure is that it is normally adopted *inaudita parte debitoris* (without hearing the debtor), that is to say without hearing the views of the defendant. The reason for this is to avoid a situation whereby, if the debtor had been given prior notice that a precautionary measure was to be introduced affecting his assets, he might engage in fraudulent acts aimed at frustrating the intention of that measure, thereby jeopardising the basic, primary purpose of the precautionary measure which is that of safeguarding the subsequent enforcement of the plaintiff's rights. Consequently, and with a view to avoiding this risk, the judicial regulations operate this precautionary instrument as a right of the plaintiff, the latter having to fulfil all the legal requirements, and without hearing the defendant. In this way the rights of the defendant are not jeopardised because he is able to state his grounds for opposition to the measure in question, but only after that measure has been granted by the judge.

General principles

Spanish law has established the precautionary system as an ancillary instrument to which recourse may only be had when there is a reasonable and well-grounded fear of a loss which might be sustained by the object of the dispute. If it is possible in some other way, ie by some tangible financial means, to obtain compensation from the defendant, this course of action will be followed by means of a guarantee or deposit, and it will not then be necessary to go ahead with adopting the precautionary measures. Therefore mechanisms are laid down for ensuring this subsidiary nature of the precautionary measure prior to its adoption (such as requiring certain basic prerequisites of the plaintiff when he files the claim), or subsequent to its adoption (such as a guarantee being given on the part of the debtor in the event that the precautionary measure is discharged at a later date).

Another general principle is the aspect of the urgency and flexibility of the precautionary procedure. For this purpose the Law of Civil Proceedings stipulates a number of essential time limits or periods which must be strictly adhered to, and which, if not observed, will result in the plaintiff forfeiting the right to resort to the precautionary measure. Thus, if, for instance, the plaintiff requests a preventive embargo on the debtor's assets, but fails to file the claim within 20 days of the date of the request for the precautionary measure, the latter will cease to have any effect and the plaintiff will be ordered to pay the procedural costs and to compensate the defendant.

Requirements

The Spanish system of judicial regulations contains a number of prerequisites or essential requirements in order for any precautionary measure to be granted by the judge, and without which the plaintiff is not permitted to institute such action. These prerequisites are of a general character, common to all precautionary measures, namely:

(1) *Fumus boni iuris*—a Latin expression which means the 'semblance of a right'. It presupposes that the plaintiff, when seeking the precautionary measure, has some initial documentary evidence to demonstrate that the right he is claiming is valid and really exists, both with regard to the subject matter of the proceedings and with regard to its object. The mere semblance, or likelihood, of a right is sufficient for justifying the request for a precautionary measure.

(2) *Periculum in mora*—this refers to all instances in which there is

a perceived risk of the disputed object being lost. The validity of such instances will be assessed on a case-by-case basis by the judge.

However, this law does give some basic guidelines: in the case of an embargo, *periculum in mora* will apply as a result of any action on the part of the debtor which produces a situation of insolvency; on the other hand, if the request is for the movable asset in question to be placed in deposit, *periculum in mora* will not be determined by general insolvency, but by the defendant's conduct with respect to the movable asset.

(3) *Plaintiff's guarantee*—as said above, the precautionary measure is intended to advance, in some way, the eventual enforceable judgment from the outset of the proceedings by granting the plaintiff a privilege in advance. For this reason (and in order to cover this initial advantage, as well as making provision for covering any damages or losses incurred by the defendant in the event that the judgment is awarded in favour of the latter), it is normally required that the plaintiff provide a guarantee or security which the judge will determine on the basis of the circumstances of the actual case.

However Spanish procedural law allows for the possibility of the plaintiff not giving a guarantee or security in the event that the plaintiff's solvency is well known. In practice the judge tends to require that the party requesting such a measure provides the aforesaid guarantee or security.

(4) Finally, given the instrumental and ancillary nature of the precautionary measure, Spanish procedural law requires the existence of a principal or primary action, such that if the measure had been requested earlier, a claim must be filed within a specified period of time or the measure will become invalid.

Categories of precautionary measures

Under substantive Spanish law, due primarily to the absence of co-ordinated regulations, it is no easy matter to classify precautionary measures. For this reason doctrine and jurisprudence are in disagreement over the point at which the boundaries occur between precautionary measures and other proceedings and safeguards which cannot properly be classified as precautionary measures.

In an effort to seek a clarification of precautionary measures we can distinguish three groups: the first of these covers those proceedings which, though not recognised as such by law, have been traditionally regarded as precautionary by jurisprudence and doctrine; in the second group we can include other actions which, though regarded as precautionary initiatives, their nature is subject to debate, even though they are geared towards facilitating and/or protecting the enforcement of a subsequently recognised right; and finally we have those actions which are recognised as having a precautionary nature by special laws.

In light of the above, and in general terms, we can draw up the classification described below.

Precautionary measures

These include all those judicial proceedings which the law, as well as legal doctrine and jurisprudence, recognise beyond any doubt as being of a precautionary nature, and which have all the recognised characteristics of such measures, namely that they are provisional, instrumental, homogeneous and not subject to hearing the views of the debtor party.

These can be divided up into two main groups:

Precautionary measures which are aimed at securing a monetary judgment
The basic precautionary measure par excellence is the Preventive Embargo. This measure is governed by arts 1397 *et seq* of the Law of Civil Proceedings.

Precautionary measures aimed at securing non-monetary judgments in connection with obligations to perform or not perform certain actions and obligations to hand over a given item
We can further divide this group into two sub-groups:

(a) Unnamed precautionary measures, governed by art 1428 of the Law of Civil Proceedings, which includes all those actions which are necessary, in the eyes of the judge, for safeguarding a future non-monetary judgment. This is something of a mixed bag because it is likely to be applied in many different cases, and this has introduced confusion into legal doctrine when it comes to defining the actual boundaries between various precautionary measures.
(b) Typical precautionary measures, which are basically:

Preventive notification of claim   governed primarily by art 42 of the Mortgage Law.

This takes the form of filing a statement with the Registry of Property relating to judicial procedures affecting a title which is or could be registered, for the purpose of notifying third parties acting in good faith.

Submission and depositing of a movable item   which is primarily governed by art 499 of the Law of Civil Proceedings.

This precautionary measure would apply, for instance, in cases where the owner of computer equipment enters into a hire purchase agreement with a buyer; the buyer fails to keep up the payments and once the period for settlement of the obligation has come to an end, the owner submits a claim for the outstanding debt or for repossessing the computer equipment which has not been paid for. In the latter case, and in light of the risk that the debtor might jeopardise his rights, the plaintiff/owner asks for the depositing, or impounding, of the equipment in question for as long as the judicial proceedings last.

Judicial intervention involving disputed assets   summed up in arts 1419–1427, inclusive, of the Law of Civil Proceedings.

For example, the owner of a commercial forest files a claim against the user thereof. Because of the risk that the user might fell trees indiscriminately in the forest, the owner, as a precautionary measure, asks that action be taken to prevent the user from engaging in any further operations while the proceedings last.

The appointment of a joint administrator by the partners (of a partnership or unlimited company)   governed by the Law of Civil Proceedings, art 2162, which envisages the possibility that, in the event of a company administrator or manager misusing his powers, the partners may call for the appointment of a joint administrator by the judge:

In a case referred to in art 307 of the Code, those members who believe that the person responsible for administering and running the company is misusing his powers, and who wish to appoint a joint administrator, shall submit a written communication to the judge, asking him to obtain information on the person in question, and having established that their fellow partner is misusing his powers, to appoint a joint administrator of their choice.

The majority view tends to extend the definition of precautionary measures to procedural actions adopted on the basis of a judgment by default, governed by art 762 of the Law of Civil Proceedings. (Under Spanish law a judgment by default refers to proceedings in which the defendant fails to appear, with the result that the judgment goes ahead in his absence.) These actions manifest themselves in a situation where the judge, having received the plaintiff's request, orders an embargo on the defendant's immovable assets and the retention of movable assets, when the latter has been in default (by failing to appear in court to defend his/her case), in so far as this expedient is necessary to safeguard the object of the litigation. They are precautionary measures in the sense that they are homogeneous, instrumental and accessory to the primary dispute, and their aim is to ensure the subsequent effectiveness of the enforcement.

Other safeguards of a non-precautionary nature

There exist under Spanish law a number of safeguards which can be invoked in advance by the owner of a right in order to guarantee the effective protection thereof. They are not precautionary measures in the true sense, but do have characteristics in common with the latter in so far as they are subordinate to a primary action. The following are examples:

Proceedings for the proving of facts   governed by arts 497–502 of the Law of Civil Proceedings, which constitute a series of measures of a preliminary nature aimed at investigating what is later to be proved in the judicial proceedings. This is the case where a partner or joint owner, as plaintiff, calls for the documents and accounts relating to the defendant company or association (art 497.5), or calls for the evidence in advance, governed by art 502 of the Law of Civil Proceedings.

Article 497 of the Law of Civil Proceedings:

Preparation for the hearing of any action may take the following forms:

(1) By the potential plaintiff asking for a sworn statement from the party against which the claim is to be made, relating to any fact relevant to the latter's identity, if, in the absence of such information, it would not be possible to proceed with the action.

(2) By requesting the presentation of the movable item which is the object of the real or mixed action which it is planned to bring against the party in possession of the item.

(3) By requesting that a claimed heir, joint heir or legatee produce the will, codicil or testamentary memorandum of the person who has left the inheritance or legacy.

(4) By the buyer requesting from the vendor, or vice versa, in the event of an eviction, that he produce the title deeds or other documents relating to the property being sold.

(5) By a partner or joint owner requesting the production of documents and company/association accounts from another partner or from a joint owner who

has these in his possession, where applicable with the relevant settlement of rights.

In any of these cases the judge will accede to the request if he deems that it is based on a well-founded case. If it does not fall into one of these categories he will automatically reject it. If the judge's ruling has the effect of rejecting the claim, an appeal may be lodged.

Article 502 of the Law of Civil Proceedings:

Apart from those cases contemplated in art 497, a claimant may not call for the statement of [the other party's] position, information from witnesses or any other form of evidence, except in the event of the advanced age of a witness, where there is the fear of imminent death, or in the event of an imminent departure to a place with which communication would be difficult or slow, or where there is some other compelling reason, that is to say in instances where the plaintiff runs the risk of losing his rights due to the absence of the necessary information, in which case the judge shall give instructions for examining the witness or witnesses in those circumstances, the examination taking the form laid down in the relevant articles of this Law. These pieces of evidence are to be attached to the file of documents when the claim is filed.

These are measures aimed at investigating the facts which are the object of litigation, but they are not strictly precautionary because their purpose is not that of providing protection for a right in order to facilitate its subsequent enforcement. Their purpose is actually that of investigating disputed facts.

Special judgments   such as the obtaining of provisional allowances, bans on destructive work and possessory action for retention and recovery of assets, which, although they also provide temporary protection of a right, do not require a subsequent main action dealing with the merits of the case.

The absence of any characteristic requirement, such as that of the instrumental or accessory nature of the measure, has meant that the majority view is to deny that this procedure has any precautionary measure status.

As an example of a ban on new work we might consider the case of the owner of a property whose property rights are jeopardised by the construction of another property adjacent to his own property. In this case the owner is entitled to invoke this ban for suspension of the new work on the part of the owner or contractor, with the warning of the demolition of any work which is carried out if the construction work continues.

Article 1663 of the Law of Civil Proceedings:

Once the request for a ban on new works has been submitted, the judge will issue his ruling, instructing the owner of the work to suspend it in the state in which it is found, under threat of the demolition of any further work carried out, and calling the parties involved to a hearing with the least possible delay, once three days have passed since notification of this measure, and advising them that at the hearing they will be expected to submit the relevant documents in support of their positions.

The claim must be accompanied by a copy of same on ordinary paper which will be given to the defendant together with the summons.

Moreover, legal doctrine also allows for the possibility of certain measures of a personal nature, such as the arrest of a bankrupt or debtor, being regarded as precautionary measures. However the absence of the necessary characteristic of similarity or homogeneity between the action of arresting the party involved and the final enforcement of a judgment would indicate the opposite.

Brief reference to special laws

With the introduction of the Spanish Constitution in 1978, and the subsequent development of the legal protection of constitutional rights, new legislative texts have come into being aimed at regulating the adoption of precautionary measures in specific areas.

In this connection Organic Law No 1 of 5 May 1982, concerning the Right of Honour, Personal and Family Privacy and One's Personal Reputation, provides for the adoption of precautionary measures aimed at securing the immediate cessation of unlawful interference with honour and privacy, and recognition of the right of reply, publication of judgments and orders to pay compensation for losses or damages caused.

Similarly, Law No 11 of 20 March 1986 on Patents, which stipulates the possibility of the owner of a patent requesting the following precautionary measures in the event of an infringement of his rights or the reasonably grounded fear that such an infringement will take place: cessation of the actions which are an infringement of his right; an embargo on the items produced or imported in violation of his rights, as well as on the means used exclusively for such production or for carrying out the patented process; and the transformation of the items produced or means of production or their destruction where this is essential as a way of avoiding infringement of the patent.

Law No 22 of 11 November 1987, concerning the protection of intellectual property, which makes provision for the judge, in the event of an infringement or where there are reasonable grounds for fearing an infringement, to allow the following precautionary measures:

intervention and depositing and/or confiscation of the revenue obtained from the unlawful activity; the suspension of the activity of reproduction, distribution and public dissemination; and the seizure of copies produced and of equipment and materials used for their production.

Along the same lines we have the Law on Trade Marks, Law No 32 of 10 November 1988, which governs the right of ownership of a trade mark; where such rights are violated the judge may order the cessation of actions which are an infringement of the right in question, order that compensation be paid for losses and damages, and order that all the necessary measures be taken to prevent the violation from continuing, and in particular that all products, packaging, cases, advertising materials, labels or other documents in which the trade mark has been unlawfully used, be withdrawn from sale.

Spain also has Law No 16 of 17 July 1989, concerning the Protection of Competition, art 45 of which regulates the possibility of the Court of Competition Protection adopting precautionary measures, either automatically or at the request of the interested parties.

Article 45 of the Law on the Protection of Competition:

Article 45—Categories and Procedures for their implementation:

(1) Once this measure has been initiated, the Department [responsible for the enforcement of competition law] may at any time, either automatically or at the request of the interested parties, propose to the Court of Competition Protection the precautionary measures necessary for ensuring the effectiveness of the resolution which is adopted, and in particular the following:
(a) orders for the cessation of an activity or for the imposition of certain conditions so as to avoid any damage which might be caused by the conduct which the measure involves;
(b) a security deposit of any type, except a personal one, and deemed sufficient by the court for covering compensation for any damage or losses which might be caused.
In the event that it is the interested parties who propose the adoption of precautionary measures, the Court may call for a security deposit.

(2) It will not be possible to introduce precautionary measures which could cause irreparable losses to [one of] the interested parties, or which would mean the infringement of basic rights.

(3) The Court will hear the interested parties within five days and will resolve the matter in three [days], regarding the appropriateness of the measures.

(4) The Court, either exercising its own jurisdiction or at the request of the Department, may impose fines with the guarantees, and in the sum envisaged, in art 11, with a view to ensuring compliance with the precautionary measures.

(5) The Department may propose to the court at any time during the course of implementation of the measure—either automatically or at the request of a party—that the precautionary measures be suspended, modified or revoked

in light of the intervening circumstances or circumstances which could not have been envisaged when the measure was first adopted.

The precautionary measures that may be adopted include orders for the cessation of activities or the imposition of certain conditions, with a view to avoiding the damage or loss which could be caused by the introduction of the precautionary measure itself, as well as obtaining a security deposit considered to be sufficient for covering any damages or losses which might be caused. A special feature under this law is the imposition of a ban on the adoption of precautionary measures which might cause (one of) the interested parties irreparable losses, or which would involve the violation of basic rights.

Other peculiarities of this law are: the possibility of the Competition Protection Court imposing fines to ensure that there is compliance with the precautionary measures, and regulation of the possible modification of the precautionary measures by the court, either automatically or at the request of the party. The precautionary measures adopted have a maximum period of six months' validity and come to an end, in any event, when the court issues its final ruling.

Recently Spain has seen the introduction of Law No 3 of 10 January 1991, concerning Unfair Competition, which makes provision for the judge—whenever there is an instance of unfair competition or the imminent likelihood thereof—to order the provisional cessation of that activity and the adoption of the precautionary measures he deems appropriate, provided that the request is submitted by the duly authorised person who will be liable for any damages caused if the main action on the merits fails.

As regards procedural regulations, all these special laws refer in a general and supplementary sense to the procedure laid down in the Law of Civil Proceedings for the regulation of Unnamed Measures (art 1428).

Regulations governing competence

Due to the multiplicity of courts that exist in our country, the Spanish judicial regulatory system makes use of regulations governing competence to determine the court to which a matter is to be assigned. In this connection a distinction is normally made between three types of competence: *functional competence*, aimed at determining to which order or level of courts each phase of the proceedings is to be assigned; *objective competence*, aimed at determining, from among the courts of the same level or area of competence, to which of them a given matter should be referred; and finally *territorial competence*, which assigns certain matters to each of the courts of the first level.

There are in Spain four jurisdictional structures: civil jurisdiction (which deals with all civil and commercial matters), criminal jurisdiction, administrative jurisdiction and social jurisdiction, which deals with labour law, industrial relations and social security matters. (This chapter is confined to a study of civil jurisdiction. As far as the other orders of jurisdiction are concerned—criminal jurisdiction, litigious/administrative jurisdiction and social jurisdiction—these have only been mentioned to indicate their existence.)

As far as civil jurisdiction is concerned, the Organic Law of Judicial Power lays down certain criteria governing competence in art 22 of that law, with reference to such matters as obligations, movable assets, consumer contracts, etc. Among these matters there are also regulations applying to the adoption of precautionary measures or safeguards.

Article 22 of the Organic Law of Judicial Power states:

In the Civil Order the Spanish Courts will have competence: . . . (5) When it is a case of adopting provisional measures or safeguards with respect to persons or assets found in Spanish territory, and which must be fulfilled in Spain.

Accordingly, once the competence of Spanish judges has been established in connection with a dispute, it is necessary to determine the objective competence. Pursuant to Law No 38 of 28 December 1988, concerning Demarcation and Judicial Level, the following judicial bodies are distinguished in the civil order: the courts of first instance in each judicial district; the Provincial Court of Appeal (courts of second instance) which are located in each provincial capital; and the higher bodies— the High Courts of Justice of the Autonomous Communities, the Supreme Court, as the venue for appeals, and the Constitutional Court which protects the rights granted by the Spanish Constitution. In addition, in the case of the adoption of precautionary measures relating to disputes over matters of the protection of competence, there is the Court for the Defence of Competence.

Normally the adoption of a precautionary measure is sought before a Judge of First Instance in the appropriate judicial district. It is also possible to seek the adoption of precautionary measures at the Provincial Court of Appeal when the primary or initial action has reached that level.

As far as territorial competence is concerned, the competent judge will be the one to whom the parties have expressly submitted themselves. In the absence of an express or implicit submission, the Law of Civil

Proceedings, in the general provisions of art 62.3, stipulates that the competent body for the adoption of precautionary measures is the judge at the Court of First Instance in the place where the immovable assets are located; in the case of movable assets or livestock, or mixed actions, the competent judge is the one for the place in which the assets are located or the domicile of the defendant is situated, at the choice of the plaintiff (art 62.2 and 62.4 of the Law of Civil Proceedings).

Finally it should be pointed out that all regulatory provisions on competence apply in the event of the request for the adoption of precautionary measures being made before submission of the main claim, since if it were made subsequent to submission of the claim, when the primary action was still pending, the competent judge would be the one who is dealing with that primary action.

Application

Under Spanish law there are no special requirements in terms of the legal representation of parties in order for them to be allowed to request precautionary measures.

If the request is made before the main action, the Law of Civil Proceedings, in art 4.4, does not require that the plaintiff be represented by a professional solicitor, justifying this by the urgency of the case. In order to submit a request for a precautionary measure it only requires the signature of the plaintiff for the request to be valid. Once the request has been granted, however, any attempt to arrive at a solution must bear the signature of a solicitor. Nevertheless in practice a request for precautionary measures is usually submitted by an *Abogado* (practising lawyer) and a *Procurador de los Tribunales (Procurador)*, even though this is not an essential requirement. A *Procurador* is a legal professional whose role is to act as agent of the parties in their dealings with the court.

On the other hand, if the request is submitted at the same time as the main action, or once the lawsuit has started, the legal representation required will be that which applies to the primary suit. Normally, ordinary Spanish legal proceedings require that the parties be represented by an *Abogado* and *Procurador*.

Moreover, and with reference to the *Abogado*, there is no legal requirement for any particular specialisation. It is sufficient that he be a graduate in Law and that he be enrolled on the register of lawyers in the place where the lawsuit is to be conducted.

Practice and procedures

Under Spanish law there is no unified set of regulations laying down, in general terms, the procedures to be followed in order to adopt a precautionary measure, although for each precautionary measure there are certain concrete procedural rules. The most comprehensively regulated precautionary measure is the preventive embargo, to which other precautionary measures, such as the depositing of assets, are referred.

However an analysis of the different procedural rules reveals that all precautionary measures contain the following intrinsic characteristics:

(1) A precautionary measure is a procedure characterised by its summary nature and brevity. The measure is granted without going into the details of the matter, and it is based essentially on the documentary evidence submitted by the plaintiff.

(2) The underlying basis for the precautionary measure is *periculum in mora*, hence the urgency which characterises the adoption of a precautionary measure. The concept of *periculum in mora* is a danger to the final judgment being rendered ineffective due to the length of the court proceedings.

(3) The precautionary measure is dependent on the declarative procedure (the main action), and is secondary to it. However, it is not static, and if the circumstances leading to its adoption change, the precautionary measure is also altered.

(4) Frequently the precautionary measure is granted by the judge *inaudita parte debitoris* without hearing the debtor party, that is to say without the defendant being involved.

Despite these common characteristics, under the Spanish legal system each precautionary measure has its own peculiarities, and we need to refer to these if we are to really understand the procedural rules which apply under Spanish law.

We will now therefore give a brief analysis of each of these measures one by one, starting with the preventive embargo since that is the most common.

Securing a monetary judgment: the preventive embargo

The most widely used precautionary embargo under Spanish law is the preventive embargo, governed by arts 1397–1418 of the Law of Civil Proceedings. This takes the form of a measure which ensures the enforcement of a judgment ordering a party to hand over a monetary sum, affecting or taken from the assets owned by the defendant. The purpose is to prevent actions which would make this difficult or impossible to enforce at a later stage.

Normally the preventive embargo guarantees the securing of monetary judgments, but this does not mean that it is an inappropriate measure in terms of non-monetary obligations. Indeed, obligations to perform or not perform certain actions can be combined with an obligation to give a certain asset to be converted into a monetary debt in the event that the debtor is unable to fulfil the obligation expected of him. In these cases there is nothing to preclude a request for a preventive embargo in order to guarantee the monetary obligation to pay the monetary equivalent of the performance/service which is no longer possible.

Prerequisites

The essential prerequisites for the granting of a preventive embargo are a document *fumus boni iuris, periculum in mora,* a security deposit and dependence on a primary action.

The first prerequisite is the existence of a document which is sufficient for meeting the requirements of *fumus boni iuris* (meaning a *prima facie* likelihood of a strong case), from which the existence of the debt can be deduced. This debt may be in hard cash or in kind, and according to the majority view, it must be a liquidated amount.

Article 1399:

The preventive embargo may apply both to debts in hard cash, and to debts in kind. In the second case it will be the plaintiff's responsibility, for the purposes of the embargo, to fix the cash amount which is the equivalent of his claim, using as a basis for calculation the average price the debt in kind has on the market in that area, without jeopardising the establishing of this credit at the corresponding hearing.

Article 1400.1 of the Law of Civil Proceedings:

In order to grant a preventive embargo it will be necessary:

(1) That the request be accompanied by a document indicating the existence of the debt ...

Article 1401:

If the title submitted is enforceable, the preventive embargo may be granted at once.

When the title substantiating the debt is one of those contained in points 1, 4, 5 and 6 of art 1429, and it does not exceed 50,000 Pesetas, a preventive embargo will be granted without the need for meeting the requirements of point 2 of art 1400.

If the title submitted is unenforceable without recognition of the debtor's signature, it may still be granted but at the risk of the party which ultimately loses the main action.

In the event that the debtor has not been able to sign, and another person has done so at his request, the preventive embargo may still be granted on behalf of, and at the risk of, the creditor, provided that, having been summonsed twice, at a twenty-four hour interval, to swear on oath to the accuracy of the document referring to the debt, the debtor fails to appear to make this sworn statement.

Once the document has been recognised, even if the debt is denied, the preventive embargo may be granted as above.

The second requirement for a preventive embargo is *periculum in mora*: this means any circumstance which leads one to believe that the debtor may at any time engage in fraudulent acts which could result in the insolvency of his assets, to the loss of the plaintiff.

Article 1400.2 of Spanish procedural law lays down a series of cases in which the existence of such a risk is presumed:

(a) That the defendant is a foreigner who is not naturalised in Spain. (The decisive factor is the nationality of the debtor. For this reason Spaniards resident abroad will not be included under this category. As regards legal entities, the determining factor, for establishing their nationality, will be the domicile of the registered office, and the nationality of the shareholders will be of no relevance. This requirement has been criticised by legal doctrine, on the grounds that it is discriminatory and goes against the equality of civil rights between Spaniards and foreigners.)

(b) That, although he is Spanish or a naturalised foreigner, he has no known domicile or property, or no industrial, agricultural or commercial establishment in the place in which the claim is to be filed against him. (This point must be interpreted in the sense that the debtor has no domicile in the place where the claim is to be filed. Property here is interpreted to mean immovable property. It is required that the domicile, the immovable property or any form of commercial, agricultural or industrial establishment must be within the territory of the Court of First Instance to which the claim is to be submitted.)

(c) That he has disappeared from his place of domicile or establishment without leaving anyone in his place, or the latter does not know his whereabouts, or again that there are sufficient reasonable grounds for believing that he will hide or undersell his assets to the detriment of the creditors. (Jurisprudence interprets this as meaning the debtor is absent from his place of domicile for an extended period of time. In the event that he leaves another person in charge of the establishment or place of residence, it will be necessary that this person is unaware of the whereabouts of the debtor. As far as 'hiding on the part of the debtor' is concerned, this is interpreted as the intention of the debtor to keep his whereabouts unknown.)

With respect to these requirements it should be pointed out that they are considered on their own, and not accumulatively. Moreover, the person or party to which these circumstances apply must be the defendant.

The requirement which has given rise to the greatest number of interpretations is the last one: 'that there are sufficient reasonable grounds for believing that he will hide or undersell his assets to the detriment of the creditors'. This requirement assumes the existence of a desire and intention on the part of the debtor to hide or undersell his assets, this requirement being interpreted as a subjective element. (The judgment of the Provincial Court of Appeal of Caceres, dated 2 March 1985 states: 'Article 1400 of the Law of Civil Proceedings stipulates two requirements for granting of the preventive embargo: firstly, in an objective sense, it makes reference to a document substantiating the debts, and secondly, in a subjective sense, it makes reference to the will/intention of the debtor; the legislator describes how this works by expounding various cases which can be regarded as instances of *periculum in mora*'.) However, there is a more flexible trend among those involved with jurisprudence, which is of the view that it is not essential that there be an intention on the part of the debtor to cause a loss to his creditors, but merely that there is the risk of such an effect being the result of the debtor's actions. (The judgment of the Provincial Court of Appeal of Barcelona, dated 8 July 1976 states: '... The words "will hide or undersell his assets to the detriment of the creditors" are not to be interpreted as meaning an intentional aim, but as referring to the actual reality of a situation where it can be seen that when the judgment is enforced, assuming this to be awarded against the debtor, there are not actually any assets with which to implement that judgment'.)

As regards the facts or actions constituting this conduct it is sufficient that these be actions which make it probable, in the opinion of the judge, that the debtor is leaning towards taking action to hide or undersell his assets. Actions classified as constituting *periculum in mora* are the transfer or mortgaging of the debtor's immovable property, the cessation of his industrial activities, or the abandonment of his productive assets.

The third prerequisite for a preventive embargo is a security deposit, to cover the damages and losses, when the party requesting the measure has no known solvency. The amount of the security deposit will be fixed at the judge's discretion, taking into account the circumstances of the case.

Article 1402 of the Law of Civil Proceedings:

In the cases referred to in the last three paragraphs of art 1402, if the party requesting the embargo has no known solvency, the judge must ask him for a security deposit sufficient to cover any losses and costs which may ensue.

The fourth prerequisite for a preventive embargo is dependence on a primary action. A preventive embargo may be requested prior to, at the same time as, or following the filing of a claim. If it is requested in advance, the claim must be filed within 20 days of the request and in the claim the plaintiff must refer to the request for the preventive embargo.

Purpose of the preventive embargo

The preventive embargo relates to the assets comprising the property of the plaintiff, and may take the form of: immovable assets (by means of filing the preventive embargo with the Registry of Property); movable assets, livestock, public securities and cash; the debtor's credits or rights with third parties; or vessels.

Procedures

Submission of request   The request for an embargo may be submitted:

(a) prior to submitting the claim—provided that the debt is greater than 500,000 Pesetas, and that the claim is filed within a maximum of 20 days and in that claim the plaintiff makes reference to the embargo he has requested. If these requirements are not met the embargo will be cancelled, with the possibility that the defendant will be awarded compensation for any damage and loss;
(b) at the same time as the claim—this will appear in the written claim itself, following the request for the primary relief (Petition), and will take the form of an additional petition;
(c) after the claim has been filed—in this case the request will be handled at the same time as the main action but independently.

Competence   We must make a distinction here between whether the request is submitted before the main claim or while judgment is pending.

Before the main claim, and in the absence of an express submission, competence will belong to the Judge of First Instance in the place where the assets which are the subject of the embargo are located.

Problems arise when the assets to which the preventive embargo refer are located in different judicial districts. In this case, according to some authorities, any of those districts may be competent to handle the matter, at the choice of the plaintiff. Another group of legal theorists, however, are of the view that in these cases consideration must be given to the personal nature of the action and thus the competent court will be that of the domicile of the defendant or the place in which the primary obligation is to be performed, at the choice of the plaintiff.

For practical reasons it is normal for the embargo request to be submitted to the court which will subsequently handle the primary action/ claim.

While judgment is pending, the competent court is the Court of First Instance where the primary action is being dealt with. If the primary action is being handled by a second instance court, the latter would be competent, and not the Court of First Instance. This follows the principle of the ancillary nature of the precautionary measure.

Form of the request   The embargo request, if submitted at the same time as the claim, will be incorporated in the latter. However, if it is made in advance of the claim, the Law of Civil Proceedings does not specify the form it is to take. Based on systematic interpretation legal theorists are of the view that it must be a written document containing the plaintiff's petition, appropriately founded or substantiated, and accompanied by the documents necessary for substantiating the right being claimed.

Development of the procedure and resolution   Once the request has been submitted, and assuming it is prior to the claim, a judicial ruling on the embargo will be issued. If, on the other hand, the request comes after or at the same time as the claim, there will first be a judicial ruling (known as a *providencia*) on the claim in a separate document, and then a judicial ruling on the request for a precautionary measure.

In order to implement the principle of *inaudita parte debitoris*, the defendant will not be notified of the request for adoption of the precautionary measure. (Article 1403 of the Law of Civil Proceedings: 'If the judge deems the creditor's request acceptable, he will award the preventive embargo with the urgency that the particular case calls for, and he will implement it without hearing the debtor or allowing any appeal . . .'.) However, if the measure is requested in the claim document, the debtor will receive a copy of this document, whereby he will become aware of the request for the precautionary measure. Nevertheless the principle of not hearing the defendant will continue to be observed because the debtor is not permitted to submit any statement before the precautionary measure is adopted. Moreover, in the context of *periculum in mora*, the embargo is granted immediately and as a matter of some urgency.

The judicial settlement or resolution may take the form of acceptance or rejection. In order to assess the applicability of the precautionary measure, the judge will consider arguments of form (ie whether the procedural periods and deadlines have been complied with, the competence of the court, etc) and arguments as to valid grounds for the request (ie an analysis of the existence of the necessary prerequisites for adopting the precautionary measure). In addition the judge will fix the amount of the security deposit which must be provided by the plaintiff in the event that he lacks known solvency. If the request is rejected, the plaintiff may appeal through the appropriate means.

If an embargo is granted, it will be officially issued, provided that the plaintiff has arranged for the security deposit, where applicable. Spanish legislation does not stipulate a period in which this embargo is to be exercised, but given its urgent nature, it is expected that the court will exercise the embargo without delay.

An embargo on immovable assets will take the form of a judicial mandate which the Registry of Property will record as a preventive note. An embargo on movable assets and livestock will take the form of the depositing thereof with the person designated by the plaintiff and accepted by the court; as for credits, public securities and cash, if they have been deposited with a banking establishment or a similar institution, they will be held at that establishment or otherwise deposited as in the case of movable assets, having obtained adequate guarantees from the depositary. If the object of the embargo is credits or rights which are in the possession of a third party, the third party will be ordered not to make any payment to the defendant.

Once an embargo has been adopted the debtor may take the following courses of action:

(1) Provide a security deposit or surety whereby the embargo would no longer apply. This is what is known as the *invalidation of the preventive embargo*. An embargo may also be lifted if the debtor pays the outstanding debt, but this would also suppose the end of the primary action.

(2) Oppose the embargo, as soon as he receives notification of the

embargo having been granted, requesting that it be declared of no effect and that he (the debtor) be awarded compensation for damages and losses. This opposition of the embargo must be drawn up in a separate document, using the procedure laid down for such action.

The judicial resolution will become binding if the defendant fails to oppose it within five days after having been served notice or—if he has opposed it—in cases where the decision in response to the opposition is merely to confirm the effect of the embargo.

Securing a non-monetary judgment

This general concept covers various possibilities, and is aimed at securing those judgments which involve specific items, and for those cases in which protection is being sought for the performance or non-performance of a certain action or service.

In those cases where the court is being asked for a judgment aimed at obtaining the handing over of given objects, Spanish law provides for the preventive notification of a claim, the production and depositing of a movable item, and the intervention in the administration of litigious matters.

For those cases where what is being sought is the performance of some action, or refraining from certain actions, Spanish law provides the following general action: unnamed precautionary measures or indeterminate precautionary measures.

Securing a judgment for the handing over of certain items
Preventive notification of a claim   Under Spanish law there are a number of assets, legal situations and rights which are subject to officially publicised registration. In order to ensure this registration-related protection, the precautionary measure has been introduced as a means aimed at protecting the interests of any third parties acting in good faith. It makes use of provisionally limited registries which publish pending litigation involving a property/asset which is or could be registered.

The regulation of this precautionary measure is basically contained in art 42 of the Mortgage Law.

Article 42 of the Mortgage Law:

Those entitled to request preventive notification of their rights in the corresponding registry are:

(1) A person who is taking legal action over the ownership of immovable property, or over the establishment, declaration, modification or cancellation of any property right.

(2) A person who obtains a favourable embargo which has become effective with respect to the immovable assets of the debtor.

(3) A person who, in any lawsuit, obtains an enforceable judgement against the defendant, and which must be put into effect by means of the expedients laid down in the Law on Civil Proceedings.

(4) A person who, having requested performance of some obligation in an ordinary lawsuit, obtains a judgment, as provided by law, ordering the seizure of, or preventing the disposal of, immovable assets.

(5) A person who proposes to file a claim with a view to obtaining any of the judicial rulings contained in art 2, point 4 of this Law.

(6) The heirs of an estate, with respect to their inheritance rights, when there is no particular allocation between them of the tangible assets, shares or indivisible parts thereof.

(7) A legatee who has no right, under law, to bring an action.

(8) A renovation creditor, for as long as the renovation work lasts.

(9) A person who submits to the Registry any title which cannot be registered, due to the absence of some remediable requirement or because the Registrar is unable to do so.

(10) A person who for any other reason is entitled to request preventive notification, in accordance with this and other laws.

The preventive notification of a claim may be sought in connection with claims involving the introduction of lawsuits with respect to property, immovable assets or movable assets which are subject to registration, personal lawsuits having some connection with registration, claims having some registration significance, or claims involving disqualification.

The necessary requirements for entitlement to request this precautionary measure are the normal ones (*periculum in mora*, *fumus boni iuris* and the provision of a security deposit), but with the special condition here that the primary claim must relate to situations or matters which are registered or could be registered.

As far as the procedure is concerned, the measure is applied for once the claim has been filed and the judgment is pending, or it is included in the claim document itself. Again the defendant is not heard.

The special features of this measure perhaps lie in the fact that the judicial ruling is limited to issuing instructions to the Public Registry to make the appropriate entry. The Registrar has the right to examine the document submitted and to check the competence of the court, the formalities called for in said document and any possible obstacles to registration, but he may not go into the details of the case.

Production (display) and depositing of a movable item This is governed by art 499 of the Law of Civil Proceedings, in the chapter devoted to Preliminary Procedural Matters, and is construed as the precautionary measure corresponding to the procedure for the production of the movable object in question.

Article 499 of the Law of Civil Proceedings:

In case 2 of art 499, if, when the movable object is produced the plaintiff declares that it is the one for which he intends to file a claim, this will be noted in the case documents kept by the court and the object will be left in the possession of the party that has produced it, the latter being warned that he must keep it in the same state until the dispute is resolved.

Again at the request of the plaintiff the object in question may be deposited if the requirements of art 1400 apply for the introduction of a preventive embargo. This depositing of the object in question will be at the risk of the party requesting the procedure, which will become invalid, incurring compensation for losses, if that party fails to submit his claim within thirty days.

The preventive measure ordered in para 1 of this article will also become invalid if the claim is not filed within the specified time limit.

The precautionary measure takes the form of securing a movable object, ie the object of the dispute, through the handing over thereof to a depositary, guaranteeing its safe-keeping by removing it from the debtor's possession. The actual production of the object is only carried out as a preliminary for the purpose of proving the liability of the defendant. The precautionary measure as such is the depositing of the item, although the two component activities are very closely related.

The prerequisites for this measure are again those applying to all precautionary measures, with the special feature that the law lays down that this measure may only be adopted when the object of the proceedings involves claims on ownership of property including rights over chattels (real property actions).

As far as the procedure is concerned, this is governed by the same procedural rules as the preventive embargo, with the following special features: if the request pre-dates the claim, the latter must be filed within a maximum of 30 days; furthermore, the judicial ruling must state who the depositary is to be—this may be the creditor himself or a third party of good faith.

The Spanish legal system also contains another provision similar to the depositing of items/assets, though broader in scope, known as sequestration. This measure is distinct in that it can apply to all types of goods/assets, movable or immovable, provided that they are specific, and it can apply to real property and combined proceedings, as well as personal proceedings. As far as the procedure is concerned, this precautionary measure is governed by the provisions laid down in the unnamed measures governed by art 1428 of the Law of Civil Proceedings.

In summary, what is being sought both through the sequestration and the depositing of assets is that the item produced and deposited as the object of the proceedings must retain the same characteristics, or must not deteriorate until the final judgment is obtained.

Judicial intervention over disputed assets   This precautionary measure is used when the aim is to ensure the integrity of a company, property asset or immovable asset which is the subject of commercial operations, so as to guarantee the continuation of the relevant activities while the dispute lasts.

It is governed by arts 1419–1427 of the Law of Civil Proceedings.

Article 1419 of the Law of Civil Proceedings:

A person who, in submitting documents to substantiate his rights, brings an action for the possession of mines, and mountains, whose main resources take the form of trees, or for the possession of plantations, industrial or craft establishments, may request that the administrative authorities intervene in connection with the disputed assets.

There is only passive involvement by the possessor of the disputed assets and the one who is operating them, and the measure seeks to avoid any action which might have a prejudicial effect on those assets. The precautionary measure takes the form of the appointment of a Judicial Controller who will monitor and supervise the actions of the debtor for as long as the proceedings last.

Legally, the object of the precautionary measure is the possession of mines, and mountains whose main resources take the form of trees, plantations, or industrial or craft establishments; this listing is exhaustive, and the principle is not extended to other cases.

The special procedural features of this measure are that the debtor is obliged to inform the Controller of all the activities he is engaged in in connection with the operation of the relevant establishment. However, the Controller's intervention is not meant to restrict the powers of the debtor; the latter may continue to exercise those powers, and even dispose of the assets which are the object of the dispute. Thus the Controller's activities are limited primarily to overseeing the actions of the debtor. The latter must inform the Controller of all his administrative activities, and carry them out with his consent.

In the event that the debtor fails to inform the Controller of his activities, or engages in any activities without the Controller's consent, it will be for the judge to decide whether or not those actions are acceptable. If the judge takes the view that the actions in question are not acceptable, he may impose a criminal sanction on the defendant, even if those activities are legally binding in dealings with third parties who have acted in good faith.

The appointment of the Controller will be made before the judge determines whether such intervention is necessary. The Controller is appointed by agreement between the parties; in the event of disagreement the creditor will nominate four persons from whom the debtor must select one; if there is still a problem with that selection, the judge will appoint a person from among the four proposed, his choice being governed by the one 'who pays most tax'. (This is interpreted as the most solvent person out of the four proposed by the plaintiff.)

Once elected, and within 24 hours of the appearance of the parties, the judge will issue the appropriate judicial ruling as to whether or not the intervention is to be ordered. In the event of this precautionary measure being adopted, the judge will approve the appointment of the Controller and order the defendant to refrain from any administrative actions that do not have the Controller's consent. The defendant may provide a security deposit in order to have this control lifted.

Securing obligations to perform or refrain from performing certain actions

Under Spanish procedural legislation there is a category referred to by legal theorists as unnamed or indeterminate measures: art 1428 of the Law of Civil Proceedings. In fact the indeterminate or unnamed measures covered by this article represent a mechanism which enables the judge to adopt all the necessary safeguards for the purpose of guaranteeing the effectiveness of the execution of the subsequent judgment.

Article 1428 of the Law of Civil Proceedings:

When written evidence is submitted in support of an action, and this clearly shows an obligation to perform or refrain from performing certain actions, or to hand over certain, specific items, the judge may, at the request of the plaintiff, and on the latter's responsibility, adopt those measures which, according to the circumstances, he deems necessary for ensuring the effectiveness of the judgment which will be pronounced in resolving the aforesaid action.

The party requesting these measures must provide a sufficient security deposit in advance, but not a personal surety, in order to cover any compensation for damages and losses.

These measures may be requested either before or after a claim is filed. If they are requested before, the claim must follow within eight days of the request being granted.

The competent judge will be the one who deals with the primary action, for which purpose a separate document must be drawn up.

The defendant may oppose the measures sought or ask for those granted to be lifted, either because he considers them inapplicable, or because he undertakes to provide compensation for the damages and losses which might be caused by the plaintiff and provides a security deposit or bank guarantee sufficient for meeting those requirements.

Once these claims have been made, the judge will summon the parties to appear before him in order to hear their cases, to admit any relevant evidence and, in the three days that follow, to issue a ruling in the form of a judgment against which an appeal may be lodged. The same procedure will be followed for resolving disputes which may arise in connection with the precautionary measures once they have been granted.

The security deposit referred to in the above sections may be any of those categories of surety admitted by law, with the exception of a personal surety.

In essence, then, this is a general precautionary system, which gives the judge full powers of discretion in terms of the granting of those measures which will safeguard non-monetary obligations in general.

Article 1428 governs those requirements which are essential for the adoption of this precautionary measure, and which are the prerequisites common to all measures: the existence of a document substantiating the right for which protection is being sought and the provision of a security deposit by the plaintiff to cover any possible compensation for damages and losses. With respect to *periculum in mora* on the part of the debtor, it is not required that there exists a risk, but in practice, where there is no such risk, the judge is certain to reject the precautionary measure.

With regard to the general principle of precautionary measures referred to as *inaudita parte debitoris*, there is perhaps a 'gap in the law': the aforesaid article provides for the possibility of opposition on the part of the defendant against the measures sought, which means that the debtor would have knowledge of those measures before they were adopted.

In addition to opposing the request, the defendant may seek the invalidation of the precautionary measure by depositing a security deposit or guarantee sufficient for covering any damages or losses.

The procedure here is faster than in the case of the other precautionary measures:

(a) the request may be submitted at any time, but if it is submitted before the claim, the latter must be filed within a maximum period of eight days;

(b) in the event of the defendant opposing the measure, the judge will summon the parties to appear before him and to hear their evidence, after which he will issue his ruling within three days.

The range of measures which the judge may grant in this context is very broad and varied: it may take the form of ordering the debtor not to engage in certain activities, granting a preventive embargo to safeguard obligations to perform certain actions, or the depositing of movable assets (titles/securities, shares, bonds, etc), and the appointment of an administrator or controller.

Costs of the action

In Spain the costs incurred in judicial proceedings are referred to as Procedural Costs, regulated in general terms by art 523 of the Law of Civil Proceedings and more specifically in arts 421–429 of that same Law. They cover costs incurred in all types of judicial activities which have been carried out during an action or lawsuit (pleadings, letters rogatory, the fees of experts, mediation costs, official costs, etc), as well as the fees of the parties' *Abogados* and *Procuradores*.

Article 523 of the Law of Civil Proceedings:

In declaratory judgments the costs of the action at first instance will be payable by the party whose claims have been totally rejected, unless the judge, after due consideration, comes to the view that there are exceptional circumstances which justify his not imposing this requirement.

If acceptance or rejection [of the request] is partial, each party will pay his own costs and half the common costs, unless there are valid grounds for requiring that they be paid by one of the parties due to his having resorted to litigation too rashly.

If the defendant complies with the request before contesting it, there will be no imposition of costs, unless the judge, after due consideration, is of the view that there has been bad faith on the part of the defendant.

When, in implementation of the provisions of paragraph one of this article, costs are to be paid by the defeated litigant, the latter alone will be required to pay a sum from the part corresponding to lawyers', experts' and other officials' fees which is not subject to tariffs, which does not exceed—for each of the parties which have obtained the pronouncement—one third of the costs of the action; for this purpose claims which cannot be fixed will be valued at one million Pesetas. This limitation will not apply when the judge finds that the litigant ordered to pay the costs acted too rashly.

The judge will be the one who, in his judgment, determines which of the parties, or in what proportion, if it involves both of them, is to pay said costs. The assessment of costs will be fixed in the corresponding court by the secretary or clerk who acted in the dispute, once costs have been awarded. The parties will be informed of the assessed costs within three days in either case, so that they can state their agreement or disagreement with those costs. If there is any disagreement, the assessed costs may be challenged through the normal process.

The different possibilities for the awarding of costs in a precautionary procedure are as follows.

(1) If the precautionary measure is granted, and the debtor is found to be in the wrong, he will be ordered to pay the procedural costs incurred as a result of the adoption of the precautionary measure, and if he has caused the plaintiff some loss, he must also pay compensation for such damages and losses.

(2) If the measure has been rejected, the plaintiff must bear the costs incurred in connection with his request.

(3) If the measure has been granted, but it subsequently becomes invalid, either because of the debtor's opposition, or because the measure is lifted due to the right in question being declared invalid, the plaintiff will be ordered to pay the costs incurred in adopting the measures, in addition to paying the defendant compensation for damages and losses.

Development of the law

In order to carry out an adequate study of precautionary measures under Spanish law it is necessary to take account of the development which is taking shape, day by day, through the judgments pronounced by the courts, for in the final analysis the judges are the ones who keep the law alive by constantly updating it. If this were not the case, substantive law, which rests on written laws, would gradually become obsolete and irrelevant, and more importantly it would be completely divorced from everyday life.

For these reasons, and in order to avoid a progressive alienation between the law and the individual, as the representative of society at large, we would encourage legal practice to endeavour to update the written laws through the constant use of judgments which are the embodiment of current thinking in society.

Under the Spanish legal system (given that the main body of legislation in the area of precautionary measures is the Law of Civil Proceedings of 1881, amended on various occasions, but still obsolete in many respects), the judgments pronounced by the courts are elements in the task of producing a study of the precautionary measures.

The development of Spanish jurisprudence in terms of the application of precautionary measures in civil proceedings is characterised by its progressive adoption of a broader approach, through a less literal interpretation. Among other things, civil legal practice has contributed to defining the concept of the precautionary measure, as well as to establishing the characteristic prerequisites applying to all types of precautionary measures.

Juan Barthe

United Kingdom

England and Wales

Introduction

The ability to obtain urgent and speedy relief is an essential part of a lawyer's armoury. Injunctions have increasingly attracted public attention in recent years as they have been used as a weapon, for example, against trade unions in industrial disputes and by the British Government in their attempts to restrain publication of the *Spycatcher* book. Applications for injunctive relief frequently receive national press coverage and the commercial world now expects its lawyers to be able to obtain injunctions quickly whenever serious damage is threatened to its business.

An injunction is an extremely effective remedy as it is an order of the court requiring a party to do a specific act or acts or to refrain from doing a specific act or acts. The High Court has the power to grant an injunction, either interlocutory or final, in all cases in which it appears to the court to be just and convenient to do so (s 37(1) of the Supreme Court Act 1981). The High Court has an extremely wide discretion in deciding on the terms of any injunction and imposing any terms and conditions as the court thinks just. This section will only deal with the courts in England and Wales. English law is applied by the courts of Northern Ireland and Scotland has its own independent courts and legal system, which are briefly examined later in this chapter. There is no Code of Civil Procedures in the English courts, unlike in other EC Member States; instead procedural rules and principles are contained in the statutory *Rules of the Supreme Court*. This chapter will consider:

(a) the nature of interlocutory relief;
(b) the structure of the courts within England and Wales;
(c) the criteria for obtaining an interlocutory injunction;
(d) the practice and procedure for obtaining interlocutory injunctions generally;
(e) Mareva injunctions;
(f) Anton Piller orders; and
(g) alternative pre-emptive remedies other than injunctions.

The nature of interlocutory injunctions

Types of injunction

In view of the length of time it takes for the majority of cases to reach a trial the position of the parties frequently needs regulating pending trial and this is the sole purpose of interlocutory proceedings. Very often a good result at the interlocutory stage leads to a settlement. There are various types of injunctions as follows.

Interlocutory

This is a provisional injunction taken at an earlier stage of the proceedings. It will usually last 'until the trial of the action or further order', ie until the other party applies for a discharge.

Interim

This is a provisional injunction which will last for only a specific period of time, for example, 'until 10.30 am 16 June or as soon as Counsel may be heard'. The terms 'interim' and 'interlocutory' are used in practice interchangeably although strictly speaking they do have different meanings. In practice an application is usually made for an interim injunction to last for a limited period of time until the application for the interlocutory injunction can be heard after the parties have exchanged affidavit evidence and the application is ready to be heard.

Quia timet injunctions

This is to prevent an apprehended legal wrong although no wrong doing has yet occurred. An application for a *quia timet* injunction should be made if a party fears that a wrong will be done to him and he cannot afford to wait for it to happen and then take action after the event. The plaintiff will need to show that damage to his business is certain or very likely. All injunctions, whether perpetual, interlocutory, interim or *quia timet* will be either mandatory or prohibitory.

Mandatory

This requires a party to do a specific act or acts. These are positive rather than negative orders. Examples would be an order for delivery up of goods, an order for delivery up of infringing materials or documents and a trade union being ordered to give instructions to its members to cease taking industrial action.

Prohibitory

This requires a party to refrain from doing a specific act or acts, for example, infringing the plaintiff's copyright materials or causing a nuisance to someone's property, or disposing of an asset.

The scope of injunctions

In the field of intellectual property, injunctions can restrain breach of copyright, infringements of patents and trade marks, breach of confidence, passing off and unfair competition.

In the field of employment law, injunctions may be used to restrain an ex-employee from breaking the terms of a restrictive covenant in his contract of employment or from using confidential information acquired during the course of his employment.

In trade union law, injunctions can be used to restrain an unofficial strike without a ballot, certain forms of unlawful picketing and secondary action.

In company law, injunctions are frequently obtained to restrain *ultra vires* acts by the company and the presentation of a winding-up petition by a creditor, for example if an outstanding debt is disputed.

In the area of real property, injunctions can restrain the disturbance of an easement or a right-of-way, building works carried out in breach of a covenant and nuisance by noise vibration or pollution.

In the field of contract, injunctions can restrain somebody from acting in breach of contract.

General principles

A discretionary remedy

The grant of an interlocutory injunction is a remedy that is both temporary and discretionary. The court must be satisfied that there is a real probability that if steps are not taken to preserve a party's interests and rights then irreparable damage may be done. The protection of the legitimate interests of the plaintiff will be paramount. An interlocutory injunction, being a discretionary remedy, is also an equitable remedy. There are a number of factors which the court will take into account when exercising its discretion which will be looked at in detail below.

Adequacy of damages

Generally an interlocutory injunction will not be granted if damages are an adequate remedy, ie damages will not compensate the plaintiff at trial. It is, however, quite rare for damages to be the only available remedy. An example may be in an action for infringement of copyright if the infringer offers to pay royalties at the full rate under the terms of the copyright owner's standard licence.

Acquiescence

This will occur when the owner of a right stands by in such a manner, when seeing a person do, or about to do, an act infringing his right, so as to induce that person committing the act into believing that the owner of the right consents to it, for example an owner lets a builder construct on his land. In such a case the owner of the right cannot later complain about the act and any attempt to obtain an interlocutory injunction will probably fail.

Delay

Any potential plaintiff must avoid undue delay in applying for an injunction. This is known as the concept of laches. If there has been undue delay then the court must decide whether the defendant has been prejudiced by the delay and will suffer any injustice as a result of the delay and will consider the nature of the acts done by the defendant in the interval. For example, in a passing-off action, the defendant may have continued to set up and establish his business, commenced trading and incurred considerable expense during the period of delay.

Structure of the courts

A civil action in England and Wales may be commenced either in the High Court or the county court.

The High Court

The High Court is divided into three divisions namely the Queen's Bench Division, the Chancery Division and the Family Division. The choice of Division depends on the nature of the work. Most actions may be commenced in the High Court irrespective of the value or nature of the claim. However, the High Court has powers to move proceedings to the county court.

High Court matters are dealt with either at the Central Office of the High Court at the Royal Courts of Justice in London or in one of the 136 District Registries. The powers of the District Registry are limited and varied. There are eight so-called 'Chancery District Registries' which have jurisdiction to issue proceedings and may deal with interlocutory proceedings in both the Queen's Bench and Chancery Divisions. All other District Registries may only deal with Queen's Bench interlocutory applications. As far as Chancery Division matters are concerned these District Registries have jurisdiction only to issue proceedings.

This chapter will concentrate on the procedures in the High Court in London but brief mention is made here of the jurisdiction of the District Registries of the High Court and of the county courts to give injunctive relief.

District Registries of the High Court

In addition to the Royal Courts of Justice in London, an application for an injunction may also be made to certain District Registries. With a few exceptions an injunction must be granted by a High Court judge either sitting in Chambers or in open court. Therefore an application to obtain an injunction outside London must be made to a District Registry where a judge of the High Court is sitting. Most District Registries will only have a Registrar who hears minor applications. The District Registries where a High Court judge sits are listed below.

The benefits of obtaining injunctive relief out of a District Registry for those practising some distance from London are obvious. However, only a handful of District Registries can grant injunctions and even these may not always be able to grant relief as a matter of urgency, for example outside court hours. There is no significant difference in procedure between the High Court in London and the District Registries.

District Registries—interlocutory applications to a judge

All District Registries have a District Registrar whose powers are the same as a High Court Master.

A District Registrar or High Court Master has limited powers to grant an injunction as follows:

(1) Where the terms are agreed by the parties to the proceedings in which the injunction is sought. (Ord 32, r 11(2).)

(2) Where the injunction is ancillary or incidental to a Charging Order. (Ord 50, r 9.)

(3) Where the injunction is ancillary or incidental to an Order for the appointment of a receiver by way of equitable execution. (Ord 52, r 1(3).)

Otherwise, an application for an interlocutory injunction must be made to a District Registry at which a High Court judge is sitting. Such places are determined in accordance with directions given by or on behalf of the Lord Chancellor (Courts Act 1971, s 2(2) and s 4(6)). The procedure to be followed at each District Registry will not vary greatly and it is advisable to make enquiries to the District Registry in question. However, the following general rules must be applied.

Chancery Division

At present the Chancery Division of the High Court sits in Liverpool, Manchester, Preston, Leeds, Newcastle upon Tyne, Birmingham, Bristol and Cardiff District Registries.

Where a Chancery cause or matter is proceeding in a District Registry which is not one of the above, any interlocutory application should be made to the nearest District Registry where there is a judge who exercises Chancery jurisdiction.

Queen's Bench Division

Queen's Bench Division hearings in Chambers take place in Manchester, Liverpool, Leeds, Birmingham, Cardiff and Bristol.

As in the Chancery Division, where an action is proceeding in a District Registry which is not listed above, a summons should be issued at the nearest District Registry where a High Court judge sits.

Before the issue of such a summons however the party should enquire at the registry whether the state of business will permit the matter to be heard there, or whether the summons should be issued in the Central Office or elsewhere.

Urgent applications

Where injunctive relief is sought as a matter of extreme urgency it should be noted that District Registries do not benefit from the Duty Judge System which operates in London. Outside London, if the necessity for an injunction arises during court hours, the Listing Clerk should locate and arrange an appointment with the nearest High Court judge. At other times, urgent applications must be made to the Royal Courts of Justice in London.

County court

The county court's jurisdiction has recently been extended by the Courts and Legal Services Act 1990. The Act provides that claims up to £25,000 may be dealt with in the county court. Where the claim is for personal injury, if the value of the claim is under £50,000 it must be dealt with by the county court.

The powers of the county court regarding injunctions have also recently changed as a result of the County Court Remedies Regulations 1991. Previously, the county court's jurisdiction was limited to the granting of injunctions relating to land or under specific statutory authority or where there was a claim for money or other relief.

Since 1 July 1991 a county court judge may grant an interlocutory injunction:

(a) Restraining a party from moving from the jurisdiction of the High Court assets located within that jurisdiction; or

(b) restraining a party from dealing with assets whether located within the jurisdiction of the High Court or not.

In the exercise of its powers the county court must grant the injunction for the purpose of making an order for the preservation, custody or detention of property which forms or may form the subject matter of proceedings.

Legal team

In England and Wales the legal profession is divided into solicitors and barristers. As a general rule, only barristers have rights of audience before High Court judges, and solicitors only have rights of audience in relation to mainly procedural hearings, before High Court Masters. Solicitors will therefore concentrate on the preparation of a case whilst barristers are specialist advocates. However, both solicitors and barristers will work closely together when preparing the papers for any interlocutory proceedings and barristers, as well as solicitors, will draft affidavits, as well as the court pleadings and other documents. It is important to note that any application for an interlocutory injunction will therefore involve the use of at least two lawyers: a solicitor and a barrister (known as counsel).

Criteria for obtaining interlocutory injunctions

Features

Not a trial

The first and most essential principle to appreciate in any application for an interlocutory injunction is that the court cannot decide the merits of the case as it will not have all of the relevant evidence before it. It will decide on the impression created by the affidavit evidence. The interlocutory hearing therefore is not a trial of the merits of the case.

Although the hearing of the application for an interlocutory injunction is not a trial of the case, in many cases the action will go no further and will settle shortly after the hearing. The real advantage of making an application for an interlocutory injunction is that the dispute is likely to be resolved on a once and for all basis. For example, in intellectual property infringement actions, about 95 per cent of cases do not proceed beyond the interlocutory stage. If the plaintiff obtains the interlocutory injunction the defendant may well lack either the financial resources and/or the resolve to fight on to a trial. Similarly, an unsuccessful plaintiff, if it loses at the interlocutory stage, is unlikely to want to continue to trial particularly if the plaintiff could not satisfy the court that it had an arguable case.

Affidavit evidence

Applications for interlocutory injunctions are dealt with by way of affidavit evidence. There will be no oral evidence and there is very rarely any opportunity for the cross-examination of witnesses. The sole purpose of the affidavits will be to assist the court in determining the outcome of the interlocutory application. Indeed, it may well be that the plaintiff has not even served a Statement of Claim when making the application for an interlocutory injunction and so the court will not usually be in a position to assess the pleadings (the formal statements of case) of each party.

Undertaking as to damages

If the plaintiff obtains an interlocutory injunction, he must give an undertaking to the court that if the case proceeds to a trial, and the plaintiff fails to obtain a perpetual injunction, and therefore the interlocutory injunction is discharged, then he will be able to, and undertakes to, compensate the defendant for any losses incurred as a result of the interlocutory injunction being ordered. This is known as the cross-undertaking as to damages and this will be inserted automatically in any interlocutory injunction unless the judge specifically states otherwise.

One of the main considerations for every plaintiff to consider, before making an application for an interlocutory injunction is whether it can afford to take the risk of being wrong at trial. As the plaintiff must give a cross-undertaking in damages, the plaintiff must consider firstly whether it can support the cross-undertaking and provide satisfactory evidence to the court of its financial status, and secondly what losses the defendant is likely to suffer if an interlocutory injunction is granted and then discharged at trial.

The plaintiff must take into account the possibility of successfully obtaining an interlocutory injunction, the case not being settled and proceeding to a trial, and subsequently losing at trial and having to pay not only the legal costs of the action but also damages to the defendant as compensation to the defendant for the interlocutory injunction being wrongly granted.

The plaintiff will usually have to exhibit its most recently audited accounts in order to show the court that it is 'good for the money' and if there are any doubts about the plaintiff's solvency then the plaintiff may be ordered to pay a sum into court or provide a bond or guarantee which can be provided by the plaintiff's holding or associated company. If the plaintiff does obtain an interlocutory injunction but subsequently loses at trial then the court will probably order an enquiry into damages to assess the amount of damages to be paid to the defendant. This will be dealt with in more detail below (see p 300).

The main action

Every plaintiff who applies for an interlocutory injunction must also commence a legal action, by issuing a writ or originating summons, which will determine the merits of the case. The interlocutory proceedings will be ancillary to the main action. An application for an interlocutory injunction can be issued at any time during the main action or at the same time as the writ is issued at the start of the main action. In certain circumstances an *ex parte* injunction can be granted before proceedings have been issued but only if the plaintiff undertakes to the court to issue a writ immediately after the hearing.

The '*American Cyanamid*' test

The House of Lords in *American Cyanamid Co v Ethicon Ltd* [1975] AC 396; 1 All ER 504 set out guidelines for the courts to follow when determining applications *inter partes* for interlocutory injunctions.

The criteria laid down by Lord Diplock should be seen in the context of the fundamental principle that the discretion of the court cannot be fettered by any rules which would inhibit the flexibility of the remedy of interlocutory relief. Nevertheless, these guidelines still remain the leading source of law on the subject.

The four guidelines are as follows.

Does the plaintiff have an arguable case?

The prospects of the plaintiff winning at trial should be investigated only to a limited extent. The interlocutory application does not take the form of a preliminary trial. The court only needs to consider whether the plaintiff has any real prospect of succeeding in his action for a permanent injunction at trial. The court must decide whether the plaintiff has an 'arguable case'. However, it is true to say that the merits of the case do inevitably have an important psychological effect on the judge.

The court should not assess whether the plaintiff has a *prima facie* case. The court is not in a position to resolve any conflict of evidence as to the facts in the affidavits. Nor is the court in a position to decide difficult questions of law. The conflict of evidence should be determined at trial, when the witnesses will give oral evidence and will be cross-examined by the other party's counsel.

If, and only if, the plaintiff has passed the first test and has shown that he has an arguable case and that there is a serious question to be tried, will the court go on to consider the other guidelines laid down by Lord Diplock.

Are damages an adequate remedy?
Lord Diplock stated (at p 408B–C):

the court should first consider whether, if the plaintiff were to succeed at the trial in establishing his right to a permanent injunction, he would be adequately compensated by an award of damages for the loss he would have sustained as a result of the defendants continuing to do what was sought to be enjoined between the time of the application and the time of the trial. If damages ... would be an adequate remedy and the defendant would be in a financial position to pay them, no interlocutory injunction should normally be granted, however strong the plaintiff's claim appeared to be at that stage.

The relevant factors which the court must take into account when considering this test are as follows:

(a) can damages adequately compensate the plaintiff for any temporary damage to its business, ie between the injunction application and the final hearing of the trial?
(b) is the plaintiff in a financial position to give a satisfactory cross-undertaking in damages?
(c) is the damage to the plaintiff's business likely to be irreparable?
(d) will the damage to the plaintiff or his business between the injunction application and the trial be outside the scope of pecuniary compensation, ie will he suffer loss for which money cannot compensate him?
(e) will the defendant be able to satisfy a future judgment? If, for example, the defendant is abroad and subject to exchange control limits, it is unlikely that damages could ever be said to be an adequate remedy;
(f) can the defendant provide security to cover any award of damages? For example, they may be able to pay an appropriate sum into a bank account in the joint names of the solicitors for each side. In a breach of copyright case a sum could be paid into a joint account representing a realistic level of royalties and the court may decide that an award of damages could ultimately be an adequate remedy;
(g) can the plaintiff's losses be directly attributed to the defendant's actions? One of the obvious difficulties any plaintiff has is in showing that any loss was caused directly by the defendant's wrongdoing. For example, the plaintiff's loss of turnover could be caused by any number of other reasons such as economic recession, exchange control factors, etc.

If there is any doubt as to the adequacy of damages as a remedy to either party then the court will consider the question of the balance of convenience.

The balance of convenience

This test would be better described as the 'balance of the risk of doing an injustice'. The court will consider whether more harm will be done to one or other party by granting or refusing the injunction. For example, if an ex-employee breaches a non-competition covenant with a former employer, would more harm be caused to the former employer's business (if an injunction is not granted) or to the former employee (if an injunction is granted and he loses his job and is unemployed until the trial of the action).

Some of the factors to consider on the question of balance of convenience are as follows:

(a) in an intellectual property infringement action, the defendant may be selling goods of an inferior quality in competition with the plaintiff and the reputation of the plaintiff's goods may generally suffer in addition to any lost sales by the plaintiff;

(b) the defendant may be depriving the plaintiff of its position in the marketplace;

(c) the interests of third parties should be taken into account: for example, the customers of an ex-employee who has solicited work from those customers, in breach of restrictions in his contract of employment with his former employer, may only be willing to place an order with the ex-employee's new business and not with his former employer.

If the arguments on the balance of convenience are evenly matched, the courts will consider the *status quo*.

This means that the court will wish to preserve as far as possible the state of affairs existing prior to the litigation until the rights of the parties have been determined in the action. For example, if a defendant is prohibited temporarily, ie until the trial of the case, from doing something which he has not done before, or has only recently started doing, then the effect of the interlocutory injunction is to postpone the date of the defendant being able to embark on his intended course of action. If a defendant has an established enterprise, and any injunction will cause him great damage, it is always much more difficult to preserve the *status quo* by granting an interlocutory injunction when the defendant is prohibited or significantly prohibited from carrying out his business, or an important part of his business, as a result of an interlocutory injunction.

The *status quo* is the state of affairs which existed during the period immediately preceding the issue of the writ and the Notice of Motion or a summons.

Only as a last resort, but very frequently in practice, to decide the balance of convenience, will the court consider the strength of the merits of each party's case. It is often the case that each party will state in the affidavit evidence that it will suffer substantial disadvantage if the interlocutory decision goes against that party. Faced with both parties claiming such irreparable disadvantage the courts may have to consider an assessment of the relative strengths of the two parties' cases based on the affidavit evidence. However, one other factor which may be decisive will be if there is a wider public interest in the outcome of the application. For example, the plaintiff may allege that a drug marketed by the defendant infringes the plaintiff's patent. The defendant may argue successfully that the drug has life saving qualities and that it was greatly in the public interest not to restrain the sale of such a drug at the interlocutory stage (*Roussel–UCLAF v JD Searle & Co* [1977] FSR 125).

It is quite possible for a plaintiff to have a very strong case on the merits but still lose at the interlocutory stage if the balance of convenience favours the defendant (or if the plaintiff cannot provide a satisfactory cross-undertaking in damages).

Special factors

Lord Diplock stated in *Cyanamid* that 'I would reiterate that, in addition to those to which I have referred, there may be many other special factors to take into consideration in the particular circumstances of individual cases'.

In certain special cases the court will apply 'special factors'. For example, the court will require the plaintiff to show a *prima facie* case 'being a stronger test than the "arguable case" test'. Examples are as follows:

(1) Trade union disputes: Section 7(2) of the Trade Union and Labour Relations Act 1974 specifically states that in any application for an interlocutory injunction, if the defendant was acting in contemplation or furtherance of a trade dispute, then the court must consider the likelihood of the defendant succeeding at the trial of the action in establishing the matters which would give rise to a defence. This is clearly a different approach from the normal *American Cyanamid* guidelines.

(2) If there is no dispute on the facts: it should not be necessary to apply the 'balance of convenience' test.

(3) In an action against a local authority: the local authority should only be restrained by an interlocutory injunction from exercising its statutory powers if the plaintiff can show that it has good prospects of succeeding at trial, and this will require a careful consideration of the merits of the plaintiff's case.

(4) In passing-off actions: for the obvious reason that an interlocutory injunction may force the defendant to change its name and invest time, money and effort in building up a reputation and goodwill under a new name and with a new business direction. The courts in certain cases have indicated that the strength of the plaintiff's case should be examined in greater depth than merely deciding whether there is a serious issue to be tried.

(5) Restraint of trade cases: sometimes an interlocutory injunction will have the practical effect of putting an end to the action because of the harm caused to the losing party by the grant or the refusal of the injunction application. Generally *American Cyanamid* guidelines should not apply where the case is unlikely to go to a trial.

In a series of recent restraint of trade cases, the Court of Appeal has considered whether the *American Cyanamid* principles should apply.

The following problems have been highlighted in these sorts of cases:

(1) The first main problem is that by reducing the burden on employers from showing a *prima facie* case to only an arguable case, this has permitted employers to obtain interlocutory injunctions in more instances than had previously been the case. The defendant may be temporarily, if not permanently, out of a job with a company in competition with the plaintiff.

(2) It cannot normally be established at an interlocutory hearing whether the defendant is, or is not, in breach of a restrictive covenant in his contract of employment. However, if he is ordered to leave the competing firm then competition may be stifled, and the ex-employee may be out of a job without the plaintiff being able to show that there had been a breach of covenant. The ex-employee will probably not get his job back by the time of the trial, therefore rendering any trial redundant unless the defendant wishes to pursue a claim for damages.

(3) Further, the plaintiff is likely to have deeper financial resources and the defendant will simply not be able to afford to proceed with the case to trial.

For these reasons, in cases where the plaintiff is seeking an injunction to enforce a restrictive covenant in an ex-employee's contract, the plaintiff will often need to show more than an arguable case and can expect a closer examination of the strength of his case than would have been the case if the court had followed conventional *American Cyanamid* guidelines.

The plaintiff will not only have to be confident of satisfying the criteria to obtain an interlocutory injunction but will also need to comply with the complicated practices and procedural rules which apply in respect of all interlocutory applications.

Practice and procedure

Should notice be given to the defendant of the application?

There are three types of interlocutory injunctions.

Ex parte injunctions

In most circumstances this will mean that no notice is given to the defendant of the application and he is not represented at the hearing of the plaintiff's application.

An application will be made *ex parte* only in cases of extreme urgency. The court must be satisfied that the delay caused by proceeding in the ordinary way, and giving sufficient notice to the defendant (ie giving the defendant two clear days' notice), would or might entail irreparable serious damage to the plaintiff.

The plaintiff must need the court's protection immediately, sometimes within hours. In certain situations there will also be a requirement of secrecy whereby the main reason for applying *ex parte* will be, not only urgency, but the need to prevent the defendant from having any notice of the application. Secrecy will be needed if, for example, there is a risk of destruction of documents or the removal of assets from the jurisdiction if the defendant receives notice of the application.

In certain situations there may be an *inter partes* hearing (with both parties represented) but due to the pressure of court business a full hearing cannot take place and the court is minded to adjourn the application. In this situation if the plaintiff cannot afford to wait for the adjourned hearing, then the plaintiff may apply *ex parte* and seek an interim injunction for a fixed and limited period of time, until the full *inter partes* hearing can take place on a date convenient to the court and to the parties. Such an application is referred to as being *ex parte* only because relief may be given by the courts in the absence of a full *inter partes* hearing and a full exchange of affidavit evidence.

Ex parte on notice

Certain applications may require urgency but no secrecy is required, ie the defendant is unlikely to do a wrongful act between the time of being notified of the application and the hearing of the application. Notice can be given to the defendant or the defendant's solicitors, shortly before the *ex parte* application is made. The plaintiff's solicitors will normally telephone the defendant's solicitors and ask for undertakings on the telephone within a short space of time, perhaps even within two hours. If no undertakings are forthcoming then the plaintiff's solicitors will notify the defendant's solicitors that an application will be made *ex parte* later that day (or the following day). The defendant can be represented at the hearing despite the fact that the application will strictly be an *ex parte* application.

In a trade union dispute statute requires that all reasonable steps must be taken for giving notice of the application to the relevant trade union, failing which the application cannot be heard.

Inter partes injunctions

If there is no desperate urgency, and the plaintiff can afford to wait several days for the injunction, then proper notice (ie two clear days) should be given to the defendant of the application, and the defendant should not only be represented at the hearing but should have sufficient time to prepare affidavit evidence prior to the hearing. If the plaintiff has been aware of the defendant's wrong-doing for some time (even a few days), then it will be difficult, if not impossible, for the plaintiff to justify an *ex parte* application.

General principles on *ex parte* applications

If the application is extremely urgent it can be made on the basis of affidavit evidence alone with an undertaking by the plaintiff to issue the formal application (in the form of a Notice of Motion or a summons) and the writ after the hearing. Alternatively, if the application is so urgent that there is no time to even prepare affidavit evidence then the plaintiff's solicitors and Counsel can simply take any relevant documents to the court and make the application by presenting those documents to the court. In such a case the plaintiff's solicitors must undertake to swear an affidavit forthwith after the hearing setting out all facts and documents disclosed to the court.

Ex parte applications should be made not only promptly and without delay, but a plaintiff must also ensure that all the material facts are laid before the court. *Ex parte* injunctions will usually be interim injunctions and the court will fix an interim return date when there will be a full *inter partes* hearing. Alternatively, the court may order that the defendant can apply to discharge the injunction on giving 24 hours' or 48 hours' notice to the plaintiff.

Which division of the High Court?

The High Court has three divisions: Chancery Division, Queen's Bench Division and Family Division. There are also various different sections within the divisions. For example, the Queen's Bench Division has a Commercial Court (specialising in commercial and banking matters) and an Official Referees Court (specialising in cases of complicated technical evidence, such as construction cases and computer cases). The Chancery Division, for example, has a special Companies Court which will deal with all winding-up petitions.

The Chancery Division will deal with, *inter alia*, patents, registered designs, copyright cases, passing off, bankruptcy, the sale of real property, the execution of trusts and all matters involving the High Court jurisdiction under the various Companies Acts.

The Queen's Bench Division deals with personal injury cases, applications for judicial review, Admiralty cases and the majority of contractual disputes.

Differences in procedure between the Chancery Division and Queen's Bench Division

Chancery Division
Inter partes hearings Applications will be made by issuing a Notice of Motion and will be heard in an open court. The hearing will therefore be open to the public and the press. It is possible for the hearing to be *in camera*, if, for example, an application is made for an Anton Piller order (a search and seize order: see p 315).

When serving a Notice of Motion at least two clear days' notice must be given to the defendant. For example, if a Notice of Motion is served before 4.00 pm on Tuesday, then Wednesday and Thursday will be the clear days and the Motion may be heard on Friday at the earliest. On the first hearing day of the Notice of Motion (the return date) the court will only hear applications which will not last for more than two hours.

If the application is likely to exceed two hours then the Motion will be adjourned as a 'Motion by Order' to the earliest available date. Further, if there has been insufficient time for the defendant to prepare any affidavit evidence, the application will be adjourned to be heard at a later date and the court will give directions for the exchange of affidavit evidence before the matter can be heard.

The plaintiff must lodge two copies of the writ and two copies of the Notice of Motion.

In most cases, therefore, the first return date of an *inter partes* application will be treated as an application for directions from the court and will not be an effective hearing. If a motion is adjourned as a 'Motion by Order' then a certificate, signed by all Counsel concerned, of the estimated length of the hearing, must be lodged with the Clerk of the Lists before the date of the hearing of the Motion can be fixed.

Ex parte hearings   As regards *ex parte* applications, these can be heard in the Chancery Division at 10.30 am and 2.00 pm each day or, if urgent, during the course of the day. There is no need to lodge any papers with the court before the hearing but the plaintiff's solicitors should notify the Clerk to the Motions Judge or, if he cannot be reached, the Listing Clerk that an application will be made.

Queen's Bench Division

Inter partes hearings   All hearings will be in Chambers and so they are private and will avoid publicity. Applications will be made by issuing a summons and, as in the case of a Notice of Motion in the Chancery Division, at least two clear days' notice should be given to the defendant. On the first hearing date the court will only hear applications of up to 30 minutes, failing which a special appointment must be obtained from the Judge in Chambers. It is possible to obtain a special appointment when the summons is first issued thereby avoiding the necessity of the first hearing date being adjourned. In both Divisions, Saturdays, Sundays, Bank Holidays, Christmas Day and Good Friday do not count as clear days.

In the Queen's Bench Division, applications will be in Room 98 of the High Court, and in the Commercial Court before a Commercial Judge in Chambers.

The plaintiff must lodge before the hearing the pleadings (if any), affidavits, summons, an estimate of the length of the hearing and any relevant order made in the action.

These papers must be lodged at least two days before a general list appointment (ie not more than 30 minutes) or five days before a special appointment. Affidavits used at previous hearings should be bespoken from the court and new affidavits lodged.

Ex parte hearings *Ex parte* applications will be heard at 10.00 am and 2.00 pm each day. If an application is made at 10.00 am then the relevant papers (being the writ, affidavit evidence and draft minutes of order) must be lodged with the court by 3.00 pm the previous day. If, in a case of even greater urgency, the application must be made that day, the papers should be lodged with the court by 9.30 am (for a 10.00 am hearing) or before 12.30 pm (for a 2.00 pm hearing). In cases of extreme urgency, where the shorter time scale applies then the plaintiff's Counsel will have to certify that such a short timetable is appropriate.

Ex parte applications outside normal court hours

The normal court hours are from 10.00 am until 4.00 pm. In certain situations *ex parte* applications can be made outside court hours, for example, to prevent circulations of newspapers to the public in the morning. The High Court operates a duty judge system. A judge will be on call overnight and the plaintiff can telephone a High Court security number. The duty judge will have jurisdiction to hear applications in all Divisions and can, if necessary, hear the application at his private residence or anywhere he chooses. If the injunction is extremely urgent, the judge, if he is on duty overnight, can even grant an injunction over the telephone.

Exchange of affidavit evidence

Affidavit evidence must set out the facts in support of each party's case and (in respect of the plaintiff's affidavit evidence) the facts giving rise to the necessity for interlocutory relief. The party should swear the affidavit evidence, and in the case of a plaintiff company, the affidavit should if possible be sworn by a director of the company with first hand knowledge of the relevant facts. If this is impossible or inconvenient then the solicitor may swear the affidavit, but he should confirm why it is inconvenient for the party to swear it. The deponent to the affidavit must confirm the source of his information and belief when stating all facts outside his knowledge.

The defendant must normally have enough time to serve affidavit evidence in reply to the plaintiff's affidavits before the effective hearing.

If he has insufficient time to do so, then the defendant will ask the court to adjourn the hearing of the plaintiff's application to allow the defendant sufficient time to prepare affidavit evidence in reply.

The plaintiff may swear further affidavit evidence in rejoinder to the defendant's affidavit evidence, and the exchange of affidavit evidence can continue up to the hearing date. After the first return date, if the application has been adjourned to be heard at a later date, the court will probably give directions for the exchange of affidavit evidence and if either party wishes to serve any affidavits in addition to those ordered in the directions, then leave will be required from the court.

In the Queen's Bench Division a special appointment can be obtained when the summons is issued, and the first hearing date should therefore be effective. However, in the Chancery Division, if the application is to last more than two hours, the application is likely to be ineffective at the first hearing.

Obtaining a hearing date

The difficulty in obtaining an effective hearing date is one of the main obstacles to a plaintiff obtaining speedy injunctive relief. It is very often the case that on the first hearing date, in both the Chancery and the Queen's Bench Divisions, the application will have to be adjourned for one of the following reasons:

(a) insufficient time to hear the application; or
(b) even if the hearing is estimated to last within the specified time restrictions, the court may have numerous other cases in the list to be heard that day and the plaintiff's application will have to be relisted to be heard on another date;
(c) the parties have not had sufficient time to exchange affidavit evidence and so the court will give appropriate directions.

If the first hearing is adjourned for any of the above reasons, it can often be several weeks, or even months (particularly in the Chancery Division) before a suitable date can be found when the court has sufficient time to hear the application and when Counsel for both parties is available. In these circumstances a plaintiff must rely on being able to persuade the court that his application is so urgent that some form of interim injunction should be granted at the first hearing until the application can be heard at a later date.

The discharge of injunctions before trial

An interim or interlocutory injunction can be discharged at any time on the application of the defendant or any interested party or, in the case of an *ex parte* order obtained improperly, by the court exercising its discretion at any subsequent *inter partes* hearing. However, the courts now generally prefer not to discharge an interlocutory injunction (particularly if it was granted at an *inter partes* hearing) before the trial of the case and so the defendant in these circumstances may have to wait until the trial to apply for a discharge of the injunction.

Examples of possible grounds for a discharge of the injunction are as follows.

(1) Non-disclosure of material facts: there is a long line of cases whereby the courts have held that any order must be discharged if the plaintiff has failed to make full disclosure of any material matters at an *ex parte* hearing.

(2) The defendant, in certain circumstances, may have new evidence and be able to satisfy the court that the plaintiff, when it obtained the *ex parte* injunction, failed to show that there was a serious issue to be tried (or, in special cases, that it had a *prima facie* case). In the case of a Mareva injunction, which will be considered in more detail at p 305, if the defendant can show that there is no risk of its assets being moved from the jurisdiction or being dissipated, or that the continuing effect of the injunction is oppressive, the Mareva injunction can be discharged.

(3) In the event that the law has changed (perhaps as a result of a recent decision from the Court of Appeal) since the date of the injunction.

(4) An injunction can be discharged if circumstances have changed since the date the injunctive relief was given.

(5) If the plaintiff has failed to pursue its case to trial expeditiously: for example, the plaintiff has sat back and allowed the damaging effects of the injunction to take effect, without pursuing the case to trial.

(6) If the injunction was granted on terms and those terms have not been fulfilled, for example, if the plaintiff has breached any of its undertakings to the court (to issue a writ forthwith or serve papers personally on the defendants), the injunction may be discharged.

(7) If the defendant has doubts about the undertaking as to damages, an application to discharge may be made.

However, in all of these cases, the defendant should be aware of the plaintiff's ability to immediately apply for a fresh injunction if the previous injunction is discharged. For example, an interlocutory injunction may be discharged on the grounds of non-disclosure of material facts but the plaintiff may then be able to demonstrate, at the conclusion of the same hearing, before the same judge, an urgent requirement for a fresh injunction, upon identical or similar terms.

Appeals

At the hearing of the interlocutory application, if the court dismisses the application for the interlocutory injunction, then the plaintiff can appeal to the Court of Appeal. In this situation, the court must decide whether the successful party (the defendant) ought to be free to act despite the pending hearing of an appeal. The court must balance the need to avoid granting an injunction which would inflict greater hardship on the defendant, with the need to make sure that the plaintiff's appeal (if it is successful) is not unenforceable because of irredeemable action taken by the defendant in the interim period.

The appeal against interlocutory decisions, if urgent, can sometimes be heard within hours. For example, in the case of *Gouriet v Union of Post Office Workers* [1977] QB 79, the plaintiff issued a writ and applied for an injunction at 3.45 pm on a Friday afternoon. The judge rejected the plaintiff's application at 5.30 pm. The Court of Appeal sat at 10.30 am the following Saturday morning and granted the plaintiff an interlocutory injunction.

The plaintiff's cross-undertaking and enquiry into damages

General points

Generally the undertaking by the plaintiff as to damages ought to be given on every interlocutory injunction. The court must consider the essential justice of the plaintiff's case. Even if the plaintiff has limited financial ability, the plaintiff may, in certain circumstances, still be able to obtain the injunction even if the cross-undertaking in damages is of limited value.

If the plaintiff is outside the jurisdiction the plaintiff may well be asked to give some form of security to the court, by lodging a sum of money with the court, in order to support the cross-undertaking in damages. Any injunction is likely, in these circumstances, to be conditional on the plaintiff providing the security within a specified time limit.

Even if the plaintiff is within the jurisdiction, security may still have to be given in order to fortify the cross-undertaking.

Enforceability

The undertaking is enforceable, when the court orders an enquiry as to damages that are due to be paid to the defendant. This will arise in the following circumstances:

(a) if the plaintiff has failed at trial;
(b) if the injunction is discharged before trial on the defendant's application; or
(c) if the defendant appeals after the trial against the injunction being given and the appeal is successful.

The timing of the enquiry into damages

The enquiry will usually be made after the trial even if an injunction is discharged at an interlocutory stage as there will be no final finding of facts.

In certain circumstances the defendant may pursue an enquiry into damages before the trial if the defendant can establish that the injunction should never have been granted in the first place and the judge is satisfied that the position will not change after discovery of documents.

An enquiry into damages will almost invariably be ordered if an injunction is discharged.

On the enquiry the defendant should be compensated by being paid all approximate and natural damages arising from the plaintiff's undertaking, in the same way as if there had been a breach of contract by the plaintiff and the defendant is being compensated for all damages arising from the breach of contract. To obtain an award of damages the defendant must establish a *prima facie* case that the injunction was the exclusive or primary cause of the damage it has suffered.

Sanctions

If the defendant breaches an injunction the defendant will be in contempt of court. The plaintiff can commence committal proceedings to commit the defendant to prison as long as the plaintiff has satisfied certain procedural requirements. If the defendant is a company, the injunction should be endorsed with a Penal Notice warning a director of the company of the consequences of failing to comply with the terms of the injunction and then the order must be served on that director personally. It is also possible to commence committal proceedings against aiders and abettors of a breach of an injunction and not solely against the defendant. Personal service of the injunction order should also be effected against any individual defendant, and the order should again be endorsed with a Penal Notice addressed to that defendant.

Any individual defendant, or director of a defendant company, served with an injunction endorsed with a Penal Notice can therefore be sent to prison for a fixed or indefinite period of time until the contempt of court is purged.

In many cases, a defendant may decide to give undertaking(s) to the court, in identical or similar terms to the injunction(s) sought by the plaintiff, rather than contest the plaintiff's application. Any undertakings given to the court, by the defendant, are treated as 'voluntary injunctions' and a breach of an undertaking to the court by a defendant attracts the same sanctions as a breach of an injunction. Furthermore, personal service of the injunction on the individual defendant, or a director of a defendant company, will not be necessary if undertakings are given voluntarily to the court, or if the defendant is present in court when the injunction was made.

Generally, when a Motion for Committal is heard, the court will usually fine the person in contempt and only in rare cases will he/she be sent to prison.

Finally, when an injunction is obtained *ex parte*, it should be served personally on the defendant company's registered office, and not in the post (Ord 45, r 7 of the Rules of the Supreme Court).

Interlocutory costs orders

When the court hears an application for an interlocutory injunction the court is not in a position to decide the final outcome of the case. For this reason the court does not automatically adopt a 'winner takes all' attitude and accordingly the following options are available to the court:

(1) *'Costs in the cause'*   The costs of the interlocutory proceedings will be paid by the losing party at the trial of the action when the final award of costs is made.

(2) *'Plaintiff's costs in the cause'*   If the plaintiff is awarded costs at the trial these will automatically include the costs of the interlocutory proceedings. However, if the plaintiff loses at trial each party will pay its own costs in relation to the previous interlocutory proceedings. The same applies in reverse if the order is 'defendant's costs in the cause'.

(3) *'Plaintiff's costs in any event'*   No matter what award is made at trial, when the case is finally decided, or settled, the plaintiff will be paid the costs of the interlocutory proceedings by the defendant or vice versa if the order is 'defendant's costs in any event'.

(4) '*Plaintiff's costs forthwith*' This means that the defendant must pay the plaintiff's costs immediately without waiting for the outcome of the trial of the action. Such orders are rare. The same applies in reverse if the order is 'defendant's costs forthwith'.

(5) '*Costs reserved*' The court has decided not to deal with costs at the conclusion of the interlocutory application and instead the judge at a subsequent hearing will be expected to decide who should be responsible for these costs.

(6) '*No order as to costs*' Each side pays its own costs and will not be able to recover these costs at a later date whatever the outcome of the trial of the case.

The position is more straightforward when the court determines responsibility for costs at the conclusion of a trial. In the vast majority of cases the trial judge will order either the plaintiff or defendant to be responsible for the other's costs. The judge can order the losing party to pay only a proportion of the successful party's costs, for example two-thirds or a half. There may be some tinkering with this to the extent necessary to reflect orders made on interlocutory applications before the trial.

In the majority of interlocutory applications, if the plaintiff succeeds, the usual order will be 'plaintiff's costs in cause', and if the plaintiff fails the usual order is 'the defendant's costs in cause'.

If the action never comes to a trial, and the case settles after the interlocutory proceedings, or at any other stage before trial, then it is unlikely that the successful party at the conclusion of the interlocutory proceedings will be paid its costs by the other party, depending of course on the terms of settlement.

A plaintiff should bear in mind, that if it simply discontinues the action at any stage in the proceedings it will have to pay all of the defendant's costs to date and honour its undertaking as to damages.

Some additional relevant points regarding costs are as follows:

(1) The court may order a party to pay costs on an indemnity basis, for example if the plaintiff pursued an application totally unreasonably or without any merit. This will usually mean that the plaintiff will pay the whole of the defendant's costs (or vice-versa as the case may be), as long as they have been reasonably incurred, whereas if a party pays costs 'on the standard basis' (the usual basis for costs) the successful party will probably recover only about 75 per cent of its costs after they have been taxed by the court.

(2) If the court does order costs to be paid by the losing party, the

costs will be taxed (assessed) by the courts, unless the parties can agree on the amount of costs between them.

(3) In any proceedings where a defendant makes a 'without prejudice' offer, for example to give certain undertakings to the court, the defendant can state in the letter that the offer is being made 'without prejudice save as to costs'. This means that the defendant reserves the right to make submissions on costs to the court if the without prejudice offer is rejected and the court makes an order on terms similar to those offered in the without prejudice letter.

Security for costs

A defendant can obtain an order for security for costs against any plaintiff who is ordinarily resident out of the jurisdiction of the courts. Security cannot be obtained from a defendant unless he has filed a counterclaim and then only in respect of the likely costs incurred in defending that counterclaim. Security for costs is not automatic against a foreign plaintiff and the court will consider the likelihood of the plaintiff succeeding at trial. Furthermore, the rule may be relaxed in the case of plaintiffs normally resident within the European Community. Security for costs can also be obtained on other limited grounds, for example if it can be shown that the plaintiff is in financial difficulty and is likely to be unable to pay any costs order in favour of the other party at trial.

Summary

It can be seen that there are many obstacles a plaintiff has to overcome in order to obtain an injunction speedily in the English courts. Even if he has not only an arguable case, but also a very strong case on the merits, he must be able to:

(a) support the cross-undertaking in damages;
(b) satisfy the court that the balance of convenience favours the grant of an injunction;
(c) obtain an early hearing date after affidavits have been exchanged with the defendant, unless an interim injunction can be obtained at the first hearing 'for directions' or relief can be obtained on an *ex parte* basis.

Mareva injunctions

Introduction

A Mareva injunction is the means of preventing a defendant dissipating or concealing his assets so as to make a judgment against him worthless or difficult to enforce. In England the origins of this type of injunction arose in 1975 in the case of the *Mareva Compañia Naviera SA v International Bulkcarriers SA* [1981] and [1975] 2 Lloyds Rep 509, (CA). Applications are almost always made *ex parte*.

The Mareva injunction has been described as one of the two nuclear weapons of the law by Donaldson LJ (*Bank Mellat v Mohammed Ebrahim Nikpour* [1982] Com LR 158). It enables the seizure of assets so as to preserve them for the benefit of the creditors. It does not give any charge in favour of any particular creditor, including the plaintiff. There is no priority given over other creditors.

The practice of giving Mareva injunctions has now expanded from cases where there was a risk of foreign defendants transferring assets abroad (as in the original Mareva case) to cases involving the assets of any person or company, foreign or otherwise. The procedure has received the recognition and approval of Parliament. Section 37(3) of the Supreme Court Act 1981 provides as follows:

The power of the High Court . . . to grant an interlocutory injunction restraining a party to any proceeding from removing from the jurisdiction of the High Court, or otherwise dealing with, assets located within that jurisdiction shall be exercisable in cases where that party is, as well as in cases where he is not, domiciled, resident or present within that jurisdiction.

The words 'otherwise dealing with' will cover any case where there is a danger that the assets will be decimated within the jurisdiction as well as removed out of the jurisdiction. A Mareva should be granted where it appears likely that the plaintiff would recover judgment against a defendant for a certain or approximate sum and there are reasons to believe that the defendant has assets within the jurisdiction to meet the judgment, wholly or in part, but might deal with them, whether by removal out of the jurisdiction or disposing of them within the jurisdiction so that they were not available or traceable when the judgment was given against him.

Mareva injunctions now have enormous benefits for a plaintiff in that they protect the prospective fruits of litigation. In commercial litigation the emphasis has now moved away from trials towards interlocutory proceedings. The Motions List in the Chancery Division, as well as the

Judge in Chambers List in the Queen's Bench Division, is full of applications for obtaining, varying and discharging Mareva injunctions. The ease with which plaintiffs can obtain Mareva injunctions has been exacerbated by the following factors.

(1) There will usually be no trial or final judgment in most cases and so the evidence set out in the affidavits will never be tested under cross-examination or at trial. A judge will base his decision on the facts set out in a plaintiff's affidavit at the initial *ex parte* hearing. It is extremely hard for a defendant to later contradict the facts set out in the plaintiff's affidavit to the extent where he must not only weaken the plaintiff's case but actually destroy it in order to show the plaintiff does not even have a good arguable case. The courts may well be reluctant to even entertain an application to discharge a Mareva if only the 'balance of convenience' test is being challenged.

(2) The plaintiff's solicitor, by diligently policing the Mareva, can significantly restrict the defendant's business. The plaintiff's solicitor will have the ability to refuse consent to any variation of the order which would allow any unusual payments by the defendant for non-business purposes.

(3) If the plaintiff's solicitor does refuse consent for certain payments the defendants will have to make an application to vary the Mareva which may be difficult and it may take time to obtain a hearing date. The plaintiff's solicitor may consent to the payment shortly before the hearing date, if he fears that the Mareva will be varied, but in the mean time the plaintiff's solicitor may have caused considerable damage to the defendant's business by the delay.

(4) The defendant's solicitor in turn, must consider very carefully the question of 'what is an asset?' when advising the defendant who will be at risk of being in contempt of court if he deals in or disposes of any asset which he did not believe, or was not advised, came within the ambit of the Mareva order.

However, Mareva injunctions should comprise adjacent proceedings and should not be treated by a plaintiff as a substitute for a full trial of the case. The plaintiff must proceed speedily with the case after obtaining a Mareva. In the case of *Lloyds Bowmaker Ltd v Britannia Arrow Holdings plc* (1987) *The Times*, 19 March the Mareva was discharged as the plaintiff's solicitors had still not set the case down for trial two and a half years after obtaining the Mareva.

The basic principles for obtaining a Mareva injunction

The basic rules of procedure for obtaining any *ex parte* injunction, as explained above, apply to Mareva cases as they do to other types of *ex parte* injunctions. However there are additional guidelines and features to be noted. The Court of Appeal has suggested the following guidelines in the case of *Third Chandris Shipping Corporation v Unimarine SA* [1979] QB 645 at 668:

(a) the plaintiff must make full and frank disclosure of all material matters;

(b) the plaintiff must set out particulars of his claims against the defendant and must clearly state the points which are likely to be made against these claims by the defendant. If the defendant is being asked to disclose documents, the affidavit should address itself to the possibility of the defendant being able to rely on the privilege against self-incrimination;

(c) the plaintiff must have a good arguable claim for a certain or approximate sum;

(d) the plaintiff must state why he believes the defendant has assets in the UK;

(e) full details must be given as to the belief that there is a risk of the assets being removed (or dissipated);

(f) the plaintiff must give a cross-undertaking in damages to be supported by a bond or security as may be necessary.

The Mareva injunction takes effect from the moment it is pronounced, on every asset of the defendant which it covers. Everybody notified of the injunction must take whatever steps necessary to preserve the defendant's assets. If anybody with knowledge of the injunction does not preserve the defendant's assets he may be guilty of contempt of court ie interfering with the course of justice.

Guidelines for the plaintiff to give full and frank disclosure to the court

Guidelines for giving full and frank disclosure were given by the Court of Appeal in 1987 in *Brink's Mat v Elcombe* (1987) *The Independent*, 25 June. The enquiries which the plaintiff should make will depend on the circumstances of each case.

(1) If there has been a breach of any of the duties of a plaintiff to make full and frank disclosure, the court must deprive the plaintiff of any advantage derived from a breach of the duty of disclosure.

(2) In relation to any application to discharge the Mareva by a defendant based on non-disclosure of material facts the success of such an application will depend on the importance of the facts to the issues to be decided.

(3) If there is an application to discharge a Mareva the courts may continue the Mareva or alternatively discharge it. If it is discharged the plaintiff can immediately apply for a new Mareva as soon as the defendant's application to discharge has been concluded and the court does have a discretion to grant a new Mareva if the circumstances require it.

(4) The materiality of facts must be decided by the courts and not the plaintiff and its lawyers.

Although the plaintiff does have a paramount duty to disclose all material facts when applying for a Mareva injunction the court does have a discretion to uphold a Mareva even if there has been a misrepresentation. In *Lagenes Ltd v It's At (UK) Ltd* (1987) *The Times*, 12 March the court held that it had a discretion to refuse or discharge an *ex parte* order which had been obtained on the basis of misleading statements even when those statements had not been made innocently. In this case the defendants applied to discharge certain *ex parte* injunctions, including a Mareva, obtained by the plaintiff on the grounds that each of them was granted upon material non-disclosure and/or material misrepresentation by the plaintiffs in respect of their profitability and financial affairs.

Statements had been given in support of the plaintiff's cross-undertaking in damages. While some of the statements could not be characterised as innocent misrepresentation the court was not prepared, in the absence of cross-examination of the deponent, to find that there had been an attempt deliberately to mislead the court. However, the court did find that the misleading statements were grossly negligent and highly reprehensible. Subsequently the plaintiff apologised to the court and provided a bond for £125,000 in favour of the defendant in respect of costs and the cross-undertaking in damages.

Having examined all the facts, the Court of Appeal decided that the Court of First Instance, when making the original order, could have made the same Mareva order which it did in fact make, if proper disclosure had been made and that if adequate security had been given by the plaintiffs then the same order would almost certainly have been made.

The Court of Appeal decided that it would be wholly disproportionate to the plaintiffs' offence of providing inadequate information as to its financial circumstances, to discharge the Mareva order and therefore remove the protection to the plaintiffs afforded by the Mareva.

This is an important decision and demonstrates the wide discretion that the court has on all interlocutory applications. The principle of proportionality as to the plaintiff's failure to give full and frank disclosure and the potential harm to the plaintiff if the Mareva is discharged is an important one.

Practical guidelines relating to banks

The Mareva takes effect on banks, from the moment it is served, on every asset of the defendant which will be covered by the terms of the Mareva. Everyone acknowledging a Mareva has to do what he reasonably can to preserve such assets or else he will be guilty of contempt of court as an act of interference with the course of justice if he assists in their disposal.

Priority over customers
The receipt by a bank of notice of a Mareva which affects a customer's account, means the bank may override the customer's instructions regarding that account and makes it unlawful for the bank to honour the customer's cheques.

Identifying the accounts
The bank must be told with as much certainty as possible what it has to do. The plaintiff should identify the bank accounts by specifying the branch and number and type of the account or any other asset with as much precision as possible. In practice the plaintiff's solicitors will probably telephone the bank as soon as a Mareva is obtained and follow up the telephone call with a letter sent by facsimile both to the relevant branch and to the Head Office. The Head Office of the bank will probably carry out a search in other branches to ascertain whether any other account is held by the defendant. If a request is made to the bank to conduct a search to ascertain whether assets of the defendant are held by any of the bank's branches, then the plaintiff's solicitor should give an undertaking to pay the bank's costs in doing so when obtaining the Mareva. The plaintiff should also inform the courts of the names of the banks to whom notice will be given.

The Mareva should specify the maximum amount claimed by the plaintiff and therefore the maximum value of the defendant's assets which should be frozen. The assets may consist solely of the money in the defendant's bank account or a combination of money in the bank and other assets.

Expenses

However, the defendant must be given the use of funds for 'normal living expenses', and/or 'normal business expenses' and the Mareva should specify the relevant amount and a special account should be opened. For normal living expenses approximately £600 per week is an amount frequently specified to be paid to a defendant depending on his anticipated or main outgoings. It should be noted that the Mareva can extend to the money the defendant has in a joint account. The Mareva will also attach to money held in a bank account in a foreign currency but the bank should convert this money to sterling at the buying rate and freeze the relevant equivalent sterling amount of the money held.

The defendant should also be able to pay certain money from his bank accounts to his solicitors for legal costs although again a limit may be imposed.

Letter of credit

Money paid under the terms of a Letter of Credit should only be frozen if the money is paid into the account(s) which is (are) the subject of the Mareva. However, in situations other than money being paid into the frozen account, a bank must honour the terms of a Letter of Credit which involve contractual obligations to third parties.

Cheque guarantee card

Similarly, a bank must honour payments made to third parties, prior to the date of service of the order, under a cheque guarantee card. After service of the order, the bank should, if possible, take steps to cancel the card or the order should provide for the bank being able to cancel the card.

The position of third parties in relation to frozen accounts

A third party can probably interfere if its rights are substantially and unwarrantedly interfered with.

When a third party asserts rights to an asset frozen by a Mareva injunction the court can either order an investigation of the third party's rights as a preliminary issue or it may decide not to make any interlocutory decision pending the outcome of the trial of the case.

Third party creditors

Generally the Mareva should only be varied to allow a payment to a third party creditor where:

(a) cheques are drawn to an account which is in credit at the date of the injunction;
(b) if there is evidence to show the state of the account at the date of the injunction; and
(c) if the third party has an outstanding debt due to be paid by the defendant.

The third party must therefore prove that prior to the injunction the third party creditor had an existing right to be paid from that particular source. It would normally be in these circumstances that a third party creditor would be able to successfully apply to vary the Mareva: the right of a third party creditor in relation to a contract with the defendant should normally prevail over the plaintiff's desire to seize the defendant's assets to protect himself prior to the day of judgment.

Banks

Therefore a bank, upon whom a Mareva is served, will be entitled to intervene and ask for the injunction to be varied if it wishes to enforce contractual rights against the funds which came into being prior to the injunction, generally without having to make full disclosure as to the state of the defendant's accounts with the bank (the *Oceanica* case in 1983).

This case also held that:

(a) a bank can apply to vary the injunction in order to exercise its usual right of set-off in respect of principal and interest due on loans to a defendant company subjected to a Mareva;
(b) a bank would be allowed to meet any liabilities which it may incur on confirmed letters of credit opened at the request of the defendant before notification of the injunction.

Orders made ancillary to a Mareva

In addition to the basic Mareva order itself (which will freeze the defendant's assets), a plaintiff will usually obtain various ancillary orders as follows.

An order for discovery

The defendant will be ordered to file an affidavit making full disclosure of all his assets. This will normally be limited to the defendant's English assets. Defendants will not normally be made to disclose particulars of their foreign assets unless there are special grounds such as where the plaintiff's claim relates to the ownership of certain assets.

Ignorance of all of the defendant's assets by a plaintiff should not be allowed to inhibit the purpose of the Mareva order and so discovery is an essential component of all Mareva orders.

Tracing orders

The court can make interlocutory orders designed specifically to ascertain the whereabouts of assets. For example, the court can order interrogatories (in the form of questions about the defendant's assets) to be served on the defendant which must be answered by the defendant or, (in the case of a defendant company) by its employees or directors.

The difficulty of tracing funds is recognised by the courts and tracing orders can be given in wide terms. In one case a firm of accountants was instructed to prepare a schedule setting out the identity and whereabouts of all assets, including property and money, wherever they were located, held or retained by one of the defendants who had to pay the accountants' fees and co-operate fully with their investigation.

Delivery up of property

This will only be ordered if there is some evidence or inference that the property has been acquired by the defendant as a result of his wrong doing, and that the defendant, unless there is an order for delivery up, is likely to dispose of the property.

An order for cross-examination of the defendant

In cases where the defendants appear determined to put their assets beyond the reach of the plaintiffs then a defendant can be cross-examined on the affidavits which he has filed (for example in relation to discovery) so that the court can ascertain the true extent and location of their assets. Such an order is extremely rare.

Limits on Marevas

Marevas will not usually be granted for the purposes of executing a judgment but a Mareva can be continued to assist in the execution of a judgment. It is only possible to apply for a Mareva after a judgment has been given if the plaintiff can produce evidence that the defendant intends to dispose of, or dissipate, his assets after the judgment has been given.

The defendant, if he wishes to obtain a discharge of a Mareva, can offer to pay money into court or provide a bond or guarantee that the plaintiff's debts will be met. This is often an effective way for defendants to dispose of a Mareva.

The plaintiff should also be aware of the possible defences open to a defendant seeking to challenge a Mareva:

(1) A defendant can argue that the plaintiff did not have a good arguable case or failed to disclose material facts or failed to demonstrate that there was sufficient evidence of any risk of the defendant disposing of or dissipating his assets.

(2) A defendant can argue that the continuing effects of a Mareva are oppressive and the court would then consider the 'balance of convenience' and whether the hardship of the grant of the Mareva outweighs any advantage to the plaintiff.

The plaintiff will also need to show to the court that the defendant has assets of approximate value to the value of his claim. If a plaintiff has a very large claim and the defendant has fairly insignificant assets then there will be no purpose in obtaining a Mareva.

International Marevas

A Mareva can extend to assets outside the jurisdiction in exceptional cases (see for example *Babanaft International SA v Bassatne* [1990] Ch 13; [1989] 1 All ER 433; [1989] 2 WLR 232, CA; (1988) *The Times*, 2 July). In the *Babanaft* case the Court of Appeal confirmed that English courts could grant a Mareva type injunction affecting assets held abroad. The Court of Appeal stated that such cases might be rare and it was held that:

(1) Even in the case of an injunction granted after judgment it should not be unqualified so as to affect foreign third parties. If it did this would involve an exorbitant exertion of extra-territorial jurisdiction over foreign third parties and as such the injunction could not be controlled or policed by the English courts.

(2) A Mareva extending to assets abroad could state that third parties will not be affected by the injunction.

(3) The injunction may be qualified by a provision stating that the

third parties will not be affected by the injunction save to the extent that the injunction may be enforced by the relevant local courts.

The following principles emerge from the leading cases on worldwide Marevas (*Republic of Haiti v Duvalier* [1989] 1 All ER 456 CA; *Derby & Co Ltd v Weldon* [1989] 2 WLR 276 and the *Babanaft* case):

(1) Third parties should not be affected by the terms of the order or have to make enquiries whether any instruction given by a defendant is or is not a breach of the order by the defendant.

(2) The English assets must be wholly insufficient to afford protection and there is a high risk of disposal of foreign assets.

(3) The defendants, such as the Duvalier family, should be sophisticated operators, with an ability to render assets untraceable and a determination not to reveal them.

(4) There should be no oppression of the defendants and exposure to a multiplicity of proceedings should be avoided.

(5) The defendants should be protected against the misuse of information gained from the ordinary order for disclosure in the Mareva.

(6) There can also be a worldwide Tracing order and so, in any international Mareva, the defendant can be ordered to disclose all his foreign assets.

(7) There have been various *Derby & Co Ltd v Weldon* cases. In *Derby & Co* (No 3) the court held that even if the defendant did not have any assets in the UK jurisdiction at all this would not necessarily be a bar to a world-wide Mareva. The court stated that there must be a prospect of the international element being recognised and enforced where the foreign assets were located. It was important that the court should not act in vain.

The damaging effects of Mareva injunctions

Based on these guidelines, the increasing willingness of the English courts to grant international Marevas should help to make London a more attractive forum for international litigation. However, Mareva orders can also be extremely damaging to a defendant's business and hinder the defendant's ability to defend the main action.

In practice banks will often freeze all accounts which they suspect may be within the ambit of the order. The banks will take a very cautious approach in respect of the defendant's ability to 'make payments in the ordinary course of business'.

The legal costs of an application to vary or discharge a Mareva can often be crippling. In cases involving Mareva injunctions there is usually an uncontrollable costs escalator and the defendant's solicitors will often ask for substantial payments of money on account of costs. If the plaintiff's solicitors refuse to consent to substantial drawings from the plaintiff's bank accounts towards legal costs, this will in practice make the case extremely difficult for the defendant to defend.

Banks are probably in need of some form of statutory protection in relation to their compliance with Mareva orders which they do not presently have. It may well be that, in future, the courts will provide for defendants to apply *ex parte* to vary Mareva orders to make certain payments, in urgent circumstances, to prevent abuse of the order by the plaintiff's solicitors. At present, the defendant's counsel usually advise against any applications to vary a Mareva being made *ex parte*.

Anton Piller orders

Introduction

Anton Piller orders allow a plaintiff to search the premises of a defendant with a view to locating and identifying, and, if appropriate, seizing infringing items or documents or evidence of the defendant's unlawful activities.

The original case is *Anton Piller KG v Manufacturing Process Ltd* (1976) Ch 55 and [1976] 1 All ER 779. In the original Anton Piller case three essential points were made:

(a) that orders should only be made in extreme circumstances;
(b) that they should be executed with great care by a solicitor of the Supreme Court;
(c) every opportunity must be afforded to the defendant to protect himself and to allow him to seek to discharge the order if he believes it has been wrongly obtained.

These three primary safeguards of the defendant have been questioned and clarified many times in recent years by the courts in order to ensure that these safeguards are as effective as they were intended to be.

An Anton Piller order is an order for the detention or preservation of the subject matter of the cause of action and the documents and articles relating to it. The plaintiff can enter the defendant's premises and search for and seize material documents and articles. The plaintiff cannot enter the defendant's premises by force and therefore the defendant has to consent to the search and seizure order being executed. They are often used in intellectual property pirating cases and in cases where employees of a company have been making secret profits from the company. Allegations of conspiracy to defraud are often made by plaintiffs applying for these orders.

The orders are always made *ex parte*, without any notice being given to the recipients. The discretion to grant an Anton Piller order is an exceptional power and is designed to deal with rogues who are unlikely to comply with any order for discovery or any *inter partes* interlocutory procedures honestly and are likely to remove or destroy evidence if they receive any notice of proceedings being issued against them. An Anton Piller order is a quick and effective way of obtaining relief, frequently accompanied by a Mareva injunction freezing the defendant's assets, and defendants rarely have sufficient financial resources and a case of substantive merit to be able to fight the action to a trial after the Anton Piller order has been executed. An Anton Piller order was intended as a wholly exceptional device but has now become quite common. It is estimated that between 50 and 100 Anton Piller orders a year at least have been made since 1980.

The evidence required and the four hurdles

In the *Anton Piller* case it was stated that an order should only be made in a case of necessity, where it is essential for justice to be done between the parties. A number of essential pre-conditions for the making of an order were laid down by the court.

(1) The plaintiff must show an extremely strong *prima facie* case.

(2) The damage, potential or actual, to the plaintiff's business, must be very serious. The damage should be verging on the irreparable.

(3) There must be clear evidence that the defendants have in their possession incriminating documents or things.

(4) There is a real possibility that the defendant may destroy such materials before an application *inter partes* can be made. The plaintiff must therefore show evidence of dishonesty on the part of the defendant.

Lord Denning also stated in the same case that an order should only be made if its execution 'would do no real harm to the defendant or his case'.

One of the main problems of Anton Piller orders, as in the case of Mareva orders, is the fact that they are always made *ex parte* without the defendant having any opportunity to put its case. The plaintiff must of course make full and frank disclosure of all material facts but it is always easier for a plaintiff to show that he has 'an extremely strong *prima facie* case' when his case in the affidavit evidence is not being countered in any way by any evidence from the defendant. As a 'search and seize' order the Anton Piller order only needs to be executed once and the damage to the defendant's business is potentially long-lasting. The evidence in support of the application is therefore frequently left unchallenged by defendants.

Additional safeguards for defendants

Nevertheless some essential safeguards have been imposed since the practice of Anton Piller orders gathered pace in the late 1970s.

(1) The order must always be explained by the plaintiff's solicitor to the defendant in 'everyday language' and the recipient, who will normally be the person in charge of the premises, can take immediate legal advice.

(2) If the recipient's solicitor tells him that he is leaving the office and will come to the house then the defendant is entitled to wait for the solicitor to arrive before permitting execution of the order.

(3) A defendant can apply immediately to discharge the Anton Piller order, before allowing execution of the order, although he will be at risk of being in contempt of court for not complying with the order if such an application is unsuccessful.

There are therefore grave risks to a defendant who decides not to comply with the Anton Piller order immediately and to seek its discharge. Further, his solicitor may be inexperienced in Anton Piller orders and may be unable to assess in the limited time available, and under great pressure from the plaintiff's solicitors to comply with the order, whether an application for a discharge will have any realistic prospects of success. By 1986 it was felt that defendants were still receiving inadequate protection from the effects of the execution of Anton Piller orders.

In the case of *Colombia Picture Industries v Robinson* [1986] WLR 540 Scott J expressed his concern that Anton Piller orders were being given far too easily. He laid down the following additional safeguards for defendants:

(1) The order must be drawn so that it goes no further than the minimum necessary to achieve the preservation of the relevant documents and articles.

(2) The plaintiff's solicitor should take copies as soon as possible of all documents removed and return the originals to the defendant within a very strict time limit, usually no more than seven days.

(3) The plaintiff's solicitor must keep a detailed record of all material taken before it is removed.

(4) No material should be taken unless it is clearly covered by the terms of the order.

(5) If the ownership of seized material is in dispute then the plaintiff's solicitor should not retain it and the disputed material should be given to neutral parties or the defendant's solicitors upon the usual undertakings being given.

(6) Affidavits in support of the application should err on the side of excessive disclosure. It is for the court to decide what is relevant and the plaintiff's solicitor will always be under a very strict duty to act scrupulously and disclose every potentially material fact.

Scott J also commented that 'the solicitor does not, and cannot be expected to, present all available evidence from the respondent's point of view'. He also noted that the execution of an order can cause severe, sometimes irreparable physical disruption to the defendant's business or daily life, and that it would be naïve to believe that this was never one of the motives behind the plaintiff seeking an Anton Piller order.

Further safeguards may now be seen in future. Following the judgment of the Vice-Chancellor in *Universal Thermosensors Ltd v Hibbern* (1992) *The Times,* 12 February the party applying for an Anton Piller order should now seriously consider providing an undertaking that the execution of the order will be supervised by a solicitor (other than the one acting for the plaintiff) who is experienced and familiar with the operation of Anton Piller orders. This solicitor should also prepare a written report on what happened and present it to the court at an *inter partes* hearing at a later date. It remains to be seen whether the courts will insist on these additional undertakings being provided in future Anton Piller orders.

The information usually sought

The plaintiffs will be looking for any documents showing the names and addresses of those involved with the defendant's business, places of manufacture, suppliers, distributors, retailers, customers, places of storage, invoices and records, documents relating to the setting up of the defendant's business (eg budgets, forecasts), drawings (in a copyright action), customer lists (in restrictive covenant cases), enquiries, purchase orders and other sales documents, quotations and VAT returns.

The plaintiff's solicitors must comply with the exact terms of the order, but they would normally be entitled to seize illicit material (such as infringing drawings in a copyright case), chattels (but not personal effects), computerised records, filing cabinets, prototypes, floppy disks and tapes, printouts of computer information and all other essential evidential documents.

If the plaintiff's solicitors do not comply they run the risk of being sued for trespass and for being in contempt of court.

Orders made ancillary to an Anton Piller order

An Anton Piller order will usually contain a number of ancillary orders. A 'state of the art' Anton Piller order will usually provide for the following:

(1) The defendant should consent to the entry into his premises and to the search and seizure of;
(a) property belonging to the plaintiff; and/or
(b) documentary or other evidence to support the plaintiff's claim.

(2) Defendants are usually asked to answer questions and disclose and produce documents. For example, the defendant will usually have to swear an affidavit within three days of the execution of the Anton Piller order, disclosing and producing all other documents which were not seized on the Anton Piller order but which come within the specified categories set out in the order.

(3) During the course of the execution of the Anton Piller order, the defendant will usually be ordered to immediately disclose the names and addresses of third parties 'mixed up' in the tortious activity (eg suppliers etc).

(4) Also during the execution of the order the defendants must disclose the whereabouts of all other illicit material.

(5) If any documents or articles are at any other premises the defendant must state exactly where they are and the Anton Piller order will then attach to the other premises (there should be a specific provision to this effect). For example, the documents may be with the defendant's accountants, preparing end of year accounts, or VAT returns, and, if so, then this should be disclosed so the search can continue at the accountant's offices.

The privilege against self incrimination

The leading case on Anton Piller orders and privilege has historically been *Rank Film Distributors Ltd v Video Information Centre* [1982] EC 380. The House of Lords in that case decided that the privilege against self incrimination could be raised to defeat that part of a composite Anton Piller order which relates to the requirement to answer questions and produce documents. The House of Lords took the view that the privilege against self incrimination did not apply to that part of the Anton Piller order that required the defendant to allow the plaintiff to seize the infringing copies of the plaintiff's films because the privilege could not override the plaintiff's proprietary rights in the infringing copies. The decision was unclear as to whether the privilege could be asserted against the plaintiff's rights to search for and seize other documentary evidence in addition to property belonging to them.

Following the *Rank Film* case, the privilege against self incrimination was of limited assistance to defendants as they could not usefully resist the 'search and seize' part of the order. The privilege against self incrimination in English law is based on the idea that no one should be obliged to give themselves away—*memo tenetur prodere seitsum.*

The *Rank Film* decision led directly to the enactment of s 72 of the Supreme Court Act 1981, which abolished reliance on the privilege against self incrimination in intellectual property litigation. In all intellectual property cases the defendant cannot assert the privilege against any part of an Anton Piller order. Therefore the whole debate concerning the defendant's ability to rely on the privilege against self incrimination, in resisting Anton Piller orders, is only relevant for cases not concerned with intellectual property infringement actions (including passing-off cases).

The law has now been clarified by a recent decision of the Vice Chancellor in *Tate Access Floors Inc v Boswell* (1990) *The Times*, 14 June. In this case the court held that the privilege against self incrimination could excuse compliance with an Anton Piller order in cases not concerned with intellectual property. There would have to be some allegation of statutory or common law conspiracy to defraud, and of some criminal activity by the defendant, for the privilege to apply. In this case an Anton Piller order was made but the defendants applied to discharge it on the basis that the order had infringed their privilege against self incrimination. They argued that if the facts alleged by the plaintiff were true, then the individual defendants were guilty of conspiracy to defraud and the documents produced or obtained under the order might incriminate them on that charge. The court held that the Anton Piller order should be discharged and the privilege against self incrimination could probably be invoked in any case involving discovery in a fraud action where, on the facts alleged by the plaintiff, there was a real risk that a defendant might be prosecuted for conspiracy and that the documents and the information sought by the order might be incriminating.

The privilege did apply to that part of the order entitling the plaintiff to enter the defendant's premises to search for and seize documents. The Anton Piller order was not discharged against the company defendants. As they were foreign companies there was no risk of their being prosecuted for conspiracy in this country. However, it seems that companies cannot avail themselves of the privilege against self incrimination nor can individual defendants claim the privilege on their behalf.

This is an important decision which seeks to address the balance between the desire to prevent defendants avoiding justice by removing or destroying the evidence and the danger that extremely draconian litigation procedures can become an instrument of oppression against individual defendants.

Contempt of court and discharge of orders

After service of the Anton Piller order the defendant can apply immediately to set aside the order. He should make the application without delay but in the realisation that if the application is not successful then he may be subject to committal proceedings for contempt of court for not complying with the order.

It has been held, that in the event of any material non-disclosure by the plaintiff, an application to discharge the Anton Piller order, after execution has already taken place, should normally be made at the trial and not at an interlocutory stage (*Dormeil Freres SA v Nicolian International (Textiles) Ltd* [1988] 3 All ER 197. In that case the Vice-Chancellor said that the court may have to consider a massive volume of affidavit evidence, much of which will have to be gone into again at trial, to deal with facts from which concluded findings cannot be made, but nevertheless to reach conclusions without full knowledge of the circumstances. If this is the case then an application to discharge an Anton Piller order at an interlocutory stage should not be made.

Any non-disclosure of material facts by the plaintiff (and therefore discharge of the order) will really only be relevant regarding the plaintiff's cross-undertaking in damages if the Anton Piller order has already been executed. Therefore the defendant will hope that the court will order an enquiry into damages, so that the defendant can be compensated for any loss, and be paid its legal costs. The actual effect of the injunction itself cannot be reversed by the discharge of an Anton Piller order.

However, an order can be discharged at an interlocutory stage if, in addition to any non-disclosure of material facts the court also decides that the order should never have been made in the first place, and/ or the defendant is in competition with the plaintiff and the defendant's reputation was suffering immeasurable harm as a result of the implied slur from the existence of the Anton Piller order; see *Lock International plc v Beswick* [1989] 1 WLR 1268.

The defendants can therefore apply to set aside the order before it is executed, or to discharge it after execution has already taken place.

Executing the Anton Piller order

The plaintiff will often have to search not only one location, but various pre-named premises. It may well be that offending documents, such as drawings, have been retained either at the home addresses of directors of a company or at the office premises. Plaintiffs will not know where the documents are and for this reason an Anton Piller order will often allow for simultaneous searches to be made against the homes of directors as well as the office premises of the company.

Simultaneous searches must be synchronised and carefully and meticulously planned. Anton Piller orders can be discharged if solicitors executing the orders do not follow the practical rules which exist as safeguards for the defendant. Not only must the solicitor executing the order be wary of all the safeguards protecting the defendant's interests, but he must also execute the order effectively and efficiently so that important evidence does not 'slip through the net'. A practical check-list for any solicitor responsible for executing an Anton Piller order is attached as an appendix and this list contains numerous practical points which apply both before and during execution of an Anton Piller order.

Alternative orders

There is a current feeling among High Court judges that perhaps the pre-conditions for obtaining Anton Piller orders have been relaxed in recent years and are in need of a thorough review so that once again Anton Piller orders are only given in rare cases.

Instead of applying for an Anton Piller order, a plaintiff who is anxious to preserve the evidence and avoid any risk of the defendant destroying or disposing of documents may apply for one of the following orders instead of an Anton Piller order:

(a) an order for delivery up: the defendant will be ordered to deliver documents and materials to his solicitors, or the plaintiff's solicitors, within a strict time scale; or

(b) an order for the listing of documents: the defendant must verify, in an affidavit, a list of all documents in his possession, custody or power, which fall within the categories of documents specified in the order. Having listed the documents, the defendant will not be able to dispose of them at a later stage of the proceedings.

Pre-emptive remedies other than interlocutory injunctions

An application for summary judgment

In England and Wales it is possible for the plaintiff to apply for summary judgment at any stage of the proceedings after the defendant has filed an Acknowledgment of Service confirming an intention to defend the action. The application can be made before or after the defendant serves a defence. The plaintiff will need to show that the defendant has no valid grounds to defend the action whatsoever. Even if the defendant has a weak defence he will be given leave to defend the action. The defendant only needs to show that there is a triable issue which should be examined at trial.

If the plaintiff is seeking an injunction, and is therefore applying for a perpetual injunction at the hearing of his application for summary judgment, then the application must be made to a judge as the High Court Masters (who normally hear these applications) have no power to grant an injunction except by consent.

At the hearing of an application for summary judgment the court will only consider the merits of the plaintiff's case. The court will not consider such issues as the balance of convenience nor will the plaintiff have to give a cross-undertaking in damages. Therefore, if a plaintiff has a strong case it may well be preferable to apply for summary judgment rather than an interlocutory injunction.

The following conditions must be satisfied:

(a) the writ and Statement of Claim must have been served on the defendant;
(b) the defendant must have acknowledged service of the writ;
(c) the plaintiff must serve an affidavit in support of the application and this must be served on the defendant not less than ten clear days before the hearing date.

If the application for summary judgment fails then the plaintiff can instead apply for an interlocutory injunction as the requirement that the defendant has no arguable defence will not then apply.

On the hearing of an application for summary judgment the court can make one of three orders:

(a) give the plaintiff leave to enter judgment;
(b) give the defendant unconditional leave to defend the action;
(c) give the defendant conditional leave to defend the action, the condition usually being a requirement for the defendant to pay money into court within a limited time period.

Speedy trial

Another alternative would be for the plaintiff to ask the court to order a speedy trial of the whole case. The court will give directions whereby the usual procedures will be expedited, strict time limits are enforced in respect of the exchange of pleadings and evidence and the date of the trial will be brought forward to an earlier date.

Judgment in default

If a defendant fails to acknowledge service of the writ, the plaintiff seeking an injunction is not permitted to automatically enter judgment in default, unlike in a case where the plaintiff is only seeking damages. Instead of entering judgment the plaintiff must file an affidavit confirming service of the writ on the defendant and then proceed with the action in the normal way.

Whether or not the defendant acknowledges service of the writ, if he fails to serve a defence within the appropriate time limits (namely, 14 days after service of the Statement of Claim unless this time is extended by consent or by way of a court order) then again the plaintiff cannot enter judgment automatically if the plaintiff is seeking an injunction. However, the plaintiff can apply by Motion (Chancery Division) or by summons (Queen's Bench Division) for judgment in default of defence.

The defendant must be given two clear days' notice of the application before the hearing date.

The court will then consider the writ and Statement of Claim and decide whether the plaintiff's pleadings are sufficient in themselves to warrant judgment being entered. The power of the court to give judgment in default of service of a defence under Ord 19, r 7, is, in any event, discretionary.

Preliminary trial

Under Ord 33, r 1, of the High Court Rules the court can order any issue to be dealt with at a preliminary trial and the hearing can be expedited if necessary. In commercial cases, this rule can be used to decide preliminary questions of law. The determination of one legal issue, which would be a final determination (subject to any right of appeal), may lead to a resolution of the whole case and so this may be an effective alternative to injunctive relief in some cases.

Nicholas Rose

Scotland

Introduction

Pre-emptive remedies in Scotland are essentially different from those in England, but the effects may be similar. In Scotland some remedies which, in England, may be discretionary, are achieved by administrative procedures in the first instance.

The only discretionary Scottish judicial remedy, in the context of commercial disputes, which results in a specific order by the court at an early stage in proceedings (other than an order for payment of money) is that of interim interdict.

Such an order is invariably made in the context of an action for a permanent order for interdict, which action may seek other remedies, such as damages, specific performance, delivery or declarator (ie a request to the court to make a finding which clarifies the rights of the parties in contention).

An interim order is usually final until recalled by the express order of the court. Such a recall may follow only if the interdicted party makes a special application to the court, or after a full trial of the issue between the parties.

Interim and final interdict are only granted where they may halt a legal wrong being done, or may prevent one which it is reasonably suspected may imminently take place.

The court will not grant an interdict (interim or final) which enforces any positive obligation. It will not, for example, order the construction of a building. It will, however, order that a building be *not* constructed, in compliance with which some positive actions may be required by those so interdicted. Interdict (as the word implies) is essentially a prohibitory order.

Examples of the scope of interdicts

The scope of interdicts frequently sought in Scotland is much the same as that discussed in the earlier section on English remedies.

General principles

As previously explained, the remedy of interim interdict is granted to prohibit continuing or apprehended acts.

The purpose of an interim interdict is to ensure that the rights of the parties are, so far as it is possible, preserved until such time as the matters in issue are properly determined. To achieve this the court will tend to pay particular attention to the balance of convenience. It will, without prejudicing the ultimate determination of the issues, attempt to make an order such as will achieve the most equitable result between the parties at a stage where the issues between the parties are incapable of determination. The *status quo* may frequently find favour, and an interim interdict granted to preserve this, particularly if that results in the avoidance of what may be irreparable damage to the party seeking the interdict.

Acquiescence and delay

Any delay in seeking an interim interdict may, if the defender has suffered prejudice, lead to a refusal of an interim order.

Structure of the courts

The Supreme Civil Court in Scotland is the Court of Session, which has its seat in Edinburgh. It does not go on circuit.

The Court of Session comprises an Inner and Outer House. The Outer House is essentially a Court of First Instance, while the Inner House, from where appeal lies to the House of Lords, exercises an appellate jurisdiction over the Outer House and the Sheriff Courts.

The Court of Session has universal territorial jurisdiction within Scotland.

Inferior to the Court of Session there exists a system of local civil courts known as Sheriff Courts with restricted local territorial jurisdiction, and very roughly equivalent to the county courts in England. There is, however, no upper financial limit to civil matters over which those courts have jurisdiction.

Both the Court of Session and the Sheriff Courts may issue interdicts, interim or final. While the Court of Session may restrain acts within the whole country, the Sheriff Courts' orders will usually only run within their local jurisdiction.

In most significant commercial disputes where interim interdict is sought it is generally the Court of Session which is the chosen Court of First Instance, as it may remove any potential jurisdictional problems, its orders are wider in their geographical effect, and, arguably, the judicial and representative expertise is more used to complex commercial litigation.

At present, in the Court of Session solicitors have no right of audience, and the solicitor will instruct a member of the Scottish Bar (advocate) to draft written pleadings and appear in court. While the relatively small Scottish Bar militates against narrow specialisation, most advocates with commercial litigation practices will be familiar with the particular problems that applications for interim interdict involve. Solicitors and advocates will work in tandem, so that a sensible division of labour, taking into account the restriction of rights of audience, is achieved. In the Sheriff Court solicitors have unrestricted rights of audience.

Criteria for obtaining interim interdict

Features

In contrast with English procedures, the requirement for affidavits does not exist in Scotland. The applicant's argument will be based on his written pleadings, supported and expanded where appropriate by *ex parte* statements by his advocate or solicitor, and any documents relevant to the application.

The relevant test

The applicant must satisfy the court that he has a proper interest in the cause, that he has suffered or reasonably anticipates some wrongful act, and that there is a proper issue for the court to try. The court will then consider, assuming it is satisfied as to these matters, the balance of convenience, which it will attempt to assess so as to do least damage to either party, while looking to the desirability of affording an effective remedy to the party who may ultimately be successful. In carrying out this difficult exercise, the Scottish courts have been more inclined to take into account the likely result of the substantive dispute between the parties than have the courts in England.

A party obtains interim interdict *periculo petentis*—he takes the risk that if his substantive case fails, and final interdict after a trial of the issues is refused, his opponent will probably have a right to recover such damages as he has sustained as a result of the interim order.

There is no requirement for cross-undertakings in damages to be given, and such procedure is regarded as unnecessary, as any rights to damages exist by virtue of the common law.

In assessing the balance of convenience, the court may, where appropriate, require either party to produce financial guarantees as a precondition to the grant or refusal of interim interdict, or require trading records to be kept so as to facilitate the ultimate assessment of damages.

In the case of a foreign applicant, arrangements may have to be made to find security for costs, either by lodging funds with the court, or by nominating an agent (or 'mandatory') who is subject to the jurisdiction of the Scottish courts and who assumes responsibility for any order for costs made against the foreign applicant. Such arrangements may be required even if the applicant has its domicile in an EC member country.

Practice and procedure

In Scotland applications for interim interdict are made without notice to the defender, unless the defender has taken steps to lodge in the appropriate court a caveat. A caveat, which is a very simple procedural step, will ensure that the defender is given the opportunity of being represented when the application for the interim order is heard. Where circumstances dictate, the court may, *ex proprio motu*, insist on the defender being heard, even in the absence of a caveat for the defender. As a matter of commercial prudence, most public authorities and commercial bodies arrange for caveats to be placed in the appropriate courts on a permanent basis, as should anyone who may suspect that they may be faced with an application for interim interdict.

In the Court of Session, urgent applications are available, in theory, 24 hours a day, seven days a week. The Sheriff Court will also entertain urgent applications. In practice most urgent applications can be heard on the day of the application being made, the assessment of urgency initially being made by senior court officials, who usually accept the representations of the applicant's legal representatives as to the urgency.

In any *ex parte* application there is a heavy professional responsibility on the representatives of the applicant not to mislead the court and to take reasonable steps to ensure the accuracy of what is said in support of the application.

Where the application for interim interdict is opposed, for whatever reason, copies of the writ and all documentary productions are made available to the defender's representative on an informal basis.

If the application is opposed, usually because a caveat has been lodged, a reasonable time, usually 24 to 48 hours, is allowed to enable the defender to arrange representation.

The fact that affidavits are not normally required, makes the preparation and hearing of opposed and unopposed applications relatively easy to organise.

Legal expenses

An award ordering payment of legal expenses will usually be made to the successful party. The recoverable expenses are usually between two thirds and three quarters of the total. The court has a wide discretion in awarding expenses, and may adjust any award to take into account, among other factors, the parties' pre- and post-litigation actions. Expenses are assessed, in the absence of agreement, by an officer of the court.

Post-interdict factors

Service of the interdict

Although not essential it is prudent to have service made by officials known as Messengers-at-Arms, for Court of Session orders, or Sheriff Officers for those made by the Sheriff Court. The order cannot safely be regarded as effective until so served.

Sanction

Any breach of interdict may constitute contempt of court. The sanctions are the imposition of a fine or imprisonment. Alternatively, a financial guarantee, which would be forfeited in the event of a further breach, may be ordered.

Variation or recall of interdicts

The defender may apply at any time to have an interim interdict recalled. If the defender was not represented when the order was made, the matter may be fully argued *de novo*. If the defender was represented, some change in circumstances would have to be argued to justify such an application.

Damages following recall of interim interdict and interdict

It is rare for damages to arise when interim interdict is recalled before a full trial, as recall usually follows the grant very rapidly. It is not, however, impossible. Any damages sought as a result of a recall of interim interdict, whether by application for recall or by recall following a full trial are recoverable by a civil action for damages for wrongful interdict. An interdict which is recalled is presumed to have been wrongfully granted.

Freezing orders

In Scotland freezing orders affecting the defender's assets can in special circumstances be made by interdict, but this is more commonly and frequently achieved by the procedures of arrestment and inhibition. Both of these are obtained without overt judicial intervention, but can subsequently be modified or discharged by judicial order in appropriate circumstances. They can be used at an early stage in the action, even, in most cases, before the defender has received notice that an action has been raised. Both orders are generally restricted to actions in which a claim for payment of money is included.

Arrestment

Arrestment freezes debts or movable property to which the defender has rights but which are held by a third party. A common example is the arrestment of the defender's bank account. The assets arrested must be held by a third party, not by the defender himself, but this is not as restrictive as it might seem. In a commercial context it is unlikely, for example, that a defender will not operate a bank account or have trade debtors. Arrestment 'on the dependence' (that is before determination) of a civil action can be an extremely inexpensive and efficient way of acquiring security. In all the Scottish civil courts, authority to arrest on the dependence of the action is automatically issued without a requirement for any special application.

Inhibition

This procedure, which is available in the same circumstances as an arrestment, allows the pursuer (plaintiff) to strike at any deeds, granted after the date when the inhibition is publicly registered, conveying or mortgaging the defender's real property in Scotland. The existence of a public record of such inhibitions ensures the efficacy of the inhibition as a pre-emptive security. It is not uncommon for the defender to offer security to achieve a suspension of the inhibition.

Search and seize orders

The availability of such orders in Scotland derives from the Administration of Justice (Scotland) Act 1972, s 1.

This empowers the court to order the preservation, custody and detention of documents and property which may be relevant to civil proceedings, extant or contemplated, and to order their production and recovery.

Where a case can be made the court may grant an order granting authority to a Commissioner (usually a senior member of the Bar) to search for and, using such force as may be necessary, seize any relevant documents or property where there is a real risk that such documents or property may be concealed or destroyed. Where justified the search and seize operation will be carried out without notice to the person who is thought to possess the property to be recovered.

The Commissioner stands in place of the court, when exercising his function, and thus his powers are very wide. He is, however, expected to exercise them with discretion. Any refusal to comply with the court's order may be dealt with as contempt of court, with sanctions of fines or imprisonment.

Any property recovered will be taken into the custody of the court in the first instance, and no access to it is possible without the court's permission.

The procedure is extremely flexible. If simultaneous searches can be justified, an additional Commissioner can be appointed.

The Scottish courts have, arguably with good reason, been cautious in granting search and seize orders. Such operations are not, for reason of expense alone, undertaken lightly. Where circumstances dictate, however, they can be carried out expeditiously, without warning, and effectively.

Scottish jurisdiction in litigation commenced in EC jurisdictions

Section 27 of the Civil Jurisdiction and Judgments Act 1982 allows the Court of Session to grant a warrant for arrestment or inhibition over assets in Scotland on the dependence of an action commenced in another part of the United Kingdom, or in another State which is a signatory of the 1968 Brussels Convention on Civil Jurisdiction and Enforcement of Judgments.

Interim interdict and search and seize orders may also be granted under this section.

David J Walker

Appendices

Appendix A

Practical checklist for lawyers executing an Anton Piller order

After the application has been made at the High Court

(1) There should be at least two people present from the plaintiff's solicitors. One person should stay after the hearing to collect the order signed by the judge (QB D) or to arrange for the sealing of the order by the court (Ch D). The other person should return to the office immediately after the hearing to organise the photocopying of documents and the practical arrangements prior to execution.

(2) The order itself must be signed by the judge and, in the QB D, retyped at the offices of the plaintiff's solicitors to include any initialled amendments made by the judge and then sealed at the court. The order must be endorsed with the relevant penal notices.

(3) Before leaving the office the plaintiff's solicitors must make sure they have sufficient copies of all the relevant documents. Copies of the Anton Piller order, the sealed writ, the affidavit and all the exhibits should be taken and there should be copies provided for:

(a) each defendant;

(b) each defendant's solicitors in the event that they may attend the execution of the order;

(c) one set of the documents should be left with Counsel in the event that an application to vary the order is necessary;

(d) another set should be left with someone in the plaintiff's solicitors' office in the event of any application to vary being made;

(e) a spare set should be taken with the solicitor who will execute the order.

(4) The Anton Piller order must be endorsed with a penal notice relating to each person to be served. The bundles for each defendant should therefore be specifically marked (with, say, a yellow tag) so that the order with the correct penal notice is served in respect of each defendant.

(5) The plaintiff must be advised both before and after the application for the Anton Piller order is made of the necessity for absolute secrecy both within their organisation and to third parties. Particularly in restraint of trade cases there may be people within the plaintiff company who are still friendly with the ex-employees/defendants and may inform them of the plaintiff's intentions.

Before execution

(1) Several people are involved in serving and executing the order. Each person must be briefed carefully on the precise rules and guidelines provided for Anton Piller orders. Each person should be taken through the Anton Piller order and each provision in the order explained carefully to every person involved in the execution of it.

(2) In the case of simultaneous searches, each team should have a team leader who should brief everyone in his team. Each team leader should memorise a copy of a 'suggested statement and introduction' when serving the order setting out the everyday language to be used explaining the order to the recipient.

(3) Before executing the order, check the premises carefully, looking out in particular for all entrances and exits.

(4) If the defendant is potentially aggressive then process servers or court bailiffs should be added to your team. Police can be used if necessary but only as an absolute last resort.

(5) If the defendant already has solicitors the plaintiff's solicitors may inform them just before serving the order (for example, on a mobile telephone) but this is not essential.

(6) In the case of multiple searches, plan for synchronising service of the orders. Each team leader should have a mobile telephone in order to communicate freely with the other teams.

(7) Consider leaving one person as a sentry outside the exit to the premises to make sure that nobody leaves.

(8) The order will usually allow for execution between, say, 7.00 am and 7.00 pm. The solicitors executing the order must then leave at 7.00 pm unless the order is varied in order to allow an extension of time.

In the absence of an extension of time or if, for example, no access to the premises is allowed before the time expires and it is necessary for the plaintiff's solicitors to return the following morning, then make sure that the premises are watched overnight, perhaps by a firm of private detectives. If necessary, use video film so that if any documents are removed from the premises overnight then the evidence can be captured on video.

During execution

(1) When searching, do not go outside the ambit of the order. Only remove documents and materials specifically stated to be within the categories of documents set out in the order.

(2) Remember to advise the recipient at each premises that he may contact a solicitor but also warn the defendant that he will be in contempt of court in the event of non-compliance with the order.

(3) Contemporaneous notes should be taken of any discussions with the defendants and/or the defendants' solicitors during the course of service and execution of the order. The discussions may be taped or someone should take a full note of everything that is said.

(4) The notes taken should include a note of the precise times of all important events: entry into the premises, commencement of execution, the time the defendant's solicitor arrives, etc.

(5) One person in the plaintiff's solicitors' team should watch everyone in the building including all exits and entrances to make sure that no documents are being hidden or removed during the course of the search.

(6) A comprehensive list of all documents and other materials taken should be made and each page of the list should be signed by both parties before the documents are removed from the premises in order to avoid dispute at a later date as to what was taken.

Appendix B

Practical checklist in relation to Mareva orders

(1) Consider how broad the terms of the proposed injunction should be to safeguard the plaintiff's claim.

(2) What particular assets of the proposed defendant should be covered by the injunction? Identify all relevant assets.

(3) Has the defendant sufficient assets in the UK to safeguard the plaintiff's claim? If not, do the circumstances justify applying for a worldwide injunction?

(4) If an application is to be made for a worldwide injunction, what foreign assets does the defendant have in other jurisdiction(s)?

(5) If it is intended to freeze bank accounts, obtain sufficient information in order to identify the bank, the address of the relevant branch and the account numbers if possible.

(6) How quickly can the defendant be served?

(7) In what manner can the defendant be served? How can the defendant's assets be protected before he is served?

(8) Consider on which third parties it is reasonably necessary to serve a copy of the injunction. In the case of banks, ascertain the address, fax number and telephone number of each relevant branch of the bank.

(9) Consider the urgency in which the application should be made. If there is a lack of time then present the draft affidavit to the court and give an undertaking to swear the affidavit after the hearing.

(10) Consider whether the defendant should be entitled to withdraw money in order to pay his legal costs and, if so, how much.

(11) Consider a reasonable amount for the defendant to pay his living expenses or business expenses as appropriate.

(12) If acting for a foreign plaintiff, bear in mind the defendant can apply for security for costs.

(13) Consider whether a provision should be made for a consensual written variation provision without recourse to the court.

(14) Consider whether any joint accounts held by the defendant should be frozen.

(15) Consider the details regarding any known letters of credit relating to the defendant.

(16) Clearly identify the assets covered and the order must make clear whether the order covers all assets held by the bank (including chattels) or just monies.

(17) Give an undertaking at the hearing to reimburse any third party, including the bank, as to expenses resulting from the order.

(18) Notify the bank prior to notifying the defendant. Serve the evidence on all relevant third parties or, alternatively, summarise the case in a covering letter to the banks and third parties.

(19) Serve the bank with a copy of the order as soon as possible, preferably by fax. Before sending the fax, telephone the bank and notify them of the terms of the order and advise them that a fax will be sent to them confirming the contents of the conversation.

(20) In the letter to the bank confirm that any money held in a foreign currency should be converted into sterling at the buying rate to the extent necessary to meet the sums stated in the order.

Index